JIRA 5.2 Essentials

Learn how to track bugs and issues, and manage your
software development projects with JIRA

Patrick Li

BIRMINGHAM - MUMBAI

JIRA 5.2 Essentials

First published: April 2013

Production Reference: 1090413

Published by Packt Publishing Ltd.
Livery Place
35 Livery Street
Birmingham B3 2PB, UK.

ISBN 978-1-78217-999-3

www.packtpub.com

Cover Image by Jarek Blaminsky (milak6@wp.pl)

Credits

Author
Patrick Li

Reviewers
Peter Callies

Sergey Markovich

Acquisition Editor
Andrew Duckworth

Lead Technical Editor
Sweny Sukumaran

Technical Editors
Lubna Shaikh

Jalasha D'costa

Project Coordinator
Shiksha Chaturvedi

Proofreader
Ting Baker

Indexer
Monica Ajmera Mehta

Graphics
Sheetal Alute

Aditi Gajjar

Production Coordinator
Shantanu Zagade

Cover Work
Shantanu Zagade

About the Author

Patrick Li is the co-founder and senior engineer of AppFusions. AppFusions is the leading Atlassian partner, specializing in integration solutions with many enterprise applications and platforms, including IBM Connections, Jive, Google Apps, Box, SugarCRM, and more.

He has worked in the Atlassian ecosystem for over five years, developing products and solutions for the Atlassian platform, and providing expert consulting services. He is one of the top contributors to the Atlassian community, providing answers and suggestions on the Atlassian user forum.

He has extensive experience in designing and deploying Atlassian solutions from the ground up, and customizing existing deployments for clients across verticals such as healthcare, software engineering, financial services, and government agencies.

I would like to thank my wife, Katherine, who supported and encouraged me along the way, especially during my relocation to San Francisco from Sydney. I would also like to thank all the reviewers for their valuable feedback, and also the publishers/coordinators, for their help in making this happen.

About the Reviewers

Peter Callies has been developing software and leading teams for over 20 years. He is currently an Agile coach, helping teams and enterprises maximize their value in their product development systems.

He has been using JIRA for three years to help manage traditional projects, plan and track work for Scrum teams, and visualize flow with Kanban.

Peter can be found on Twitter (`@pcallies`) and LinkedIn (`http://www.linkedin.com/in/petercallies`).

Sergey Markovich is currently a cofounder of Plugenta Labs, a company focusing on the development of add-ons for enterprise software, and an independent Atlassian JIRA and Confluence contractor.

In the past, he was a code wizard in several multinational corporations and startups and is a computer science bachelor.

> I want to thank my wife for her constant support in all my plans and activities and putting up with me while I work late hours.
>
> I also want to say warm words to everybody involved with Plugenta Labs. It's a real pleasure to work with them as I keep learning from them every day.

www.PacktPub.com

Support files, eBooks, discount offers and more

You might want to visit www.PacktPub.com for support files and downloads related to your book.

Did you know that Packt offers eBook versions of every book published, with PDF and ePub files available? You can upgrade to the eBook version at www.PacktPub.com and as a print book customer, you are entitled to a discount on the eBook copy. Get in touch with us at service@ packtpub.com for more details.

At www.PacktPub.com, you can also read a collection of free technical articles, sign up for a range of free newsletters and receive exclusive discounts and offers on Packt books and eBooks.

http://PacktLib.PacktPub.com

Do you need instant solutions to your IT questions? PacktLib is Packt's online digital book library. Here, you can access, read and search across Packt's entire library of books.

Why Subscribe?

- Fully searchable across every book published by Packt
- Copy and paste, print and bookmark content
- On demand and accessible via web browser

Free Access for Packt account holders

If you have an account with Packt at www.PacktPub.com, you can use this to access PacktLib today and view nine entirely free books. Simply use your login credentials for immediate access.

Instant Updates on New Packt Books

Get notified! Find out when new books are published by following @PacktEnterprise on Twitter, or the *Packt Enterprise* Facebook page.

Table of Contents

Preface

JIRA 5 was unveiled during the Atlassian Summit in 2011, the annual conference event that brings together users, partners, and experts around the world. It was at this time that we were given the first glimpse of the advancements and new direction that Atlassian is taking JIRA, the world's most popular issue-tracking software. Fast forward to 2012, and Atlassian announced its JIRA Enterprise offering and shortly after, JIRA 5.1, another monumental milestone for this amazing software. With this new release, Atlassian took JIRA to the next level, transforming it from a single software package into a complete platform that supports agile practices through plugins such GreenHopper and Bonfire, adding social aspects through features such as sharing and mentions, and a much improved user experience from the interface down to its core performance.

While JIRA 5 introduces numerous new features and enhancements, some of the more prominent changes for the old-time users are on the newly improved user interface designs. For this reason, we will assume nothing, and introduce JIRA fresh from the perspective of JIRA 5.

Packed with real-life examples and step-by-step instructions, this book will help you become a JIRA expert.

What this book covers

This book is organized into eleven chapters. *Chapter 1, Getting Started with JIRA*, starts with setting up your own JIRA, and the subsequent chapters will introduce the key features and concepts. With each chapter, you will learn important concepts such as business processes, workflows, e-mails, and notifications, and you will have the opportunity to put your newly acquired knowledge into practice by following a live JIRA sample implementation.

Chapter 1, Getting Started with JIRA, serves as a starting point for the book and aims to guide you through setting up a local copy of the JIRA application that will be used throughout the book. For seasoned JIRA experts, this will both refresh your knowledge and also introduce you to the new changes in JIRA 5. By the end of the chapter, you should have a running JIRA application.

Chapter 2, Project Management, covers how to set up projects and project-related administration tasks in JIRA. The concept of schemes will also be introduced, as it is the core concept in JIRA administration.

Chapter 3, Issue Management, covers everything related to issue creation and operations that can be performed on an issue (excluding workflow transitions). Furthermore, this chapter will gently touch on the various aspects of issues, as they are the focal point of JIRA. This chapter will also serve as an opportunity to show and allow you to set up dummy data that will be used by the sample project.

Chapter 4, Field Management, covers how JIRA collects data through the use of fields and how to expand on this ability through the use of custom fields. The chapter will then continue with the various behaviors that can be configured for fields.

Chapter 5, Screen Management, builds on the preceding chapter and explores the concept of screens and how users can create and manage their own screens. This chapter will tie in with all the previous chapters to show the power behind JIRA's screen design capabilities.

Chapter 6, Workflows and Business Processes, explores the most powerful feature offered by JIRA, workflows. The concept of issue life cycle will be introduced and various aspects of workflows explained. This chapter will also explore the relationship between workflows and other JIRA aspects previously covered, such as screens. The concept of JIRA extensions will also be briefly touched on in the sample project, using some popular free extensions.

Chapter 7, E-mails and Notifications, focuses on how to get automatic e-mail notifications from JIRA and explores the different settings that can be applied. This is a very important and powerful feature of JIRA and also a critical part of the example project for this book. This chapter will also tie in with the workflow chapter and explain in detail how JIRA manages its notification mechanism.

Chapter 8, Securing JIRA, focuses on the different security control features offered by JIRA. As this topic affects all aspects of JIRA, all previous topics will be touched on, explaining how security can be applied to each. We will also cover LDAP integration where you can hook up your JIRA with an existing LDAP system for user management.

Chapter 9, Searching, Reporting, and Analysis, will focus on how data captured in JIRA can be retrieved to provide various types of reporting features. We will also introduce the new search features introduced in JIRA 5.

Chapter 10, General Administration, covers other administration features offered by JIRA, including using add-ons and the Atlassian Marketplace. These features often do not form the backbone of a JIRA installation but can be very useful when used properly.

Chapter 11, Advanced Features, covers advanced features that can help to change your JIRA into more than just a traditional issue-tracking system. We will look at how you can run agile projects with JIRA through the use of GreenHopper, and turn JIRA into an effective feedback collection system.

What you need for this book

The installation package used in this book will be the Windows Installer standalone distribution, which you can get directly from Atlassian at `http://www.atlassian.com/software/jira/download`.

At the time of writing, the latest version of JIRA is 5.2.5.

You will also need additional software, including Java SDK, which you can get from `http://java.sun.com/javase/downloads` and MySQL, which you can get from `http://dev.mysql.com/downloads`.

Who this book is for

If you want to get started with JIRA and learn how to install, use, and manage your instances, then this is the perfect book for you.

You will need to be familiar with the basic computer operations, specifically the system on which you will use JIRA, and software project management. For the first chapter, it's assumed that you are familiar with the operating system you are going to install JIRA on.

Conventions

In this book, you will find a number of styles of text that distinguish between different kinds of information. Here are some examples of these styles, and an explanation of their meaning.

Code words in text are shown as follows: "we will be referring to this directory as JIRA_INSTALL."

A block of code is set as follows:

```
<security-constraint>
  <web-resource-collection>
    <web-resource-name>all-except-attachments</web-resource-name>
    <url-pattern>*.js</url-pattern>
    <url-pattern>*.jsp</url-pattern>
    <url-pattern>*.jspa</url-pattern>
    <url-pattern>*.css</url-pattern>
    <url-pattern>/browse/*</url-pattern>
  </web-resource-collection>
  <user-data-constraint>
    <transport-guarantee>CONFIDENTIAL</transport-guarantee>
  </user-data-constraint>
</security-constraint>
```

Any command-line input or output is written as follows:

```
mysql -u root -p
```

New terms and **important words** are shown in bold. Words that you see on the screen, in menus or dialog boxes for example, appear in the text like this: "Click on **Next** on the welcome screen."

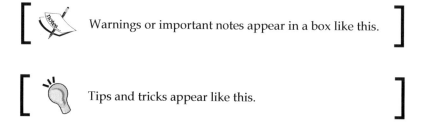

Warnings or important notes appear in a box like this.

Tips and tricks appear like this.

Reader feedback

Feedback from our readers is always welcome. Let us know what you think about this book—what you liked or may have disliked. Reader feedback is important for us to develop titles that you really get the most out of.

To send us general feedback, simply send an e-mail to feedback@packtpub.com, and mention the book title via the subject of your message.

If there is a book that you need and would like to see us publish, please send us a note in the **SUGGEST A TITLE** form on www.packtpub.com or e-mail suggest@packtpub.com.

If there is a topic that you have expertise in and you are interested in either writing or contributing to a book, see our author guide on www.packtpub.com/authors.

Customer support

Now that you are the proud owner of a Packt book, we have a number of things to help you to get the most from your purchase.

Errata

Although we have taken every care to ensure the accuracy of our content, mistakes do happen. If you find a mistake in one of our books—maybe a mistake in the text or the code—we would be grateful if you would report this to us. By doing so, you can save other readers from frustration and help us improve subsequent versions of this book. If you find any errata, please report them by visiting http://www.packtpub.com/support, selecting your book, clicking on the **errata submission form** link, and entering the details of your errata. Once your errata are verified, your submission will be accepted and the errata will be uploaded on our website, or added to any list of existing errata, under the Errata section of that title. Any existing errata can be viewed by selecting your title from http://www.packtpub.com/support.

Piracy

Piracy of copyright material on the Internet is an ongoing problem across all media. At Packt, we take the protection of our copyright and licenses very seriously. If you come across any illegal copies of our works, in any form, on the Internet, please provide us with the location address or website name immediately so that we can pursue a remedy.

Please contact us at copyright@packtpub.com with a link to the suspected pirated material.

We appreciate your help in protecting our authors, and our ability to bring you valuable content.

Questions

You can contact us at questions@packtpub.com if you are having a problem with any aspect of the book, and we will do our best to address it.

1
Getting Started with JIRA

JIRA has always been a fun to use and easy to install software, and JIRA 5 is no different. In fact, JIRA 5 has improved on its predecessors by providing a more polished and powerful installation wizard, eliminating some of the old installation steps where users had to manually edit configuration files in a text editor.

In this chapter, we will start with a high-level view of JIRA, looking at each of the components that make up the overall application. We will then examine the various deployment options, system requirements for JIRA 5, and platforms/software that are supported. Finally, we will get our hands dirty by installing our very own JIRA 5 from scratch, with the newly improved installation wizard. In the end, we will also cover some post installation steps, such as setting up SSL to secure your new instance.

By the end of this chapter, you will have learned about the following:

- The overall architecture of JIRA
- The basic hardware and software requirements to deploy and run JIRA
- Platforms and applications supported by JIRA
- Installing JIRA and all of the required software
- Post-installation configuration options to customize your JIRA

The JIRA architecture

Installing JIRA is simple and straightforward. However, it is important for you to understand the components that make up the overall architecture of JIRA and the installation options available. This will help you make an informed decision and be better prepared for future maintenance and troubleshooting.

High-level architecture

Atlassian provides a comprehensive overview of the JIRA architecture at `https://developer.atlassian.com/display/JIRADEV/JIRA+Architectural+Overview`. However, for day-to-day administration and usage of JIRA, we do not need to go into details; the information provided can be overwhelming at the first glance. For this reason, we have summarized a high-level overview that highlights the most important components in the architecture:

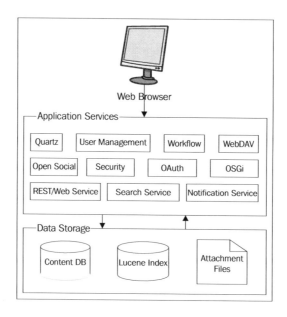

Web browsers

JIRA is a web application, so there is no need for users to install anything on their machine. All they need is a web browser that is compatible with JIRA. Since JIRA 4, JIRA has made some major changes to its user interface, and JIRA 5 has continued to improve upon this to deliver a more responsive user experience. As a result, some of the older browsers are no longer supported. The following table summarizes the browser requirements for JIRA:

Browsers	Compatibility
Microsoft Internet Explorer	8.0, 9.0 (Compatibility View is not supported)
	10 is not supported
Mozilla Firefox	Latest stable versions
Safari	Latest stable versions
Google Chrome	Latest stable versions

Application services

The application services layer contains all the functions and services provided by JIRA. These services include various business functions, such as workflow and notification, which will be discussed in depth in *Chapter 6*, *Workflows and Business Processes* and *Chapter 7*, *E-mails and Notifications*, respectively. Other services, such as REST/Web Service, provide integration points to other applications, and the OSGi service provides the base add-on framework to extend JIRA's functionalities.

Data storage

The data storage layer stores persistent data in several places within JIRA. Most business data, such as issues and projects, are stored in a relational database. Contents such as uploaded attachments and search indexes are stored in the filesystem, in the JIRA_HOME directory, which we will talk about in the next section. The underlying relational database used is transparent to the users and you can migrate from one database to another with ease.

The JIRA installation directory

The JIRA installation directory is where you install JIRA. It contains all the executable and configuration files of the application. JIRA does not modify the contents of the files in this directory during runtime, nor does it store any data inside; the directory is used primarily for execution. For the remainder of the book, we will be referring to this directory as JIRA_INSTALL.

The JIRA home directory

The JIRA home directory contains key data files that are specific to each JIRA instance. There is a one-to-one relationship between JIRA and this directory. This means each JIRA instance must and can have only one home directory, and each directory can serve only one JIRA instance. In the old days, this directory was sometimes called the **data** directory. It has now been standardized as the JIRA Home. It is for this reason that for the rest of the book we will be referring to this directory as JIRA_HOME.

It is recommended that JIRA_HOME be created separately from JIRA installation. This separation of data and application makes tasks, such as maintenance and future upgrades, an easier process.

Within JIRA_HOME, there are several subdirectories that contain vital data:

Directory	Description
data	This directory contains data that is not stored in the database. For example, uploaded attachment files.
export	This directory contains the automated backup archives created by JIRA. This is different from a manual export executed by a user; manual exports require the user to specify where to store the archive.
import	This directory contains the backups that can be imported. JIRA will only load the backup files from this directory.
log	This directory contains the JIRA logs.
plugins	This directory is where the installed add-ons are stored. In the previous versions of JIRA, add-ons were installed by copying the add-on files to this directory manually, but in JIRA 5, you will no longer need to do this, unless specifically instructed to do so. Add-ons will be discussed further in later chapters.
caches	This directory contains cache data that JIRA uses to improve its performance at runtime. For example, search indexes are stored in this directory.
tmp	This directory contains temporary files created at runtime, such as file uploads

When JIRA runs, this directory gets locked, when JIRA shuts down, it gets unlocked. This locking mechanism prevents multiple JIRA instances from reading/writing to the same JIRA_HOME directory and causing data corruption.

JIRA locks the JIRA_HOME directory by writing a temporary file called jira-home. lock into the root of the directory, and during shutdown, it will be removed. However, sometimes JIRA may fail to remove this file, such as during an ungraceful shutdown. In these cases, you can manually remove this locked file to unlock the directory, so that you can start up JIRA again.

> You can manually remove the locked file to unlock the JIRA_HOME directory if JIRA fails to clean it up during shutdown.

System requirements

Just like any software applications, there is a set of base requirements that need to be met before you can install and run JIRA, so it is important for you to be familiar with these requirements so you can plan out your deployment successfully. Note that these requirements are for a behind-the-firewall deployment. Atlassian also offers a SaaS based alternative called Atlassian OnDemand http://www.atlassian.com/software/ondemand/overview.

Hardware requirements

For evaluation purposes, where there will only be a small number of users, JIRA will run happily on a normal workstation computer that has a 1.5 GHz processor and 256 MB to 512 MB of RAM. As a matter of fact, many organizations start their JIRA from a simple desktop and eventually migrate onto a proper server hardware.

For production deployment, as most applications, it is recommended that you run JIRA on its own dedicated server. There are many factors that you should consider when deciding how much resource to allocate to JIRA, and also keep in mind how JIRA will scale and grow. When deciding on your hardware needs, you should consider the following:

- Number of users in the system
- Number of issues and projects in the system
- Number of concurrent users, especially during peak hours

It can be difficult at times to estimate these figures, so as a reference, a server running with 2.0+ GHz of dual/quad CPU and 1 GB of RAM will be sufficient for most instances with around 200 users. Starting with JIRA 5.1, JIRA has significantly improved its performance and scalability, especially for large deployments. It is now able to handle more than 250 thousand issues with ease.

Officially, JIRA only supports x86 hardware and 64 bit derivatives of it. When running JIRA on a 64 bit system, you will be able to allocate more than 4 Gb of memory to JIRA, a limit if you are using a 32 bit system. So, if you are planning to deploy a large instance, it is recommended that you use 64 bit.

Software requirements

JIRA has four requirements when it comes to software. It needs to run on top of an operating system, and a Java environment. It needs an application server to host and serve its contents, and a database to store all of its data. In the following sections, we will discuss each of these components and the options that you have to install and run JIRA with.

Operating systems

JIRA supports most of the major operating systems, so the choice of which operating system to run JIRA on becomes a matter of expertise, comfort, and in most cases, existing organization IT infrastructure and requirements.

The operating systems supported by Atlassian are Windows and Linux. There is a distribution for Mac OSX, however, it is not officially supported. With both Windows and Linux, Atlassian provides an executable installer wizard package that bundles all the necessary components to simplify the installation process (only available for standalone distribution).

There are minimal differences when it comes to installing, configuring, and maintaining JIRA on different operating systems. So, if you do not have any preferences and would like to keep the initial cost down, Linux is a good choice.

Java platforms

JIRA is a Java-based web application, so it needs to have a Java environment installed. This can be a **Java Development Kit (JDK)** or a **Java Runtime Environment (JRE)**. The executable installer that comes with Windows or Linux contains the necessary files and will install and configure the JRE for you. However, if you want to use the archive distributions, you will need to make sure that you have the required Java environment installed and configured.

JIRA 5 supports Java 6 or 1.6, from update 18 and above. If you run JIRA on an unsupported Java version, including its patch version, you may run into unexpected errors.

Java platforms	Support status
Oracle JDK/JRE	1.6 (update 18 or higher is required, update 24 or higher is recommended).
	1.7 is supported starting with JIRA 5.2.

Databases

JIRA stores all its data in a relational database. While you can run JIRA with HSQLDB, the in-memory database that comes bundled with JIRA, it is prone to data corruption. For this reason, it is important that you use an enterprise database for production systems.

Most relational databases available in the market today are supported by JIRA, and there are no differences when you install and configure JIRA. Just like operating systems, your choice of database will come down to your IT staff's expertise, experience, and established corporate standards. If you run Windows as your operating system, then you might probably want to go with Microsoft SQL Server. On the other hand, if you run Linux, then you should consider Oracle (if you already have a license), MySQL, or PostgreSQL.

The following table summarizes the list of databases that are currently supported by JIRA. It is worth mentioning that both MySQL and PostgreSQL are open source products, so they are excellent options if you are looking to minimize your initial investments:

Database	Support status
MySQL	MySQL 5.x (excluding 5.0)
	Requires JDBC Connector/J 5.1
PostgreSQL	PostgreSQL 8.3, 8.4
	Requires PostgreSQL Driver 8.4.x
Microsoft SQL Server	SQL Server 2008
	SQL Server 2005
	Requires JTDS 1.2.4 driver
Oracle	Oracle 11g
	Requires Oracle 11.2.x driver
HSQLDB	Bundled with standalone distribution

Take a special note of the driver requirements on each database, as some drivers that come bundled with the database vendor are not supported. If you are using the standalone distributions, the necessary drivers are included with JIRA.

Application servers

Unlike the previous versions of JIRA, JIRA 5 officially only supports Apache Tomcat as the application server. While it is possible to deploy JIRA into other application servers, you will be doing this at your own risk.

The following table shows the versions of Tomcat that are supported by JIRA 5:

Application server	Support status
Apache Tomcat	Tomcat 5.5.27 – 5.5.29
	Tomcat 6.0.32
	Tomcat 7.0.29 is supported starting JIRA 5.2

Installation options

JIRA comes in two distributions, the standalone and WAR distributions. Fundamentally, there are no differences between them. The major difference is that the standalone distribution comes bundled with Apache Tomcat, an in-memory database, and Java if you use the executable installer version.

As you can see, the standalone distribution comes with everything required to get JIRA installed. As mentioned earlier, the standalone distribution comes in two flavors, an executable installer and a ZIP archive. The executable installer provides a wizard-driven interface that will walk you through the entire installation process. It even comes with a Java installer to save you some time. The ZIP archive flavor contains everything except for a Java installer, which means you will have to install Java yourself. You will also need to perform some post-installation steps manually, such as install JIRA as a service. However, you do get the advantage of learning what really goes on under the hood.

The WAR distribution is for more advanced users who are familiar with the Java EE application deployment model. With the WAR distribution, you have to make the necessary changes to the configuration files, build your own deployable JIRA, and then deploy it to an application server; in this case, Tomcat. The advantage of using the WAR distribution is that it is very easy for you to version and control all the changes you make to the standard distribution files, which makes future upgrades much easier.

Installing JIRA

Now that you have a good understanding of the overall architecture of JIRA, the basic system requirements, and the various installation options, we are ready to deploy our own JIRA instances.

In the following exercise, we will be installing and configuring a fresh JIRA instance that will be ready for a small production team. We will be performing our installation on a Windows platform with a MySQL database server. If you are planning to use a different platform or database, please refer to the vendor documentation on installing the required software for your platform.

In this exercise, you will:

1. Install a fresh instance of JIRA.
2. Configure JIRA to an enterprise relational database.
3. Configure JIRA as a service so it will start automatically with the system.

We will continue to use this JIRA instance in our subsequent chapters and exercises as we build up our help desk implementation.

For our deployment, we will be using the following:

*   JIRA standalone distribution 5.2.5
*   MySQL 5.5.27
*   Java Development Kit 6 Update 33
*   Microsoft Windows 7

Installing Java

JIRA 5 requires **Java Runtime Environment (JRE)** version 6 update 18 or higher to run. If you already have a JDK installed, then you can skip this section. If you are not sure, then you can verify this by running the following command in a command prompt:

```
java -version
```

If you do not see a similar output, then chances are, you do not have Java installed. You will need to perform the following steps below to set up your Java environment.

To install JDK onto your system, simply perform the following steps:

1. Download the latest JDK from `http://java.sun.com/javase/downloads`.

     At the time of writing, the latest version of Java 6 is JDK 6 Update 39.

2. Double-click on the downloaded installation file to start the installation wizard.

3. Select where you would like to install Java, or you can simply accept the default values. The location where you install JDK will be referred to as `JAVA_HOME` for the rest of the book.

4. Create a new environmental variable named `JAVA_HOME` with the value of where you installed Java:

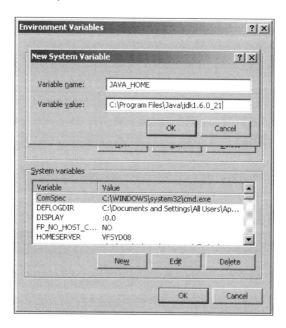

5. Test the installation by typing the following command in a new command prompt:

    ```
    java -version
    ```

This will display the version of Java installed if everything is done correctly. In Windows, you have to start a new command prompt after you have added the environment variable to see the change.

Installing MySQL

The next step is to prepare an enterprise database for your JIRA installation. JIRA requires a fresh database. If during the installation process, JIRA detects that the target database already contains any data, it will not proceed. If you already have a database system installed, then you may skip this section.

To install MySQL, simply perform the following steps:

1. Download MySQL from `http://dev.mysql.com/downloads`.

 At the time of writing, the latest version of MySQL is 5.6.10

2. Double-click on the downloaded installation file to start the installation wizard.
3. Click on **Next** on the welcome screen.
4. Select the **Typical setup** option on the next screen. If you are an experienced database administrator, you can choose to customize your installation. Otherwise, just accept the default values for all subsequent screens.
5. Once the installation is completed, make sure you select the **Configure MySQL Server now** option and click on **Finish**. This will bring up the MySQL configuration wizard:

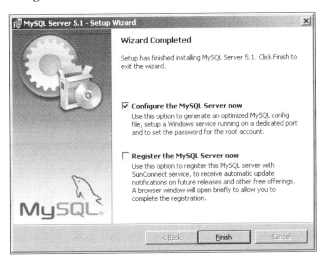

6. From the MySQL configuration wizard, select **Standard Configuration**.

7. Select both the **Install As Windows Service** and **Include Bin Directory in Windows PATH** options on the next screen. This will display the MySQL startup when the system starts up and also allow you to run the MySQL command-line tools directly:

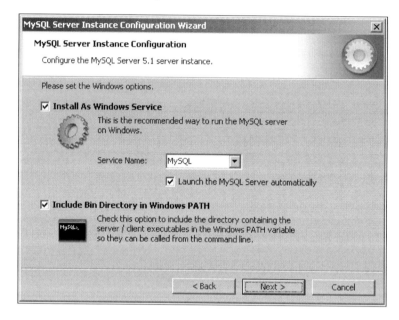

8. Configure the MySQL root user password. The username will be `root`.

9. Click on **Execute** on the next screen and MySQL will start applying the configuration options.

Prepare MySQL for JIRA

Now that you have MySQL installed, you need to first create a user for JIRA to connect to MySQL with, and then create a fresh database for JIRA to store all its data:

1. Start a new command prompt.

2. Issue the following command to connect to MySQL:

```
mysql -u root -p
```

3. When prompted for a password, enter the password you chose during configuration. This will bring up the interactive shell for MySQL.

4. Issue the following command to create a database:

```
create database jiradb character set utf8;
```

5. Here, we are creating a database called `jiradb`. You can name the database anything you like. As you will see later in this chapter, this name will be referenced when you connect JIRA to MySQL. We have also set the database to use UTF8 character encoding, as this is a requirement for JIRA. You need to ensure that the database uses the InnoDB storage engine to avoid data corruption.

6. Issue the following command:

```
grant all on jiradb.* to 'jirauser'@'localhost' identified by
'jirauser';
```

7. We are doing several things here. First, we create a user called `jirauser` and assign the password `jirauser` to him. You should change the username and password to something else.

8. We have also granted all the privileges to the user for the database `jiradb` that we just created, so that the user can perform database operations, such as create/drop tables, and insert/delete data. If you have named your database something other than `jiradb` in step 3, then make sure you change the command so that it uses your database name.

9. This allows you to control the fact that only authorized users (specified in the preceding command) are able to access the JIRA database to ensure data security and integrity.

10. To verify your setup, exit the current interactive session by issuing the following command:

```
quit;
```

11. Start a new interactive session with your newly created user:

```
mysql -u jirauser -p
```

12. You will be prompted for a password, which you have set up in the previous command as `jirauser`.

13. Issue the following command:

```
show databases;
```

14. This will list all the databases that are currently accessible by the logged-in user. You should see `jiradb` amongst the list of databases.

15. Examine the `jiradb` database by issuing the following commands:

```
use jiradb;
show tables;
```

16. The first command connects you to the `jiradb` database, so all of your subsequent commands will be executed against the correct database.

17. The second command lists all the tables that exist in the `jiradb` database. Right now, the list should be empty, since tables have been created for JIRA now, but don't worry—as soon as we connect to JIRA, all the tables will automatically be created.

Installing JIRA

With the Java environment and database prepared, you can now move on to install JIRA. Normally, there are only two steps—create and set up the `JIRA_HOME` directory and run through the JIRA setup wizard.

Obtaining and installing JIRA

The first step is to download the latest stable release of JIRA, and install the necessary files to the `JIRA_INSTALL` directory:

1. Download Atlassian JIRA from
   `http://www.atlassian.com/software/jira/download`.

   The Atlassian website will detect the operating system you are using and automatically suggest the installation package for you to download. If you intend to install JIRA on a different operating system than the one you are currently on, make sure you select the correct operating system package.

2. As mentioned earlier, with Windows, there is a Windows installer package and a self-extracting ZIP package. For the purpose of this exercise, we will use the self-extracting option as this will provide us with an insight of the steps usually hidden by the installation programs.

3. Unzip the downloaded file to your intended `JIRA_INSTALL` directory.

 Atlassian also offers installer packages for Windows and Linux, which can help you quickly get the setup.

Configuring jira-application.properties

The next step is to create the `JIRA_HOME` directory. As we have discussed earlier in the chapter, this is where JIRA keeps its data such as configurations, indexes, and attachments. It is usually a good practice to create this directory in a separate location where JIRA is installed; in other words, where the `JIRA_INSTALL` directory is:

1. Create a new directory on your filesystem. In this example, we will call it `JIRA_HOME`.

2. Open the `JIRA_INSTALL\atlassian-jira\WEB-INF\classes\jira-application.properties` file in a text editor.

3. Locate the following line:

   ```
   #jira.home =
   ```

4. Fill in the full path to your `JIRA_HOME` directory and save the file:

   ```
   jira.home = C:/JIRA_HOME
   ```

 Make sure that you remove # at the front and use a forward slash (/) instead of a backward slash (\).

The JIRA setup wizard

JIRA 5 comes with an easy-to-use setup wizard that will walk you through the installation and configuration process in four simple steps. You will be able to configure database connections, default language, and much more.

Once you complete the preceding steps, you can start up JIRA by running the `start-jira.bat` file from the `JIRA_INSTALL\bin` directory. You will see a command prompt opening up and eventually an output similar to the following screenshot, ending with `INFO: Server startup in x ms`:

```
___ Plugin System Started _____
2012-08-13 14:21:27,982 main INFO      [jira.config.database.SystemTenantDatabas
2012-08-13 14:21:28,083 main INFO      [jira.config.database.DatabaseConfigurati
2012-08-13 14:21:28,084 main INFO      [jira.config.database.DatabaseConfigurati
2012-08-13 14:21:28,087 main INFO      [jira.config.database.DatabaseConfigurati
2012-08-13 14:21:28,087 main INFO      [jira.config.database.DatabaseConfigurati
13/08/2012 2:21:28 PM org.apache.coyote.http11.Http11Protocol start
INFO: Starting Coyote HTTP/1.1 on http-8080
13/08/2012 2:21:28 PM org.apache.catalina.startup.Catalina start
INFO: Server startup in 10462 ms
```

If you see the output similar to the preceding screenshot, it means that your JIRA is up and running. Now, you can fire up your browser and point it to `http://localhost:8080` to start the setup wizard.

In the first step of the wizard, you will be asked to select **Server Language** and whether JIRA should use an internal or **External Database** connection.

The server language will determine what language will be used when users access JIRA. You will see that as soon as you make a change from the drop-down list, JIRA will automatically change its onscreen text to the selected language.

The database connection setting will determine what database JIRA will use. If you select **Internal**, JIRA will use its bundled in-memory database, which is great for evaluation purposes. If you want to use a proper enterprise database, such as in our case, you should select the **External** option.

The **Internal** option is great to get JIRA up and running quickly for evaluation purposes.

After you have selected the **External** option, the wizard will expand for you to provide the database connection details. Once you have filled in the details for your database, it is a good idea to first click on the **Test Connection** button to verify that JIRA is able to connect to the database. If everything is set up correctly, JIRA will report back with a success message, and you should be able to move onto the next step by clicking on **Next**. This may take a few minutes, as JIRA will now create all the necessary database objects. Once this is done, you will be taken to step 2 of the wizard.

In the second step, you will need to provide some basic details about this JIRA instance, and most importantly, the license key. If you have already obtained a license from Atlassian, you can cut and paste it into the **License Key** text box. If you do not have a license, you can generate an evaluation license by clicking on the **Generate an Evaluation Key** link at the bottom. An evaluation license allows you to use JIRA with its full features for three months. Once you have filled in the required properties, click on **Next** to move on to step 3 of the wizard:

Property	Description
Application Title	This is the title given to your JIRA.
Mode	**Public** will allow user signup.
	Private will disable user signup and only allow administrators to create users.
Base URL	This is the URL used to access your JIRA. It will be used for links generated by JIRA.
License Key	This is a valid license key for your JIRA. It can be either a full license or an evaluation license.

In the third step, you will be setting up the administrator account for JIRA. It is important that you keep the account details somewhere safe and do not lose the password. Since JIRA only stores the hashed value of the password instead of the actual password itself, you will not be able to retrieve it. However, there are methods for you to reset the password if you do lose it, as we will see in the later chapters. Fill in the administrator account details and click on **Next** to move on to the last step:

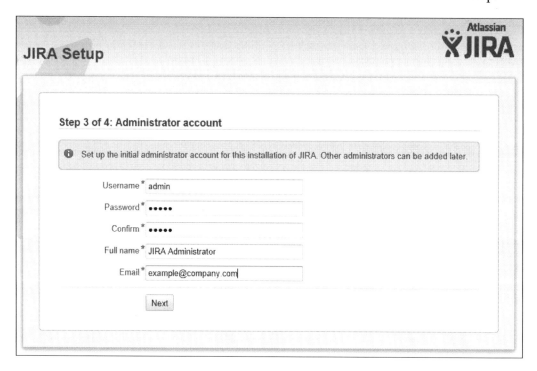

In the fourth and final step, you can set up your e-mail server details. JIRA will use the information configured here to send out notification e-mails. As you will see in *Chapter 7, E-mails and Notifications*, notification is a very powerful feature in JIRA and one of the primary methods for JIRA to communicate with the users. If you do not have your e-mail server information handy, do not worry, you can skip this step now by clicking on **Disable Email Notifications**. JIRA allows you to change your e-mail server settings anytime; we will cover the settings in *Chapter 7, E-mails and Notifications*, when we delve deeper into JIRA's notification system. After you have filled in the e-mail server details, click on **Finish** to complete the setup wizard:

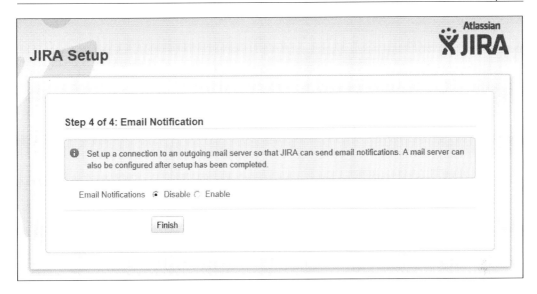

Congratulations! You have successfully completed your JIRA setup, and you will be taken directly to your new JIRA instance, with a welcome message.

Configuring JIRA as a service

Your JIRA is now installed and running, however, at the moment, if you restart your server, you will need to manually start up JIRA. In a production environment, it is usually required for applications to start up automatically when the system reboots, in events such as hardware upgrades and system patching. In Windows, this means you need to install JIRA as a service.

To configure JIRA as a Windows service, simply follow the steps below:

1. Start a new command prompt and browse to the `JIRA_INSTALL/bin` directory.

2. Run the following command:

   ```
   service.bat install JIRA
   ```

3. This will install JIRA as a Windows service. The name of the service will be **Atlassian JIRA**, followed by the name you supplied after the `install` command. So in your example, the name of the service will be **Atlassian JIRA**:

4. Verify the configuration by going to **Settings | Administrative Tools | Services**:

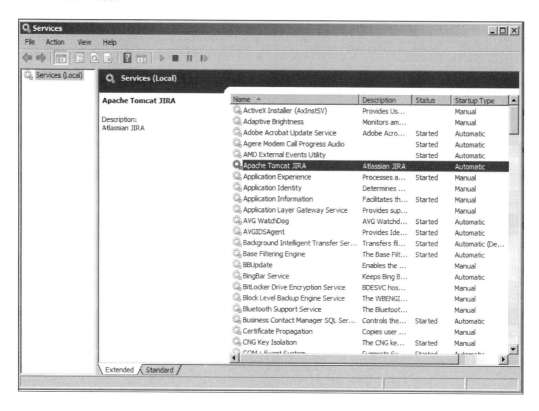

You can now start/stop/restart JIRA from the Windows services panel. You can also set JIRA to start automatically.

Post-installation configurations

The post-installation configuration steps are optional depending on your needs and environment. If you set up JIRA for evaluation purposes, you probably do not need to perform any of the following steps, but it is always a good practice to be familiar with these as a reference:

Configuring the application server

In both standalone and WAR distributions, you can configure some of the applications server settings, such as context path and port number. This is useful, for example, if you have multiple servers running on the same machine, then they can co-exist by listening on different port numbers. If JIRA is the only application running on your machine, then you may choose not to make any changes. Another reason you might want to change the port number to a standard port such as 80 instead of 8080, is so that you will not need to type in the port number as a part of the URL.

To configure the settings, locate and open the `server.xml` file in a text editor. The file can be found in the `JIRA_INSTALL/conf` directory:

```
<Server port="8005" shutdown="SHUTDOWN">
... ... ... ...
<Connector port="8080" protocol="HTTP/1.1">
... ... ... ...
<Context path="/jira" docBase="${catalina.home}/atlassian-jira"
reloadable="false" useHttpOnly="true">
```

Let's examine the relevant contents in this file:

- **Line 1**: This line specifies the port for command to shutdown JIRA/Tomcat. By default, it is port 8005. If you already have an application that is running on that port (usually another Tomcat instance), you need to change this to a different port.

- **Line 2**: This line specifies which port JIRA/Tomcat will be running on. By default, it is port 8080. If you already have an application that is running on that port, or if the port is unavailable for some reason, you need to change it to another available port.

- **Line 3**: This line allows you to specify the context that JIRA will be running under. By default, the value is empty, which means JIRA will be accessible through the URL of `http://hostname:portnumber`. If you decide to specify a context, the URL will be `http://hostname:portnumber/context`. In our example here, JIRA will be accessible through the URL of `http://localhost:8080/jira`.

Configuring HTTPS

By default, JIRA runs with standard, non-encrypted HTTP protocol. This is acceptable if you are running JIRA in a secured environment, such as an internal network. However, if you plan to open up access to JIRA over the Internet, you will need to tighten up security by encrypting sensitive data, such as usernames and passwords that are being sent, by enabling HTTPS (HTTP over SSL).

For a standalone installation, you will need to perform the following tasks:

- Obtain and install a certification
- Enable HTTPS on your application server (Tomcat)
- Redirect traffic to HTTPS

First, you need to get a digital certificate. This can be from a certification authority such as VeriSign (CA certificate), or a self-signed certificate generated by you. CA certificate will not only encrypt data for you, but also identify your copy of JIRA to users. A self-signed certificate is useful when you do not have a valid CA certificate and you are only interested in setting up HTTPS for encryption. Since a self-signed certificate is not signed by a Certification Authority, it is unable to identify your site to the public, and users will be prompted with a warning that the site is untrusted when they first visit it. However, for evaluation purposes, a self-signed certificate will suffice until you can get a proper CA certificate.

For the purpose of this exercise, we will create a self-signed certificate to illustrate the complete process. If you have a CA certificate, you can skip the following steps.

Java comes with a handy tool for certificate management called **keytool**, which can be found in the JAVA_HOME\lib directory. To generate a self-signed certificate, run the following commands from a command prompt:

```
keytool -genkey -alias tomcat -keyalg RSA
keytool -export -alias tomcat -file file.cer
```

This will create a keystore (if one does not already exist) and export the self-signed certificate (file.cer). When you run the first command, you will be asked to set the password for the keystore and Tomcat. You need to use the same password for both. The default password is changeit. You can specify a different password of your choice, but you then have to let JIRA/Tomcat know, as we will see later.

Now that you have your certificate ready, you need to import it into your trust store for Tomcat to use. Again, you will use the keytool application in Java:

```
keytool -import -alias tomcat -file file.cer JAVA_HOME\jre\lib\security\
cacerts
```

This will import the certificate into your trust store, which can be used by JIRA/Tomcat to set up HTTPS.

To enable HTTPS on Tomcat, open the `server.xml` file in a text editor from the `JIRA_INSTALL/conf` directory. Locate the following configuration snippet:

```
<Connector port="8443" maxHttpHeaderSize="8192" SSLEnabled="true"
maxThreads="150" minSpareThreads="25" maxSpareThreads="75"
enableLookups="false" disableUploadTimeout="true"
acceptCount="100" scheme="https" secure="true"
clientAuth="false" sslProtocol="TLS" useBodyEncodingForURI="true"/>
```

This enables HTTPS for JIRA/Tomcat on port 8443. If you have selected a different password for your keystore, you will have to add the following line to the end of the preceding snippet, before the closing tag:

```
keystorePass="<password value>"
```

The last step is to set up JIRA so that it automatically redirects from a non-HTTP request to an HTTPS request. Find and open the `web.xml` file in the `JIRA_INSTALL/atlassian-jira/WEB-INF` directory, and add the following snippet to the end of the file, before the closing `</web-app>` tag:

```
<security-constraint>
  <web-resource-collection>
    <web-resource-name>all-except-attachments</web-resource-name>
    <url-pattern>*.js</url-pattern>
    <url-pattern>*.jsp</url-pattern>
    <url-pattern>*.jspa</url-pattern>
    <url-pattern>*.css</url-pattern>
    <url-pattern>/browse/*</url-pattern>
  </web-resource-collection>
  <user-data-constraint>
    <transport-guarantee>CONFIDENTIAL</transport-guarantee>
  </user-data-constraint>
</security-constraint>
```

Now, when you access JIRA with a normal HTTP URL, such as `http://localhost:8080/jira`, you will be automatically redirected to its HTTPS equivalent, `https://localhost:8443/jira`.

Installing the database drivers

With the standalone distributions, JIRA comes bundled with the necessary database drivers for all the supported database systems. However, if you are using the WAR distribution or if for some reason, the database driver gets corrupted, you will need to manually obtain and install the driver.

To install a database driver, simply perform the following steps:

1. Obtain the database driver from the vendor.
2. Copy the driver (usually a JAR file) into your JIRA_INSTALL/lib directory.
3. Restart JIRA so the driver can be properly loaded.

Managing the database setup

As we have already seen, the JIRA setup wizard takes care of setting up the database connection for us during the installation process. However, there will be times when you will need to make changes to this. The database name or user credentials may have changed, or there may be a need to use a different database altogether.

When the wizard sets up your database connections, these settings are written to a file called dbconfig.xml in the JIRA_HOME directory. Now, you can edit this file directly in a text editor, or you can use a built-in GUI tool to help you with this.

 Before you make any changes, make sure you make a back up of the dbconfig.xml file, in case you need to roll back the changes.

The tool is called **JIRA Configuration Tool**, a utility application that comes bundled with JIRA. You can find the application in the JIRA_INSTALL/bin directory called config.bat. Double-click on the file to start the application.

Click on the **Database** tab once the application starts up. You will see that all the configuration options are populated with the settings you just configured:

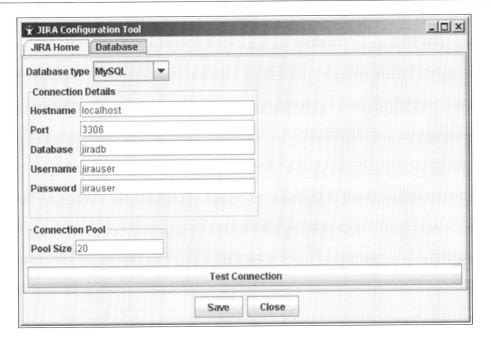

To verify that your settings are correct, make sure that the database is running and click on the **Test Connection** button. If everything is correct, you should see a confirmation message as shown in the preceding screenshot. From now on, you can use this utility application to update database configurations for JIRA, and you will know what files are being touched when changes occur.

Summary

JIRA is a powerful and yet simple application, as reflected by its straightforward installation procedures. You have a wide variety of options to choose how you would like to install and configure your copy. You can mix and match different aspects, such as operating systems, and database to best suit your requirements. The best part is that you can have a setup that is comprised entirely of an open source software that will bring down your cost and provide you with a reliable infrastructure at the same time.

Now that you have a working instance of JIRA, we will start to explore various aspects of JIRA in the following chapters, starting with projects, which are the first key components in any JIRA installation.

2
Project Management

JIRA initially started off as a bug tracking system, helping software development teams to better track and manage their projects. Over the years, JIRA has improved on its features to add support for Scrum and Kanban through the GreenHopper add-on, enabling projects to be managed via both the traditional waterfall model and newer agile methodologies.

In this chapter, we will first start with a high-level view of the overall hierarchy on how data is structured in JIRA. We will then take a look at the various user interfaces that JIRA has for working with projects, both as an administrator and an everyday user. We will also introduce permissions for the first time in the context of projects, and will expand on this in later chapters.

By the end of this chapter, you will have learned:

- How JIRA structures contents
- Different user interfaces for project management in JIRA
- How to create new projects in JIRA
- How to manage and configure a project
- How to manage components and versions

The JIRA hierarchy

Like most other information systems, JIRA organizes its data in a hierarchical structure. At the lowest level, we have **fields**, which are used to hold raw information. Then we have **issues**, which are like a unit of work to be performed. An issue will belong to one project, which defines the context of the issue. Finally, we have **project categories**, which logically group similar projects together. We will discuss each of these levels in the following sections:

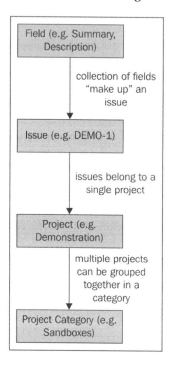

Project category

Project category is a logical grouping for projects, usually of similar nature. Project category is optional. Projects do not have to belong to any category in JIRA. When a project does not belong to any category, it is considered uncategorized. The category itself does not contain any information, as we will see later in this chapter and later chapters. Project categories can be a helpful way to organize all you projects in JIRA, especially when you have many of them.

Project

In JIRA, a **project** is a collection of issues. Projects provide the background context for issues by letting users know where issues should be raised. A project also defines various 'rules' and 'boundaries' for its issues, such as who will have permission to view the issues, and notifiy recipients when changes are made against an issue.

It is important to remember that projects are not limited software development projects that need to deliver a product. They can be anything logical, such as the following:

- Company department or team
- Software development projects
- Products or systems
- A risk register

Issue

Issues represent work to be performed. From a functional perspective, an issue is the base unit for JIRA. Users create issues and assign them to other people to be worked on. Project leaders can generate reports on issues to see how everything is tracking. In a sense, you can say JIRA is issue-centric.

We will be looking at issues in more details in *Chapter 3, Issue Management*. For now, you just need to remember three things:

- An issue has to belong to one and only one project
- There can be many different types of issues
- An issue contains many fields that hold values for the issue

Field

Fields are the most basic unit of data in JIRA. They hold data for issues and give meaning to them. Fields in JIRA can be broadly categorized into two distinctive categories, namely system fields and custom fields. They come in many different forms, such as text fields, drop-down lists, and user pickers. Fields and their related topics are discussed in more depth in *Chapter 4, Field Management*. For now, you just need to remember three things:

- Fields hold values for issues
- Fields can have behaviors (hidden or mandatory)
- Fields can have a view and structure (text field or drop-down list)

Project permissions

Before we start working with projects in JIRA, we need to first understand a little bit about permissions. **Permission** is a big topic and we will be covering that in detail in *Chapter 8, Securing JIRA*. For now, we will briefly talk about the permissions related to creating and deleting, administering, and browsing projects.

In JIRA, users with the JIRA administrator permission will be able to create and delete projects. By default, users in the `jira-administrators` group have this permission, so the administrator user we have created during the installation process in *Chapter 1, Getting Started with JIRA*, will be able to create new projects, and we will be referring to this user and any other users with this permission as **JIRA Administrator**.

For any given project, users with the **Administer Project** permission for that project will be able to administer the project's configuration settings. As we will see in the later sections in this chapter, this includes updating the project's name and description, managing the versions and components, and who will be able to access this project. We will be referring to users with this permission as **Project Administrator**. By default, the JIRA Administrator will have this permission.

If a user needs to browse the contents of a given project, then he must have the **Browse Project** permission for that project. This means the user will be able to create and view issues in that project (assume all other permissions allow for it). By default, the JIRA Administrator will have this permission.

As you have probably realized already, one of the key differences in the three permissions is that the JIRA Administrator's permission is global, which means, a user either has it or not. The Administrator Project and Browse Project permissions are project specific. A user may have the Administer Project permission for project A, but only Browse Project permission for project B. As we will see in *Chapter 8, Securing JIRA*, this allows you to set up your JIRA instance in such a way that you can effectively delegate permission controls, so you can still have centralized control on who can create and delete projects, but not get over-burdened with having to manually manage each project on its own settings. Now with this in mind, let's first take a look at JIRA from the JIRA Administrator user's view.

JIRA Administration

As we have seen earlier, users with the JIRA Administrator's permission are the only ones allowed to create and delete projects, and this is done through the JIRA Administration interface. It can be accessed as follows:

1. Log in to JIRA with a username that has the JIRA Administrator's permission.

2. Click on the **Administration** link at the top-right corner:

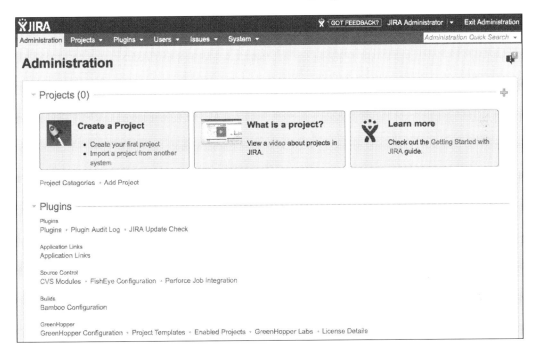

The JIRA Administration interface is where JIRA administrators can manage and control all the aspects of JIRA, including setting up projects, managing users, backing up and restoring the system, and requesting support from Atlassian, to just name a few. You can leave this interface by clicking on the **Exit Administration** link at the top-right corner.

If you are familiar with previous versions of JIRA, you will notice that in JIRA 5, this interface looks completely different. **Atlassian** has been revamping JIRA's user interface, making it cleaner and easier for the end users. In the older versions of JIRA, all the administration options are listed in a menu bar to the left-hand side, in JIRA 5 however, all the options are grouped together and laid out nicely under appropriate headings.

Creating projects

If you have a brand new JIRA, as we have, where you have no pre-existing projects, the JIRA **Administrator** interface will have three blue boxes at the top. You can click on the **Create your first project** in the first box to bring up the **Add a new project** dialog box. However, you can also use the plus sign at the right-hand side or from the **Projects** drop-down menu and select the **Add Project** menu item. All the three options will have the same effect:

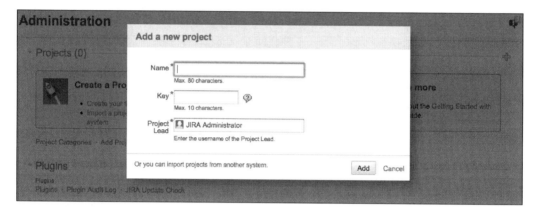

You will notice that unlike the JIRA versions, JIRA 5 will present you with a dialog box with only three fields to fill in, namely **Name**, **Key**, and **Project Lead**. All the other fields, such as notification scheme, are no longer required. As the projects are often created with the default settings, it is much more efficient to remove those settings at creation time, and you can update all the settings later, when you really need to:

Field	Description
Name	A unique name for the project.
Key	A unique identity key for the project. This key cannot be changed once the project is created. As you type the name of your project, JIRA will auto fill the key based on the name, but you can change the auto-generated key with one of your own.
	The project key will also become the first part of the issue key for issues created in the project.
Project Lead	The lead of the project. Each project can only have one lead.

Once you have created the new project, you will be taken to the **Project Administration** interface, which we will discuss in the following sections, where you, as a project administrator, can update the settings and delete the project.

Project interfaces

There are two distinctive interfaces for projects. The first interface is designed for everyday users, providing useful information on how the project is going with graphs and statistics, called **Project Browser**.

The second interface is designed for project administrators to control project configuration settings, such as permissions and workflows, called **Project Administration**.

Since when you first create a project, the first interface you see will be Project Administration, we will start our discussion around this interface and then move on to the Project Browser interface.

Project administration

The Project Administration interface is where project administrators can manage the settings and configurations for their projects. For example, you can change the project's name, select what issue types will be available for the project, and manage a list of components within the project. As we have seen earlier, any user with the Administer Projects permission for a given project will be able to access this interface.

1. Browse to the JIRA **Administration** interface.
2. Bring down the **Projects** menu from the top navigation bar and select the **Projects** menu item.

3. Select a project from the list. This will take you to the **Project Administration** interface:

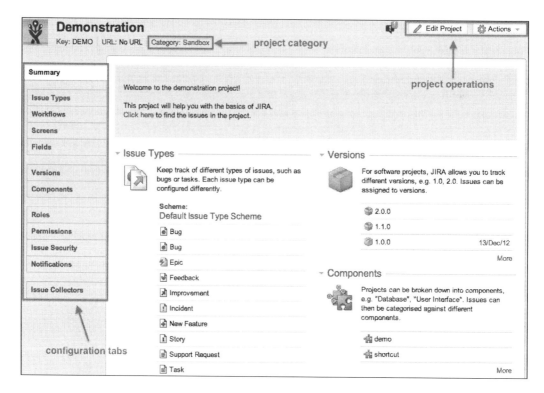

From the Project Administration page, you will be able to perform the following key operations:

- Update project details, such as project name, description, and avatar
- Manage what users see when working on the project, such as issue types, fields, and screens
- Control permission settings and notifications
- Manage the list of available components and versions

JIRA 5 has a brand new Project Administration layout. Compared to the previous JIRA versions, this new layout is more organized, and is much easier for project administrators to find out the current project configuration settings. One of the major differences, especially when compared to JIRA 3 and the earlier versions of JIRA 4, is that all settings are broken into their own individual tabs, and nicely grouped together in terms of relevance. By default, there are five tabs on the Project Administration page.

The Summary tab

The first group consists of a single tab, the **Summary** tab. On this tab, JIRA displays a single page view on all the current configuration settings for the project. Not all the settings will have their own tabs. So those that do not have a tab will also be shown here, on the **Summary** tab.

On this tab, you can edit the project's general information, such as its name and description, set the project's category, and delete the project.

The Components tab

The **Components** tab is where project administrators can manage the components for their projects. Components can be thought of as subsections that make up the full project. In a software development project, components can be various modules that the final product comprises.

In JIRA, components are project specific. This means that components from one project cannot be used in a different project. This also allows each project to maintain its own sets of components. As we will see in the later chapters, there are configuration items in JIRA where the values are shared across all projects.

A component has four pieces of information:

Field	Description
Name	This is a unique name for the component.
Description	This is an optional description to offer more explanation on what the component is for.
Component Lead	This is an optional field where you can select a single user as the lead for the component. For example, in a software project, this can be the main developer for the component.
Default Assignee	This tells JIRA when an issue is created without the assignee being selected. If the issue has a component, then JIRA will auto assign the issue to the selected default assignee.

One of the changes in JIRA 5 is that you can manage your project's components all on one tab, including create, edit, and update:

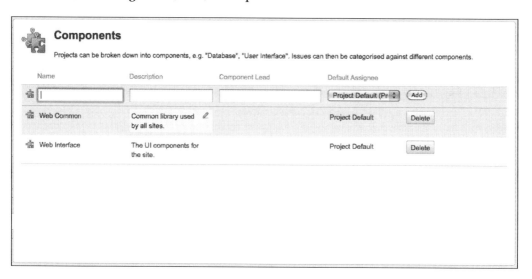

Creating components

Unlike some older versions of JIRA, you can create new components directly from the **Components** tab:

1. Browse to the **Components** tab for the target project.
2. Provide a unique name for the component. JIRA will let you know if the name is already taken.
3. Provide a short description for the new component.
4. Select a user to be the lead of the component. Just start typing and JIRA will prompt you with options that meet the criteria.
5. Click on **Add** to create the new component.

Once you have created the new component, it will be added to the list of existing components. When a component is first created, it will be placed at the top of the list. If you refresh the page, the list will then be ordered alphabetically.

Managing components

As mentioned earlier, the **Components** tab in JIRA 5 allows you to directly edit and delete the existing components. You will be able to edit specific fields of each component, without jumping through different pages.

If you want to edit a component's name, all you need to do is hover your mouse over the component's name and you will see that the name field is highlighted. Click on the name to make the field editable, make your changes, and click on **Update**. If you want to delete a component, all you have to do is to click on the **Delete** button next to the target component.

Component lead and default assignee

As explained in the preceding section, one of the useful features of components is the ability to assign a default assignee to each individual component. This means, when a user creates an issue and does not select an assignee, JIRA will be able to automatically assign the issue based on the component selected. This is a very powerful feature where in an organization, members of various teams often do not know each other. So when it comes to assigning issues at creation time, it is difficult to decide who to assign it to. With this feature, it can be set up so that the lead of the component becomes the default assignee and the issues raised can then be delegated to other members of the team.

For our demo project, each of our supported systems has a system expert, which is represented as the lead of the respective component. When the business user logs a ticket and selects a component, the ticket will go directly to the lead. This setup is also flexible enough. If the user knows who to best assign the ticket to, he or she can directly assign the ticket to the member of the team and the automatic assignment will not take place.

If the issue has more than one component with a default assignee, the assignee for the first component in alphabetical order will be used.

The Versions tab

Like the **Components** tab, the **Versions** tab allows project administrators to manage versions for their projects. Versions serve as milestones for a project. In project management, versions represent points in time. While for projects that are not product-oriented, versions may seem to be something that is less relevant, versions can still be invaluable at managing and tracking the progress of issues and work.

As with components, versions also have a number of fields:

Field	Description
Name	This is a unique name for the version.
Description	This is an optional description to offer more explanation on what the version is for.
Release Date	This is an optional date that will be marked as the scheduled date to release the version. Versions that are not released according to the release date will have the date highlighted in red.

Very similar to the **Components** tab, in JIRA 5, you can create, update, and delete versions all on the single tab. This makes managing large number of versions a much simpler job.

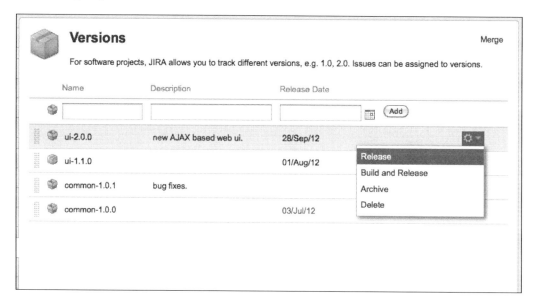

Creating versions

Creating new versions is as simple as providing the necessary details for the new version and hitting the **Add** button:

1. Browse to the **Versions** tab for the target project.
2. Provide a unique name for the version (for example, 1.1.0, v2.3). JIRA will let you know if the name is already taken.

3. Provide a short description for the new version.

4. Select the date for when the version will be released by using the date picker.

5. Click on **Add** to create the new version.

Unlike components, versions will not be ordered automatically by JIRA, so you will have to manually maintain the order. In the older versions, project managers will have to manually click on the up and down arrow keys repeatedly to move the version to the correct location. In JIRA 5, all you have to do is hover your mouse pointer over to the left of the version, and you will be able to drag the version up and down the list.

Managing versions

Just like managing components, the **Versions** tab of JIRA 5 uses the in-place editing feature. So, you just need to click on the field of the version to editor update the value and click on **Update**.

When you hover over a version, you will notice that there is a little action icon to the right. If you click on that, you will have the options to do the following:

Option	Description
Release	This will mark the version as released; meaning it is completed or shipped. When you release a version, JIRA will automatically check to make sure that all the issues are completed for the selected version. If these are incomplete, you will be prompted to either ignore those issues or push them to a different version.
	If the version has already been released, it will change to **Unrelease**.
Build and Release	This is similar to the **Release** option, but it also performs a build via Atlassian Bamboo, if there are any software codes. The version will only be released if the build is successful.
	This option is not available if the version is already released.
Archive	This will mark the version as archived; meaning that the version is stored away until further notice. When a version is archived, you cannot release or delete it until it is unarchived.
Delete	This will delete the version from JIRA. Again, JIRA will search for issues that are related to this version and prompt you if you would like to move these issues to a different version.

The Issue Collectors tab

This is in fact an add-on that is now bundled with JIRA 5.1. If you are familiar with web browsers such as FireFox, you are probably familiar with add-ons. As we will be covering add-ons in *Chapter 10, General Administration*, all you need to know for now is that they are sometimes referred to as plugins, and they are small applications that can be installed on top of JIRA to provide additional functionalities.

So, if you do not have the Issue Collectors add-on installed, you will not see this tab. The The Issue Collector add-on lets you create and add dialog boxes that can be added to any websites you may have, so users can provide their feedback and these will be captured automatically in JIRA. We will cover the Issue Collectors add-on in *Chapter 10, General Administration*, when we introduce a number of other useful add-ons that will make JIRA work harder for you.

Other tabs

There are a number of other tabs on the Project Administration interface. We will not get into the details for these tabs, as they will each be covered in their own chapters later. We will, however, take a quick tour to look at what each tab does:

Tab	Description
Issue Types	This controls the types of issue that users can create for the project. For example, this may include **Bugs**, **Improvements**, and **Tasks**.
	Issue Types will be covered in *Chapter 3, Issue Management*.
Workflows	This controls the workflow issues that we will go through. Workflows consist of a series of steps that usually mimic the existing processes that are in place for the organization.
	Workflows will be covered in *Chapter 6, Workflows and Business Processes*.
Screens	**Screens** are what users see when they create and edit issues in JIRA.
	Screens will be covered in *Chapter 5, Screen Management*.
Fields	**Fields** are what JIRA uses to capture data from users when they create issues. JIRA comes with a set of default fields, and the JIRA administrator is able to add additional fields as needed.
	Fields will be covered in *Chapter 4, Field Management*.
People	The project administrators can define roles in the project and assign users to them. These roles can then be used to control permissions and notifications.
	People will be covered in *Chapter 8, Securing JIRA*.

Tab	Description
Permissions	As we have already seen, permissions define who can perform certain tasks or have access in JIRA.
	Permissions will be covered in *Chapter 8, Securing JIRA*.
Issue Security	JIRA allows users to control who can view the issues they have created, by selecting the issue security level.
	Issue security will be covered in *Chapter 8, Securing JIRA*.
Notifications	JIRA has the ability to send out e-mail notifications when certain events occur. For example, when an issue is updated, JIRA can send out an e-mail, alerting all users who participate on the issue of the change.
	Notifications will be covered in *Chapter 7, E-mails and Notifications*.

Project Browser

We have seen the Project Administration interface, which is designed for project administrators. For most users, Project Browser is the interface they will be using with JIRA. Project Browser acts like the home page of a project, providing much useful information, such as issue statistics, recent user activities, and source control information.

To access the Project Browser interface, you first need to make sure that you have the **Browse Project** permission, and then select the project you wish to browse. The easiest way to select your project is to find your project from the projects listing.

The project category revisited

Remember at the start of the chapter, we said that project category helps you to organize and group similar projects together? Well, here is the first example where you will see how project category may be useful.

First, we will go to the projects listing where JIRA will list all the projects we have; make sure you do not do this from the JIRA Administration interface. If in doubt, check if there is an **ExistAdministration** link at the top-right corner. If you see that, then you are in JIRA Administration and you need to click on the link to exit. Now, perform the following steps to bring up the projects list:

1. Bring down the **Projects** menu from the top navigation bar.

2. Click on **View All Projects** in the menu. This will take you to the projects listing:

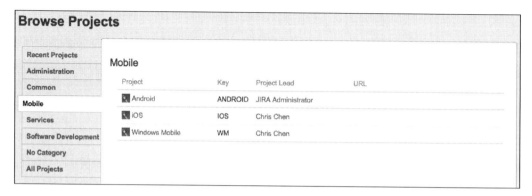

If you have set up project categories and assigned projects to them, JIRA will display your list of projects in their own categories. In our example, the projects **Android**, **iOS**, and **Windows Mobile** are in the **Mobile** category. So, when the category is selected, only those three projects will be displayed. This can be useful when you have a lot of projects and it can be difficult when you have to sort through the large list.

Browsing a project

From the project listing, if you click on the project's name, you will be taken to the Browse Project interface:

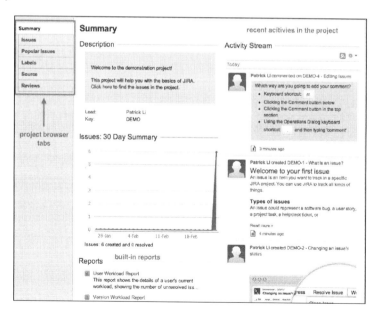

Just like the Project Administration interface, the Project Browser is made up of several tabs:

The Browser tab	Description
Summary	Displays a quick overview of the project. You can also access predefined reports and search filters directly here.
Issues	Displays a breakdown of issues in the project grouped by attributes, such as priority and status.
Road Map	Displays all the unreleased versions for the project.
Change Log	Displays all the released versions for the project.
Popular Issues	Displays a list of unresolved issues, ordered by popularity (votes).
Versions	Displays the summary of unreleased versions of the project. This tab is only available when versions are configured.
Components	Displays the summary of components and their related issues. This tab is only available when components are configured for the project.
Labels	Displays all the available labels in the project. Labels can be assigned to issues as tags.
Source	Displays change sets from Atlassian FishEye and Stash
Reviews	Displays code reviews from Atlassian Crucible.

The Summary tab

The **Summary** tab provides you with a single page view into the project you are working with. It provides you with a quick glance of the project with key information, including the following:

- Project description
- Unresolved issues that are due to be completed
- Unreleased versions due to be released
- Recently-updated issues
- Recent activities performed on the issues in this project
- Summary graph showing issue created versus issue resolved
- The **Summary** tab is also where you will be able to generate project reports and run search filters. Both, reports and filters are covered in *Chapter 9, Searching, Reporting, and Analysis*.

The Issues tab

The **Issues** tab provides users with a nice breakdown of issues within the project. Issues are broken down and grouped by several key factors, such as priority and assignee, giving users a quick overview of the project's state. For example, **Unresolved: By Assignee** lets you know how many open issues are being assigned to each user, allowing the project team to better plan their resource allocation:

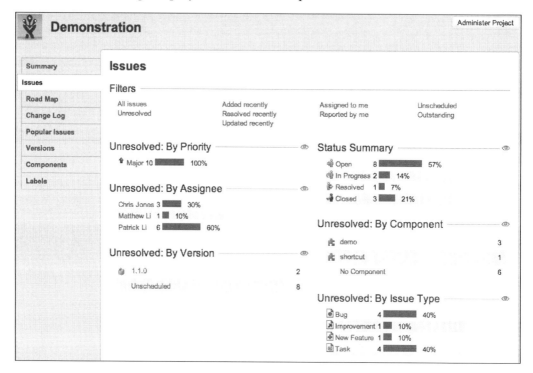

The Road Map tab

The **Road map** tab breaks down issues based on the versions they belong to. If you have set up versions in JIRA, then this tab will show you the upcoming unreleased versions and issues that need to be completed before the version can be completed.

The Change Log tab

Similar to the **Roadmap** tab, the **Change Log** tab breaks down issues based on versions. The difference is that the **Change Log** tab shows the versions that have already been released. This is very useful when you have to go back and check what has been achieved and completed for each of the past versions, providing you with a lot of changes.

The Versions/Components tab

The **Versions** and **Components** tabs list all the available versions and components that have been configured for this project respectively. If the user is also the project administrator, then there will be links for the user to add new versions and components respectively.

The Source/Reviews tab

The **Source** and **Reviews** tabs require you to have the Altassian FishEye, Stash, and Crucible applications to be installed. Once installed, the tabs will pull in data from the applications and display them. If you do not have the required applications installed and configured, the tabs will prompt you to install the applications. FishEye and Stash are great tools to manage your code repositories, from browsing code contents to reviewing commits and changes. Stash is specially designed to support DVCS repositories, such as Git. Crucible is another application from Atlassian that allows your developers to collaborate with code reviews. Installing and configuring FishEye, Stash and Crucible are beyond the scope of this book.

The help desk project

Now that we have seen all the key aspects that make up a project, let's revisit what we have learned so far and put them to practice. In this exercise, we will be setting up a project for our support teams:

- A new project category for all support teams
- A new project for our help desk support team
- Components for the systems supported by the team
- Versions to better manage issues created by users

Creating a new project category

Let's start by creating a project category. We will create a category for all of our internal support teams and their respective support JIRA projects.

Please note that this step is optional, as JIRA does not require any project to belong to a project category:

1. Log in to JIRA with a user who has JIRA Administrator's permission.
2. Click on the **Administration** link at the top-right corner.
3. Bring down the **Projects** menu and select **Project Categories**.

4. Fill in the fields as shown in the next screenshot.

5. Click on **Add** to create the new project category:

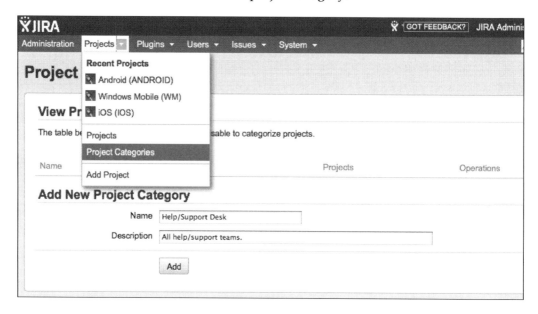

Creating a new project

Now that we have a project category created, let's create a project for our help desk support team. To create a new project, perform the following steps:

1. Browse to the JIRA Administration interface.

2. Bring up the **Add a new project** dialog box by either selecting **Add Project** from the **Projects** menu or by clicking on the little plus icon at the top-right corner.

3. Name our new project Support Desk – Global, and accept the other default values for **Key** and **Project Lead**.

4. Click on **Add** to create the new project.

You should now be taken to the Project Administration interface of your new project.

Assigning a project to a category

Having your project created, you need to assign the new project to your project category, and you can do this directly from the Project Administration interface:

1. Click on the **None** link next to **Category**, right underneath the project's name.

2. Select your **Help/Support Desk** project category.

3. Click on **Select** to assign the project:

Creating new components

As discussed in the earlier sections, components are subsections of a project. This makes logical sense for a software development project, where each component will represent a software deliverable module. For other types of project, components may first appear useless or inappropriate.

It is true that components are not for every type of projects out there, and this is the reason why you are not required to have them by default. Just like everything else in JIRA, all the features come from how you can best map them to your business needs.

The power of component is more than just a flag field for an issue. For example, let's imagine that the company you are working for has a range of systems that need to be supported. These may range from phone systems and desktop computers to other business applications. Let's also assume that our support team needs to support all of the systems. Now, that is a lot of systems to support. To help manage and delegate, we will create a component for each of the systems the help desk team supports. We will also assign a lead for each of the components. This setup allows us to establish a structure where the **Help Desk** project is led by the support team lead, and each component is led by their respective system expert (who may or may not be the same as the team lead). As we will see in the later chapters, this allows for a very flexible management process when we start wiring in other JIRA features, such as notification schemes:

1. Browse to the Project Administration interface for the `Support Desk - Global` project.

2. Select the **Components** tab.

3. Type `Internal Phone System` for the new component's name.

4. Provide a short description for the new component.

5. Select a user to be the lead of the component. Since you only have one user in your system at the moment, we will put admin as the component lead.

6. Click on **Add** to create the new component.

Creating new versions

As we discussed earlier, while versions are most applicable for projects with deliverables, they can still be helpful for tracking and reporting purposes. For our **Support Desk** project, we can use versions to represent different calendar months, and each ticket or incident raised by users will have a version number attached. This way, it will be very easy for the management to pull up a report to see how many issues are being raised for any given month:

1. Select the **Versions** tab.

2. Type August for **Version Name**.

3. Provide a short description for the new version.

4. Click on the calendar icon and select the last day for **Release Date**.

5. Click on **Add** to create the new version.

Putting it together

Now that you have fully prepared your project, let's see how everything comes together by creating an issue. If everything is done correctly, you should see a dialog box similar to the next screenshot, where you can choose your new project to create the issue in, and also the new components and versions should be available for selection too:

1. Leave the JIRA Administration interface by clicking on the **Exit Administration** link.

2. Click on **Create Issue** near the top-right corner. This will bring up the **Create Issue** dialog box.

3. Select **Support Desk – Global** for **Project**.

4. Select **Bug** for **Issue Type**.

5. Click on the drop-down arrow for **Component/s**, **Affects Version/s**, and **Fix Version/s**; the components and versions we have created earlier should be available for selection.

6. Fill in the other fields with some dummy data.

7. Click on the **Create** button to create the issue:

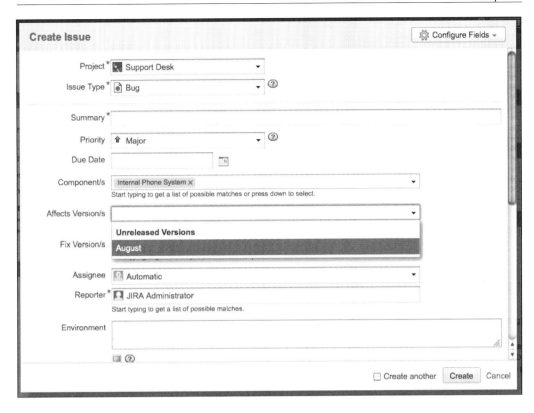

We will be exploring issues in more details in the next chapter.

If everything goes well, the issue will be created in the new project.

Summary

In this chapter, we have looked at one of the most important concepts in JIRA, projects, and how to create and manage them. Permissions have also been introduced for the first time, and we looked at three permissions that are related to creating and deleting, administering, and browsing projects.

We have been introduced to the various interfaces JIRA provides for project administrators and everyday users, the Project Administration interface, and Project Browser interface respectively.

Let's conclude this chapter by starting on our exercise to implement a support desk system. In the next chapter, you will be introduced to another important concept in JIRA, **issues**.

3
Issue Management

In the previous chapter, you saw that JIRA is a very flexible and versatile tool that can be used in different organizations for different purposes. A software development organization will use JIRA to manage its software development lifecycle and bug tracking, while a customer services organization may choose to use JIRA to track and log customer complaints and suggestions. For this reason, issues in JIRA can represent anything that is applicable to the real-world scenario. Generally speaking, an **issue** in JIRA often represents a unit of work that can be acted upon by one or more people.

In this chapter, we will explore the basic and advanced features offered by JIRA for you to manage issues. We will also look at some of the changes that JIRA 5 brings, which will make it more efficient to work with issues. By the end of this chapter, you will have learned the following:

- Issues and what they are in JIRA
- Creating, editing, and deleting issues
- Moving issues between projects
- Expressing your interest in issues through voting and watching
- Advanced issue operations, including uploading attachments and linking issues

Understanding issues

In JIRA, an issue can represent any number of things. In fact, an issue in a given project may mean something that is very different in another project. So what an issue really is depends upon the context of what project it is in, and how you choose to define and use JIRA. For example, an issue in a normal software development project would often represent a software bug, while in a help desk project it can represent a support request.

Despite all the different objects an issue can represent, there are a number of key aspects that are common for all issues in JIRA, as follows:

* An issue must belong to a project.
* It must have a type, otherwise known as an issue type, which indicates what the issue is representing.
* It must have a summary. The summary acts like a one-line description of what the issue is about.
* It must have a status. A status indicates where along the workflow the issue is at a given time. We will discuss workflows in *Chapter 6, Workflows and Business Processes*.

What does an issue look like?

As we have discussed, an issue in JIRA can be anything in the real world to represent a problem domain. It can be a software bug, a help desk ticket, or a customer request. But, what does an issue look like in JIRA? How does JIRA achieve this level of flexibility and still present it in a consistent manner?

Let's first take a look at an issue in JIRA. The following screenshot shows a typical example of an issue and breaks it down into more digestible sections, followed by an explanation of each of the highlighted sections in a table. This view is often called the **Issue Summary** or the **View Issue page**:

These sections are described in the following table:

Section	Description
Project / Issue Key	It shows the project the issue belongs to. The issue key is the unique identifier of the current issue. This section acts as a breadcrumb for easy navigation.
Issue Summary	It is a brief summary of the issue.
Issue View Options	These are the various view options for the issue. The options include **XML**, **Excel**, and **Word**.
Issue Operations	These are the operations that users can perform on the issue, such as edit, assign, and comment. These are covered in the later sections of this chapter.
Workflow Options	These are the workflow transitions available. Workflow will be covered in *Chapter 6, Workflows and Business Processes*.
Issue Details / Attributes	This section lists the issue fields such as issue type and priority. Custom fields are also displayed in this section. Fields will be covered in *Chapter 4, Field Management*.
User Fields	This section is specific for user-type fields such as assignee and reporter. Fields will be covered in *Chapter 4, Field Management*.
Date Fields	This section is specific for date-type fields such as **Create** and **Due date**. Fields will be covered in *Chapter 4, Field Management*.
Vote / Watch Issue	These are the options that allow users to vote and watch an issue.
Attachments	These list all the attachments on an issue.
Comments	These list all the comments that are visible to the current user.

Working with issues

As we have seen, issues are the center of JIRA. So, it should be no surprise that JIRA 5 (and especially 5.2) comes with many new features and enhancements for working with issues. In the following sections, we will look at what you as a user can do with issues and some of the new features in JIRA 5:

- Create/edit changes
- In-line editing
- Sharing issues
- Remote issue link

Creating an issue

When creating a new issue, you will need to fill in a number of fields. Some fields are mandatory, such as the issue's summary and type, while others are optional, such as the issue's description. We will discuss fields in more details in the next chapter.

There are several ways in which you can create a new issue in JIRA. You can choose any of the following options:

1. Click on the **Create Issue** link at the top of the screen.
2. Select the **Create Issue** option for the **Issues** drop-down menu.
3. Press *C* on your keyboard:

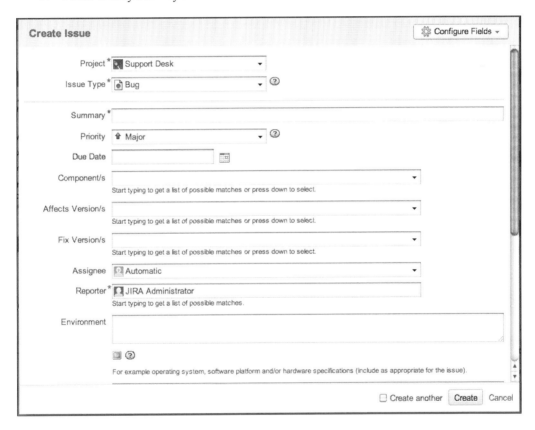

This will bring up the **Create Issue** dialog box, as shown in the preceding screenshot. As you can see, there are quite a few fields, and the required fields will have a red asterisk mark next to their names. By default, all the fields will be displayed in the dialog box.

Since only a handful of them are really required, as a user, you can actually choose to "hide" some of the optional fields by performing the following steps:

1. Click on the **Configure Fields** option at the top-right corner.

2. Select the **Custom** option.

3. Uncheck all the fields you want to hide, and check the fields that you want to show:

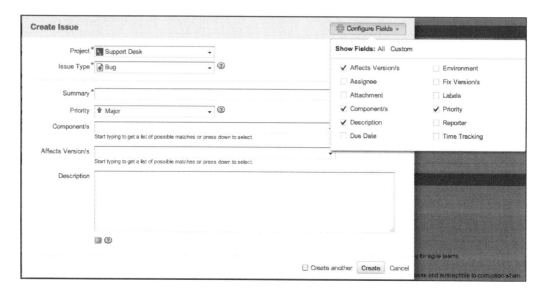

 You are only hiding or showing these fields for yourself. Only the JIRA administrator can actually hide and show fields globally for all users.

There is a new **Create another** option beside the **Create** button in JIRA 5. By ticking this option and then clicking on the **Create** button, the **Create Issue** dialog box will stay on the screen and remember what you have previously typed in. In this way, you can avoid having to fill in the whole dialog box again and will only have to update some of the fields that actually are different, such as **Summary**. With this new feature, you can rapidly create many issues in a much shorter time frame.

Editing an issue

In the earlier versions of JIRA, when you wanted to edit existing issues, you had to click on the **Edit** button, wait for the **Issue Edit** page to load, scroll down the page to find the fields you wanted to update, make the change, and finally, save the update. This works well, but if all you want to change is a single field, then all these steps may seem very inefficient.

Starting with JIRA 5.1, as a part of the effort to make JIRA easier to use and more efficient, a new feature called **in-line editing** has been introduced. With this new feature, you will be able to edit the fields while viewing the page, without ever needing to wait for extra page loads.

However, one thing to note is that the new in-line editing feature only works for fields that are present on the **View Issue** page. Generally, this means that the field needs to have a value set, but we will see in *Chapter 5, Screen Management*, how you can create different screens for viewing and editing issues. In these cases, you will need to use the classic edit option.

To edit an in-line issue, all you have to do is hover your mouse over the value for the field you want to update, wait for the **Edit** icon to show up, click the icon, and start editing:

Deleting an issue

You can delete an issue from JIRA. You might need to delete issues that have been created by mistake, or if the issue is redundant, although normally, it is better to close and mark the issue as a duplicate. We will discuss closing an issue in *Chapter 6, Workflows and Business Processes*.

 Issue deletion is permanent in JIRA. Unlike some other applications that may put deleted records in a trash bin, which you can retrieve later, JIRA completely deletes the issue from the system. The only way to retrieve the deleted issue is by restoring JIRA with a previous backup.

Perform the following steps to delete an issue:

1. Browse to the issue you wish to delete.
2. Click on the **Delete** option from the **More Actions** menu. This will bring up the **Delete Issue** dialog box.
3. Click on the **Delete** button to remove the issue permanently from JIRA.

Deleting an issue permanently removes it from JIRA, along with all of its data including attachments and comments.

Moving an issue between projects

Once an issue has been created, the issue is associated with a project. You can, however, move the issue around from one project to another. This may sound like a very simple process, but there are many steps involved and things to consider.

First, you need to decide on a new issue type for the issue if the current issue type does not exist in the new project. Second, you will need to map a status of the issue. Third, you will need to decide on the values for the fields that exist in the new project but do not exist in the current project; if those fields are set to mandatory in the new project. Sounds like a lot? Luckily, JIRA comes with a wizard that is designed to help you address all those items.

Perform the following steps to start moving an issue:

1. Browse to the issue you wish to move.
2. Click on the **Move** option in the **More Actions** menu bar. This will bring up the **Move Issue** wizard.

There are essentially four steps in the **Move Issue** wizard.

The first step is to select which project you wish to move the issue to. You will also need to select the new issue type. If the same issue type exists in the new project, it is recommended that you continue to use the same issue type:

The second step allows you to map the current issue to the new project's workflow. If the current and target projects use the same workflow, the wizard will skip this step:

The third step shows all the fields that exist in the new project but not the current project and requires a value. Again, if there are no missing fields, this step will be skipped:

The fourth and last step shows you the summary of the changes that will be applied, by moving the issue from project A to project B. This is your last chance to make sure that all the information is correct. If there are any mistakes, you can go back to step one and start over again. If you are happy with the changes, confirm the move by clicking on **Move**:

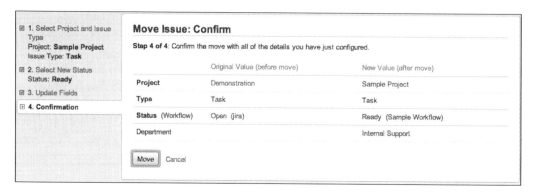

Casting a vote on an issue

The most straightforward way to express your interest in a JIRA issue is to vote for it. For organizations or teams that manage their priorities based on popularity, voting is a great mechanism to collect this information.

An example of this is how Atlassian uses JIRA (for example, `https://jira.atlassian.com/browse/JRA-9`) as a way to let its customers choose and vote what features they want to be implemented or bugs to be fixed, by voting on issues based on their needs. This allows the product management and marketing team to have an insight on the market needs and how to best evolve their offerings.

One thing to keep in mind is when voting, you can only vote ONCE per issue. You can vote many times for many different issues, but for any given issue, you have only one vote. This helps prevent a single user from continuously voting on the same issue, which may blow the final statistics out of proportion. You can, however, unvote a vote you have already casted on an issue, and vote for it again later; if you choose to do this, it will still only count as one vote.

To vote for an issue, simply click on the thumbs-up icon next to **Votes**. When you have voted for an issue, the icon will appear as colored. When you have not yet voted for an issue, the icon will appear gray.

Receiving notifications on an issue

JIRA is able to send automated e-mail notifications about updates on issues to users. Normally, notification e-mails will only be sent out to the issue's reporter, assignee, and people who have registered interest in the issue. This behavior can be changed through **Notification Schemes**, which we will discuss in *Chapter 7, E-mails and Notifications*.

You can register your interest in the issue by choosing to watch the issue. By watching an issue, you become a watcher of an issue and will receive e-mail notifications on activity updates. Users watching the issue can also choose to stop watching, thus stop receiving e-mail updates from JIRA.

To watch an issue, simply click on the **Watch** link. When you are already watching the issue, the text will be **Watching**. If you click on the link again, you will stop watching the issue. In JIRA 5, you will automatically be set to watch issues you have created:

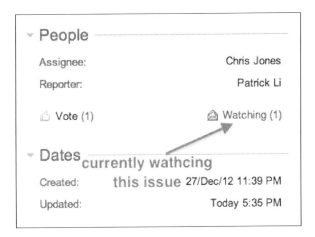

JIRA also shows how many people are actively watching the issue by displaying the total watchers next to the watch icon. You can click on the number or the **Watchers** link to bring up the **Watchers** page, which will show a list of users that are currently watching the issue.

Assigning issues to others

Once an issue has been created, the user normally assigned to the issue will start working on it. However, this does not mean that the issue will stay with the same person forever.

There are many instances where an issue needs to be reassigned to a different user. For example, the current assignee may be unavailable, or if issues are created with no specific assignees. Another example will be that issues are assigned to different people at different stages of the workflow. For this reason, JIRA allows users to reassign issues once they have been created.

Perform the following steps to assign an issue:

1. Browse to the issue you wish to assign.
2. Click on the **Assign** option in the **Issue** menu bar. This will bring up the **Assign Issue** page.
3. Select the new assignee for the issue, and optionally add a comment to provide some information to the new assignee.
4. Click on the **Assign** button.

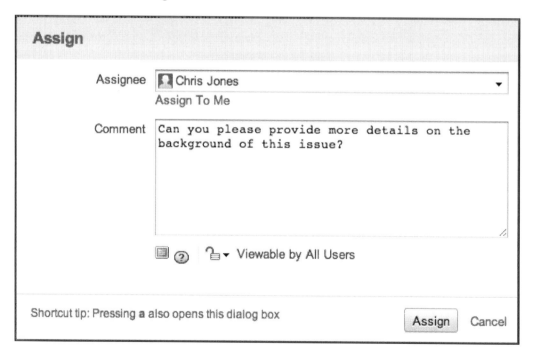

Once this issue has been reassigned, its assignee value will be updated to the new assignee. The new assignee will also receive a notification e-mail, alerting him/her that a new issue has been assigned and waiting to be worked upon. It is also possible to keep an issue unassigned. Unassigned issues do not have an assignee and will not show up on anyone's list of active issues.

Issue linking

Back in the older versions of JIRA, issues could only be linked to other issues in the same JIRA instance. In JIRA 5, Atlassian has introduced a new feature called **Remote issue links**, which lets issues be linked to any arbitrary resources. For example, for a support type issue, you can link it to a web page that contains information on how to resolve similar types of problems. Another example will be to link the issue to another issue on a different JIRA instance.

Enabling issue linking

Issue linking is enabled by default when you first install JIRA. Issue linking is configured globally, so once it is enabled, it will become available for all projects in JIRA.

You need to be a JIRA administrator in order to enable issue linking. Perform the following steps to enable issue linking:

1. Log in as a JIRA administrator user.
2. Browse to the administration console by clicking on the **Administration** link at the top navigation panel.
3. Click on **Issue Linking** under the **Issue Features** section. This will take you to the **Issue Link Administration** page.

4. Click on **Activate** to enable issue linking in JIRA:

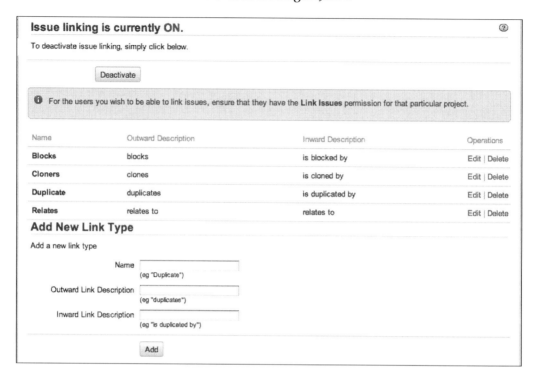

From this page, you will be able to see a list of **Link Types** available. A link type defines the nature of the link between issues. As shown in the preceding screenshot, the default **Blocks** link type defines that issue A blocks issue B. This means that issue B cannot be completed until issue A is resolved. It is important to note that issue linking does not place any restrictions on issues. So in our example, although the link states that issue B cannot be completed until issue A is done, this is not enforced and users can close issue A while issue B remains open.

All the link types shown here are for standard issue links. There are no remote issue link types. However, you do need to enable issue linking to make use of remote issue links.

Creating link types

JIRA comes with four link types by default: Blocks, Cloners, Duplicate, and Relates. As we have discussed earlier, a link type is simply a type of association or a label on the association, that describes the relationships between two issues, and so you can define your own link types in JIRA. For example, one issue can support another issue, and we can create a link type called Supports.

Perform the following steps to create a new link type:

1. Browse to the **Issue Linking Administration** page.

2. Make sure issue linking is enabled.

3. Fill in the **Add New Link Type** form. Do the following for the **Support** link type:

    1. Enter Supports for the **Name** field
    2. Enter supports for the **Outward Link Description** field
    3. Enter is supported for the **Inward Link Description** field

4. Click on the **Add** button.

Outward and inward link descriptions define what is shown when users select the type of link to use when linking two issues together. We will see an example of this in a later section. Once a new link type is added, it will be displayed in the table on the **Issue Linking Administration** page:

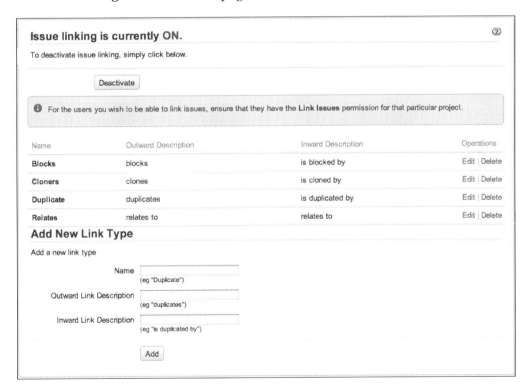

Linking other issues

Issues are often related to other issues in some way. For example, issue A might be blocking issue B, or issue C might be a duplicate of issue D. You can add descriptions to the issue to capture this information, or delete one of the issues in the duplication case, but with this approach, it is hard to keep a track of all these relationships. Luckily, JIRA provides an elegant solution for this, with the standard issue link feature.

The **standard issue link** lets you link an issue with one or more other issues in the same JIRA instance. So, you can link two issues from different projects together (if you have access to both the projects). Linking issues this way is very simple; all you need to know is whether the target issues to a link or not:

1. Browse to the **View Issue** page for the issue you wish to create a link for.

2. Select **Link** from the **More Actions** menu. This will bring up the **Link Issue** dialog box.

3. Select the **JIRA Issue** option from the left panel.

4. Select the type of issue linking.

5. Select the issues to link to. You can use the search facility to help you locate the issues you want.

6. Click on the **Link** button:

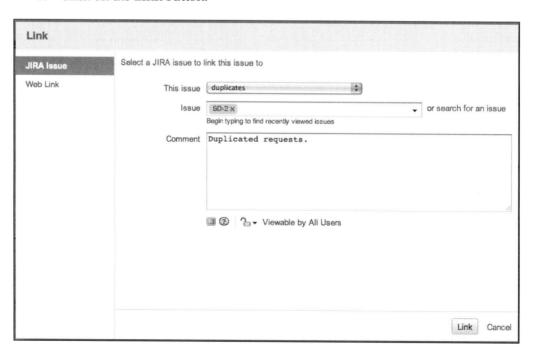

After you have linked your issues, they will be displayed in the **Issue Links** section on the **View Issue** page. JIRA will display the target issue's key, description, priority, and status.

Linking remote contents

The standard JIRA issue link allows you to link multiple issues in the same JIRA instance, the new JIRA 5 remote issue link lets you link issues from different JIRA instances, and other resources such as a web page on the Internet.

Using remote issue links is very similar to the standard issue link; the difference is that instead of selecting another issue, the URL address of the target resource is specified:

1. Open up the **Link Issue** dialog box.

2. Select the **Web Link** option from the left panel.

3. Specify the URL address for the target resource. JIRA will automatically try to find and load the appropriate icon for the resource.

4. Provide the name for the link in **Link Text** field. The name you provide here will be what is shown for the link when viewing the issue.

5. Click on the **Link** button:

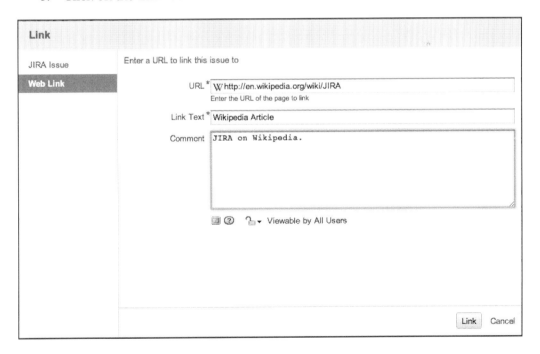

Issue cloning

When you need to create a new issue and you already have a baseline issue, JIRA allows you to quickly create it with the data based on your existing issues, by cloning the original one. Cloning an issue allows you to quickly create a new one with most of its field populated.

A cloned issue has the same values as the original issue for its fields such as description, issue type, and priority; it is a separate entity nonetheless. Further actions performed on either of the two issues will not affect the other.

When an issue is being cloned, a **Clone** link is automatically created between the two issues, establishing a relationship.

Cloning an issue in JIRA is simple and straightforward. All you have to do is specify a new summary for the cloned issue:

1. Browse to the issue you wish to clone.
2. Select **Clone** from the **More Actions** menu. This will bring up the **Clone Issue** page.
3. Type in a new summary for the new cloned issue.
4. Click on the **Create** button.

Once the issue is successfully cloned, you will be taken to the issue summary page for the newly cloned issue.

Time tracking

Since issues often represent a single unit of work that can be worked upon, it is logical for users to log the time they have spent working on it. You can specify an estimated effort required to complete an issue, and JIRA will be able to help you track the progress. JIRA displays the time tracking information of an issue in the **Time Tracking** panel at the right-hand side:

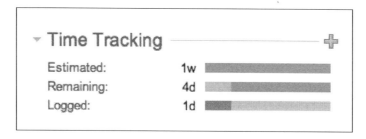

- **Estimated**: This represents the original estimated effort required to complete the issue.

- **Remaining**: This represents the remaining time for the issue to be completed. It is calculated automatically by JIRA based on the original estimate and total time logged by users. However, the user logging work on the issue, as described in the following section, can also override this value.

- **Logged**: This represents the total time logged by all users on this issue.

Enabling time tracking

Time tracking is enabled by default when you install JIRA. However, if it is disabled on your system, for example, if you have upgraded from an older version of JIRA, which has time tracking disabled by default, you can re-enable it. Perform the following steps to enable time tracking:

1. Log in as a JIRA administrator user.

2. Browse to the administration console by clicking on the **Administration** link at the top navigation panel.

3. Click on **Time Tracking** under the **Issue Features** section. This will take you to the **Time Tracking** page.

4. Click on **Activate** to enable issue linking in JIRA:

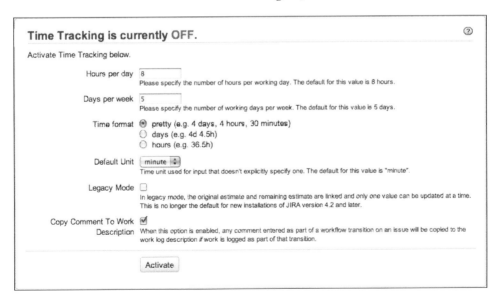

You can set several parameters on the **Time Tracking** page. As we will see in later sections, these parameters will determine the time tracking behavior for JIRA:

Parameter	Description
Hours per day	This is the number of working hours per day in JIRA. For example, if this is set to eight hours per day, when the user puts in 16 hours, JIRA will automatically convert it to two days.
Days per week	This is the number of working days per week in JIRA. For example, if this is set to five days per week, when the user puts in 10 days, JIRA will automatically convert it to two weeks.
Time format	This is the format in which JIRA will display time in the **Time Spent** field.
Default Unit	This is the default time tracking unit if the user does not supply one.
Legacy Mode	This will make JIRA use the old time tracking behavior.
Copy Comment To Work Description	This is a very handy feature, where JIRA will automatically copy comments made during a workflow transition (workflow will be discussed in *Chapter 6, Workflows and Business Processes*) that allows time logging.

Specifying original estimates

Original estimate represents the anticipated time required to complete the work represented by the issue. It is shown as the blue bar under the **Time Tracking** section.

In order for you to specify an original estimate value, you need to make sure that time tracking is enabled and the **Time Tracking** field is added to the issue's create and/or edit screen. We will discuss fields and screens in *Chapter 4, Field Management* and *Chapter 5, Screen Management*, respectively.

To specify an original estimate value, provide a value for the **Original Estimate** field on the create issue and/or edit issue screen.

Logging work

Logging work in JIRA allows you to specify the amount of time (work) you have spent working on an issue. You can log work against any of the issues, provided that **Time Tracking** is enabled and you have permission to do so. We will cover permissions in *Chapter 9, Searching, Reporting, and Analysis*.

Perform the following steps to log work against an issue:

1. Browse to the issue you wish to log work against.
2. Select **Log Work** from the **More Actions** menu. This will bring up the **Log Work** page.
3. Enter the amount of time you wish to log. Use w, d, h, and m to specify week, day, hour, and minute respectively.
4. Select the date you wish to log your work against.
5. Optionally, select how the remaining estimate should be adjusted.
6. Optionally, add a description to the work you have done.
7. Optionally, select who can view the work log entry.
8. Click on the **Log** button:

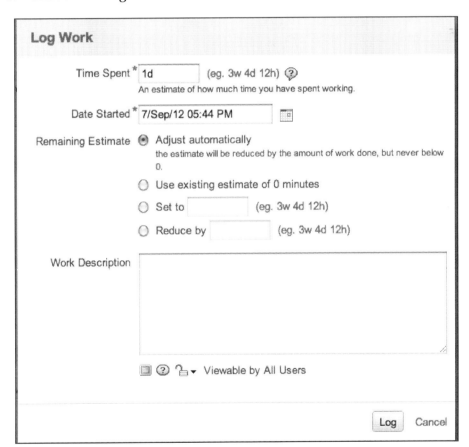

When you log work on an issue, you have the option to choose how the **Remaining Estimate** value will be affected. By default, this value will be automatically calculated by subtracting the amount logged from the original estimate. You can, however, choose other options available, such as setting the remaining estimate to a specific value or reducing it by an amount that is different to the amount of work being logged.

Issues and comments

JIRA lets users create comments on issues. As we have already seen, you will be able to create comments when assigning an issue to a different user. This is a very useful feature that allows multiple users to collaborate to work on the same issue and share information. For example, the support staff (issue assignee) may request more clarification from the business user (issue reporter) by adding a comment to the issue. When combined with JIRA's built-in notification system, automatic e-mail notifications will be sent to the issue's reporter, assignee, and any other users watching the issue. Notifications will be covered in *Chapter 7, E-mails and Notifications*.

Adding comments

By default, all logged-in users will be able to add comments to issues they can access. Perform the following steps to add a comment to an issue:

1. Browse to the issue you wish to add a comment for.
2. Click on the **Comment** option in the **Issue** menu bar. This will bring up the **Comment input** section.
3. Type a comment into the text box. The text box will adjust its size as you type.
4. Click on the **Add** button to add the comment:

Once a comment has been added, the comment will be visible in the **Comments** tab in the **Issue Activity** section:

Managing your comments

After you have added your comment to an issue, you can edit its contents, security settings, and delete it altogether. To edit or delete a comment, simply hover over the comment and the comment management option will appear to the right-hand side:

Permalinking a comment

From time to time, you will want to refer other people to a comment you have made previously. While you can tell them the issue and let them scroll down to the bottom until they find your comment amongst hundreds of others, JIRA allows you to create a quick permalink to your comment that will take you directly to the comment of interest.

Perform the following steps to create a permalink for a comment:

1. Browse to the comment you wish to permalink.
2. Hover over the comment to bring up the comment management options.
3. Click on the permalink icon. This will highlight the comment in pale blue.

You will now notice that your browser's URL bar will look something similar to `http://sample.jira.com/browse/DEMO-1?focusedCommentId=10100 &page=com.atlassian.jira.plugin.system.issuetabpanels:comment- tabpanel#comment-10100` (notice the `focusedCommendId` section after the issue key). Copy and paste that URL and give it to your colleagues; once they click on this link, they will be taken directly to the highlighted comment.

Attachments

As we have seen so far, JIRA uses fields such as summary and description to capture data. This works for most cases, but when you have complex data such as application log files or screenshots, fields become insufficient. This is where attachments come in. JIRA allows you to attach files to issues as support documents.

Enabling attachments in JIRA

Attachments are saved as files on the JIRA file server and not in the database, so you need to ensure that there is sufficient disk space to accommodate the volume of attachments for now and future growth. As attachments are not stored in the database, JIRA will not backup the files as a part of its backup process. Attachments need to be backed up separately.

Attachments are enabled by default in JIRA, so users will be able to attach files to issues as soon as JIRA is installed. However, if it is disabled for some reason, you can re-enable it. Perform the following steps to enable attachments for JIRA:

1. Log in to JIRA as a JIRA administrator.
2. Browse to the administration console by clicking on the **Administration** link at the top navigation panel.

3. Click on **Attachments** under the **Advanced** section at the bottom-right end of the page. This will take you to the **Attachment Settings** page.

4. Click on the **Edit Settings** button. This will bring up the **Edit Attachment Settings** page.

5. Select **Use Default Directory** for the **Attachment Path**.

6. Click on the **Update** button to enable attachments in JIRA.

On the **Attachment Settings** page, as shown in the following screenshot, there are a few options that you will need to configure when enabling attachments in JIRA:

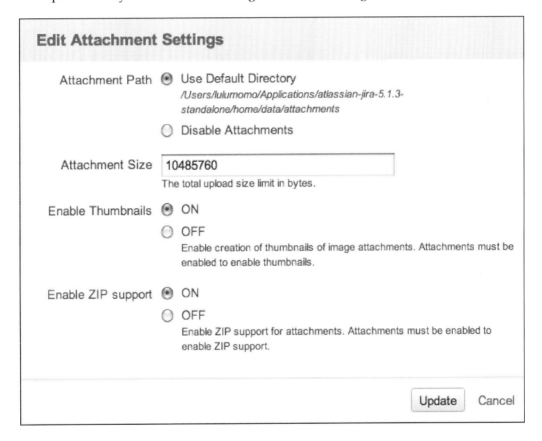

The following table summarizes the configuration options:

Options	Description
Attachment Path	This specifies the location where attachments will be stored on the filesystem. The only options are the default directory, which is inside your JIRA_HOME directory, or disabled attachments in JIRA.
Attachment Size	This specifies the maximum size of the attachment that users can upload.
Enable Thumbnails	This specifies whether or not to enable thumbnail generation when the attachment is an image.
Enable ZIP support	This specifies whether or not to enable ZIP support, which allows users to download multiple attachments as a single ZIP file, and also view the contents of ZIP attachment files.

Attachments are enabled and disabled globally across JIRA. You cannot selectively enable or disable attachment functions on a per project basis. You can, however, achieve a similar result by controlling the permission around who can attach files. Permissions are discussed in *Chapter 8, Securing JIRA*.

Attaching files

JIRA allows you to attach any arbitrary files to issues. These can be image files, Microsoft Office documents, and other binary files. Perform the following steps to attach a file to an issue:

1. Browse to the issue you wish to attach a file.
2. Select **Attach File** from the **More Actions** menu. This will bring up the **Attach Files** page.
3. Click on the **Browse** button to select the file you wish to attach.
4. Optionally, provide a comment for the attached file. The comment will be added as a normal comment to the issue.
5. Optionally, select the security level for who can see the comment.
6. Click on the **Attach** button:

 There are a few things you need to keep in mind when attaching files to JIRA:

The file name cannot contain the following characters – \, /, \ ", %, :, $, ?, and *.

Attaching screenshots

Apart from letting you attach any files to an issue, JIRA also allows you to directly attach a screenshot from your system clipboard to issues. This saves you from having to take a screenshot, save it as a physical file on the disk, and finally attach it to JIRA.

Perform the following steps to attach a screenshot:

1. Browse to the issue you wish to attach a screenshot.
2. Select **Attach Screenshot** from the **More Actions** menu. This will bring up the **Attach Screenshot** page.
3. Click on **Yes** when prompted for whether you want to trust the applet.
4. Click on the **Paste** button and the screenshot will be pasted into the panel above.
5. Enter a file name for the screenshot or accept the default name.
6. Optionally, provide a comment for the attached file. The comment will be added as a normal comment to the issue.
7. Optionally, select the security level for who can see the comment.
8. Click on the **Attach** button.

Just like attaching a file to JIRA, the same file name restriction applies to attaching a screenshot.

Issue types and subtasks

As seen earlier, issues in JIRA can represent many things ranging from software development tasks to project management milestones. Issue type is what differentiates one issue from another.

Each issue has a type (therefore the name issue type), which is represented by the issue type field. This lets you know what type of issue it is, and also helps determine many other aspects of it, such as what fields will be displayed for this issue.

JIRA comes with a set of default issue types, as shown in the following table:

Issue type	Description
Bug	A problem that impairs or prevents the functions of the product
Improvement	An enhancement to an existing feature
New feature	A new feature of the product
Task	A task that needs to be done

The default issue types are great for simple software development projects, but they do not necessarily meet the needs of others. Since it is impossible to create a system that can address everyone's needs, JIRA lets you create your own issue types and assigns them to projects. For example, for a help desk project, you might want to create a custom issue type called `ticket`. You can create this custom issue type and assign it to the Help Desk project and users will be able to log tickets, instead of bugs in the system.

Issue types are managed through the **Manage Issue Types** page. Perform the following steps to access this page:

1. Log in to JIRA as a JIRA administrator.

2. Browse to the administration console by clicking on the **Administration** link at the top navigation panel.

3. Click **Issue Types** under the **Issue Types** section at the bottom-right of the page:

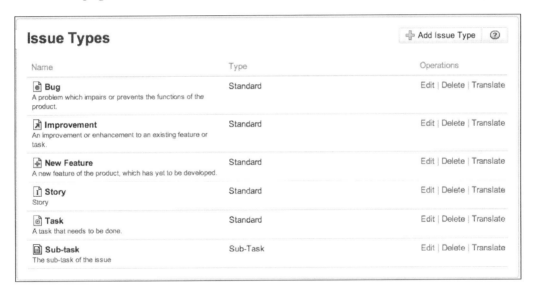

Creating issue types

You can create any number of issue types. Perform the following steps to create a new issue type:

1. Browse to the **Manage Issue Types** page.

2. Click on the **Add Issue Type** button.

3. Type a unique name for the new issue type.

4. Type in a general description for the issue type.

5. Select if the new issue type will be a standard issue type or a subtask issue type.

6. Click on the **select image** link to bring up the **Icon selection** page.

7. Select an image icon.

8. Click on **Add** to create the new issue type.

Deleting issue types

When deleting an issue type, you have to keep in mind that the issue type might already be in use; meaning there are issues created with that issue type. So, if you delete an issue type, you will need to select a new one for those issues. The good news is that JIRA takes care of this for you. As shown in the next screenshot, we delete the **Bug** issue type and JIRA informs us of the already existing three issues of type **Bug**. You will need to assign them to a new issue type, such as **Improvement**.

Perform the following steps to delete an existing issue type:

1. Browse to the **Manage Issue Types** page.

2. Click on the **Delete** link for the issue type you wish to delete. This will bring up the **Delete Issue Type** page. If there are existing issues with the issue type you are trying to delete, you will be asked to select a new issue type.

3. Select the new issue type for the existing issues. Once deleted, those issues will be automatically updated to the new issue type.

4. Click on the **Delete** button to delete the issue type:

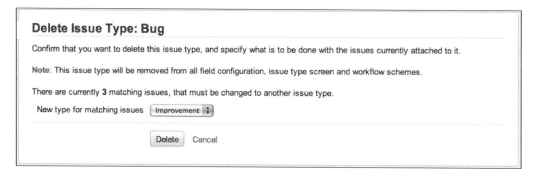

Subtasks

JIRA allows only one person (assignee) to work on one issue at a time. This design ensures that an issue is a single unit of work that can be tracked against one person. However, in the real world, we often find ourselves in situations where we need to have multiple people working on the same issue. This may be caused by a poor breakdown of tasks or simply because of the nature of the task at hand. Whatever the reason, JIRA provides a mechanism to address this problem through subtasks.

Subtasks are similar to issues in many ways, and as a matter of fact, they are a special kind of issue. They must have a parent issue, and their issue types are flagged as subtask issue types. You can say that all subtasks are issues, but not all issues are subtasks.

For every issue, you can have one or more subtasks that can be assigned and tracked separately from one another. Subtasks cannot have other subtasks. JIRA allows only one level of subtasks.

Enabling subtasks

Subtasks are enabled by default. If you have subtasks disabled for some reason, you will need to enable this feature.

Perform the following steps to enable subtasks in JIRA:

1. Log in to as a JIRA administrator user.
2. Browse to the administration console by clicking on the **Administration** link at the top navigation panel.
3. Click on **Sub-Tasks** under **Issue Types** section. This will take you to the **Sub-Tasks Administration** page.
4. Click on **Enable** to enable subtasks in JIRA.

Creating subtasks

Since subtasks belong to an issue, you need to browse to the issue first before you can create a new subtask:

1. Browse to the issue you wish to create subtasks for.
2. Select **Create Sub-Task** from the **More Actions** menu.

You will see the familiar **Create Issue** dialog box. However, one thing you will notice is that, unlike when you are creating an issue, you do not select which project to create the subtask in. This is because JIRA can determine the project value based on the parent issue. You will also notice that you can only select issue types that are subtasks.

Other than these differences, creating a subtask is no different than creating a normal issue. You can customize the fields shown on the dialog box and choose to rapidly create multiple subtasks by selecting the **Create another** option.

Once the subtask has been created, it will be added to the **Sub-Tasks** section of the parent issue. You will see all the subtasks that belong to the issue and their status. If a subtask has been completed, it will have a green tick next to it:

Issue type schemes

Issue type schemes are templates or collections of issue types that can be applied to projects. As shown in the next screenshot figure, JIRA comes with **Default Issue Type Scheme**, which is applied to all projects that do not have specific issue type schemes applied.

When a new issue type is created in JIRA, it is added to **Default Issue Type Scheme**. This means that the new issue type will be available to all the projects by default. This will become a problem when you start to have specialized projects such as help desk, and issue types such as **Bug** become inappropriate:

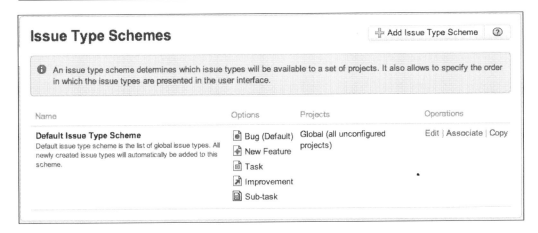

To overcome this problem, JIRA lets us group a collection of issue types together. We can also rearrange the order of the issue types within the collection so that they appear in the drop-down list in a logical manner to the users. In effect, we create an issue type scheme, a template for issue types, and their order, which can be reused and applied to one or more projects.

We will create a new issue type scheme for our example JIRA implementation later in the chapter.

Creating issue type schemes

Perform the following steps to create a new issue type scheme:

1. Log in to JIRA as a JIRA administrator.

2. Browse to the administration console by clicking on the **Administration** link at the top navigation panel.

3. Click on **Issue Types Schemes** under the **Issue Types** section. This will bring you to the **Manage Issue Type Scheme** page.

4. Click on the **Add Issue Type Scheme** button.

5. Provide a name for the new issue type scheme in **Scheme Name**.

6. Drag the issue types you want to be part of the scheme from the **Available Issue Types** list and drop them into the **Issue Types for Current Scheme** list.

7. Select a **Default Issue Type** value. Note that you can only select a default issue type after you have selected at least one issue type for the new scheme.

8. Click on the **Save** button:

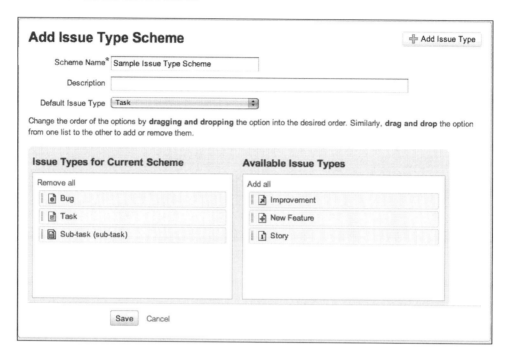

After the issue scheme has been created, you will need to associate it with the projects you want to apply the scheme to. The simplest way to do this is to click on the **Associate** link for the issue type scheme and then select the projects you want. This allows you to apply the scheme to multiple projects at once.

The Help Desk project

In this exercise, we will continue our setup for the project we have created in the previous chapter. We will add the following configurations to our project:

- A set of new issue types that are specific to our help desk project
- A new scheme to limit the selection of issue types

Creating issue types

Since our project is for a help desk support team, the default issue types that come with JIRA are not appropriate for this purpose. For this reason, let's create our own issue types and associate them to the project. For this exercise, we will create two new issue types, **incident** and **ticket**.

The first step to set up an issue type association is to create the two issue types we need, incident and ticket:

1. Browse to the **Manage Issue Types** page.
2. Click on the **Add Issue Type** button.
3. Type in `Incident` for the **Name** field.
4. Click on the **select image** link to bring up the **Icon selection** page.
5. For the ticket issue type, let's select the unused exclamation icon.
6. Click on **Add** to create the new `Ticket` issue type.

You should now see the new `Incident` issue type in the table. Now, let's add the `Ticket` issue type:

1. Type in `Ticket` for the **Name** field.
2. Click on the **select image** link to bring up the **Icon selection** page.
3. For the ticket issue type, let's select the unused documentation icon.
4. Click on **Add** to create the new `Incident` issue type.

You should see both the `Incident` and `Ticket` issue types. However, this will only make our new issue types available, but will not make them the only options when creating a new issue for our project. Default issue types, such as Bug and New Feature, which are not applicable for a help desk, are still available. By leaving them there, we are running the risk of confusing the users and allowing mistakes to be made.

If you remember from previous discussions, we can address this problem with a new issue type scheme. Let's go ahead and create one.

Creating an issue type scheme

We want to limit the issue types to be only `Incident` and `Ticket` for our `Support Desk - Global` project, but we do not want to affect the other projects that still need to have Bug and other default issue types. So, we need to create a new issue type scheme specifically for support projects, which can be used by us and other teams:

1. Browse to the **Manage Issue Type Scheme** page.
2. Click on the **Add Issue Type Scheme** button.
3. Name our new issue type scheme `Support Desk Issue Type Scheme`.
4. Drag the `Incident` and `Ticket` issue types from the **Available Issue Types** panel to the **Issue Types for Current Scheme** panel.

5. Select **Incident** as the **Default Issue Type** value.

6. Click on the **Save** button.

With the issue type scheme in place, the last step is to apply it to our
`Support Desk` project:

1. Click on the **Associate** link for **Support Desk Issue Type Scheme**.

2. Select your **Support Desk – Global** project.

3. Click on the **Associate** button to apply this issue type scheme to the project.

Putting it together

With everything created and set up, you can go back and create a new issue to see
how it all looks. If everything works out, you should see something similar to the
following screenshot:

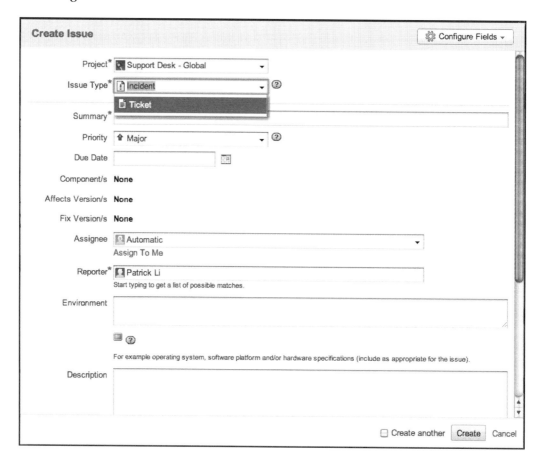

As you can see, `Incident` and `Ticket` are the only issue types that can be selected when creating a new issue for the `Support Desk - Global` project.

Summary

In this chapter, we looked at what issues are in JIRA, and explored the basic operations of creating, editing, and deleting issues. We also looked at the advanced operations offered by JIRA to enhance how you can manipulate and use issues, such as adding attachments, creating subtasks, linking multiple issues, and so on. In the next chapter, we will look at fields and what we can do with them.

4
Field Management

Projects are collections of issues, and issues are collections of fields. As we have seen in the earlier chapters, fields are what capture and display data to users. There are many different types of fields in JIRA, ranging from simple text fields that let you input alphanumeric texts, to more complicated fields with pickers to assist you in choosing dates and users.

An information system is only as useful as the data that goes into it. By understanding how to effectively use fields, you can turn JIRA into a powerful information system for data collection, processing, and reporting.

In this chapter, we will expand on our `Help Desk` project with these customized fields and configurations, by exploring fields in detail and learn how they relate to other aspects of JIRA. By the end of this chapter, you will have learned the following:

- Understand built-in and custom fields, and what they are
- Extend JIRA's ability to collect data through custom fields
- Adding behaviors to fields with field configurations
- Field configuration schemes and how to apply them to projects

Built-in fields

JIRA comes with a number of built-in fields. You have already seen a few of them in the previous chapters. Fields, such as summary, priority, and assignee, are all built-in. They make up the backbone of an issue, and you cannot remove them from the system. For this reason, they are referred to as **system fields**. The following table lists the most important built-in fields in JIRA:

System field	Description
Assignee	Specifies the user who is currently assigned to work on the issue.
Summary	Specifies a one-line summary of the issue.
Description	Provides a detailed description of the issue.
Reporter	Specifies the user who has reported this issue (although most of the time it is also the person who has created the issue, but not always).
Component/s	Specifies the project components the issue belongs to.
Effects Version/s	Specifies the versions that the issue effects are found in.
Fix Version/s	Specifies the versions that the issue will be fixed in.
Due Date	Specifies the date when this issue is due.
Issue Type	Specifies the type of the issue (for example, **Bug** and **New Feature**).
Priority	Specifies how important the issue is compared to other issues
Resolution	Specifies the current resolution value of the issue (for example, **Unresolved** or **Fixed**).
Time Tracking	Lets users specify estimates for how long the issue will take to complete.

Custom fields

While JIRA's built-in fields are quite comprehensive for basic general uses, most organizations will soon find that they have special requirements that cannot be addressed simply with the default fields available. To help you tailor JIRA to your organization's needs, JIRA lets you create and add your own fields to the system, called **custom fields**.

Custom field types

Every custom field belongs to a custom field type, which dictates its behavior, appearance, and functionality. So, when you add a custom field to JIRA, you really add another instance of a custom field type.

JIRA comes with over 20 custom field types that you can use straight out of the box. Many of the custom field types are identical to the built-in fields, but provide you with more control and flexibility that are not available with their built-in counterparts. The following tables breaks down and lists all the JIRA standard custom field types and their characteristics.

Simple fields

These fields are the most basic field types in JIRA. They are usually simple and straightforward to use, such as text field, which allows users to input any text:

Custom field type	Description
Free text field (unlimited text)	These are multiple line text-areas enabling entry for large text contents.
Number field	These are input fields that store and validate numeric values.
Radio buttons	These are radio buttons that ensure only one value can be selected.
Select list	These are single select lists with a configurable list of options.
Text field	These are basic single link input fields to allow simple text inputs of less than 255 characters.
URL field	These are input fields that validate a valid URL.

JIRA specialized fields

These fields provide specialized functions. For example, the **Date Picker** field provides you with a calendar to let you pick a date from, and **User Picker** has an auto-complete feature to help you find the user you want to select:

Custom field type	Description
Cascading select	These are multiple select lists where the options for the second select list are dynamically updated based on the value of the first.
Date picker	These are input fields that allow input with a date picker and enforcing valid dates.
Date time	These are input fields that allow inputs with a date and time picker and enforcing valid date timestamps.
Group picker	These choose a user group using a pop-up picker window.
Labels	These are input fields that allow labels to be added to an issue.

Custom field type	Description
Project picker	These select lists displaying the projects viewable by the user in the system.
Read-only text field	These are read-only text fields that do not allow users to set their data. It's only possible to programmatically set the data.
Single version picker	These choose a single version from the available versions in the project.
User picker	These choose a user from the JIRA user base via either a pop-up user picker window or through auto completion.
Version picker	These choose one or more versions from the available versions in the current project.

Multi-value fields

These fields are like their single value versions and allow you to select multiple values rather than only one. For example, the **Multi Select** field lets you select one or more values, while its singular equivalent, the **Select List** field, only lets you choose one. The only exception is the **Multi Checkboxes** field, which does not come with a singular variety:

Custom field type	Description
Multi checkboxes	These are checkboxes that allow multiple values to be selected.
Multi group picker	They choose one or more user groups using a pop-up picker window.
Multi select	They select lists allowing multiple values to be selected.
Multi user picker	They choose one or more users from the user base via a pop-up picker window.

As you can see, JIRA provides you with a comprehensive list of custom field types. In addition, there are many custom field types developed by third-party vendors (called **plugins** or **add-ons**) that you can add to your JIRA to enhance its functionality. These custom fields provide many specialized functionalities, such as automatically calculating values, retrieving data from databases directly, or connecting to an external system. Once you have installed the plugin, the process of adding custom fields from other vendors is mostly the same as adding custom fields shipped with JIRA.

We will look at plugins in *Chapter 10*, *General Administration*, and discuss where to find plugins, and how to install and manage them. The following list shows some examples of plugins that provide additional useful custom fields:

- **JIRA Enhancer Plugin**: This includes a number of custom fields that will automatically display dates when key events occur for an issue. For example, when the issue was last closed.

- **JIRA Toolkit Plugin**: This provides a number of useful custom fields, such as automatically showing you all the users that participate in a given issue, and the date when the issue was last commented on.

- **nFeed**: This provides a suite of custom fields that let you connect to databases, remote files, and web services to retrieve data and display them in JIRA.

- **CFR Part 11 E-Signature**: This lets users electronically sign issues in JIRA as they work on them; for example, approving an issue to be closed.

- **SuggestiMate for JIRA**: This provides a specialized custom field that shows similar and potentially duplicated issues when you are creating new fields or browsing existing ones.

Searchers

For any information system, capturing data is only half of the equation. Users will need to be able to retrieve the data at a later stage, usually through searching, and JIRA is no different. While fields in JIRA are responsible for capturing and displaying data, it is their corresponding searchers that provide the search functionality.

In JIRA, all the built-in fields have searchers associated by default, so you will be able to search issues by their summary or assignee, without any further configuration. For custom fields, however, you will need to specify a searcher for each custom field you add. If you do not specify a searcher, you will not be able to search data based on that field.

For all custom field types that come with JIRA, one or more searchers are available for you to choose from. You can select a searcher when you create a new custom field and later change the searcher, as we will see when we cover how to manage custom fields.

Custom field context

Built-in fields, such as priority and resolution, are static across JIRA. What this means is that these fields will have the same set of selections for all projects. Custom fields, on the other hand, are a lot more flexible.

Custom field types, such as select list and radio buttons, can have different sets of options for different projects, or different issue types within the same project. This is achieved via what is called **custom field context**.

A custom field context is made up of a combination of applicable projects and applicable issue types. When you are working with an issue, JIRA will check the project and issue type of the current issue to determine if there is a specific context that matches the combination. If one is found, JIRA will load the custom field with any specific settings such as selection options. However, if no context is found, the custom field will not be loaded.

> In JIRA, if no context can be found that matches the project and issue type combination, the custom field does not exist for the said issue.

We will look at how to set custom field contexts in a later section. What you need to remember now is when adding a custom field, you need to make sure that it has the correct context setting.

Managing custom fields

Just like built-in fields, custom fields are used globally across JIRA, so you will need to have the JIRA Administrator global permission to carry out management operations, such as creation and configuration.

JIRA maintains all the custom fields in a centralized location for easy management. Perform the following steps to access the custom field management page:

1. Log in to JIRA as a member of the `jira-administrator` group.
2. Click on **Administration** in the top menu bar.
3. Select **Custom Fields** from underneath the **Fields...** section:

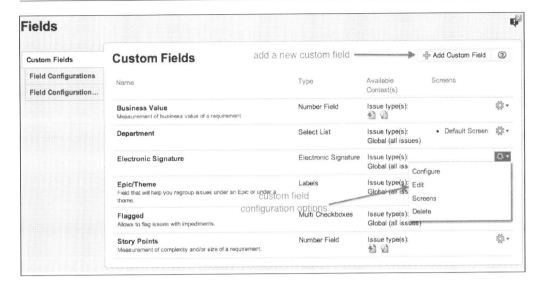

On the **Custom Fields** page, all existing custom fields will be listed. From here, you can see the name of each custom field, their type, the context they belong to, and the screens they are on.

Adding a custom field

Creating a new custom field is a multi-step process, and JIRA provides a wizard to help you through the process. There are two required steps and an optional step when adding a new custom field. You need to first determine the type of custom field, and then its searcher and context. The last optional step is to decide what screens to add the field onto. We will be walking through the following process:

1. Browse to the **Custom Fields** page.

2. Click on the **Add Custom Field** button. This will bring you to step 1 of the process where you can select the custom field type.

3. Select the custom field type you wish to add and click on **Next**. This will bring you to step 2 of the process, where you can specify other aspects of the new custom field:

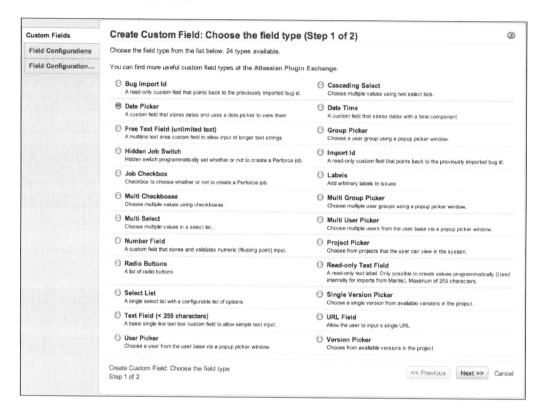

4. Enter values for the **Field Name** and **Field Description** fields. You can have multiple custom fields with the same name. However, doing so will make it harder for maintenance.

5. Select a search template, if available. All custom field types that are shipped with JIRA will have one or more search templates. If you do not wish the field to be searchable, then select **None**.

6. Select which issue types the custom field will be available for. If you select the **All issue type** option, the custom field will be available to all the issue types (assuming if it is also available for the project).

7. Select the projects the custom field will be available for. **Global context** means all the projects are in JIRA. If you select specific projects, then the custom field will only be available for issues within those projects (if it is available for the issue type):

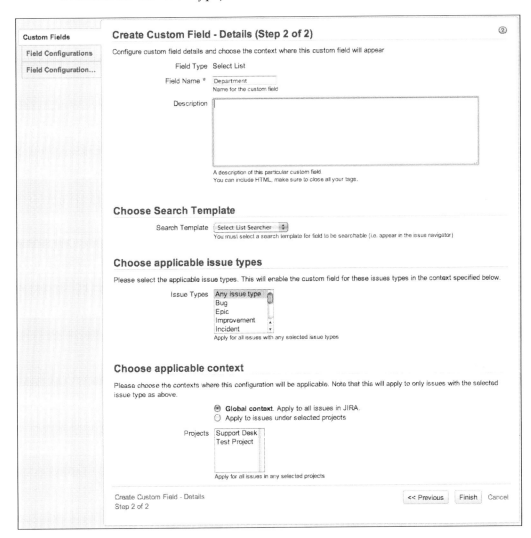

8. Click on **Finish**. This will bring you to the last step of the process, where you can specify which screen you would like to add the field onto. This step is optional, as the custom field has already been added in JIRA. You do not have to add the field onto a screen. We will be discussing fields and screens in *Chapter 5, Screen Management*.

9. Select the screens and click on **Update**:

Once a custom field has been created, you will be able to manage its configurations and settings.

Editing/deleting a custom field

Once a custom field has been created, you can edit its details at any time. You might have already noticed that there is a **Configure** option and an **Edit** option for each custom field. It can be confusing in the beginning to differentiate between the two. Configure specifies options related to custom field context, which we will discuss in the following sections. Edit specifies options that are global across JIRA for the custom field; these include its name, description, and search templates:

1. Browse to the **Custom Fields** page.

2. Select the **Edit** option by clicking on the tools icon for the custom field you wish to edit from the list of custom fields.

3. Change the custom field details.

4. Click on the **Update** button to apply the changes.

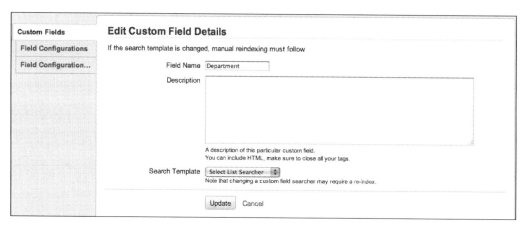

When making changes to the search templates for your custom fields, it is important to note that while the change will take effect immediately, you need to perform a full system reindex in order for JIRA to return correct search results. This is because for each search template, the underlying search data structure might be different, and JIRA will need to update its search index for the newly applied search template.

For example, if you have a custom field that did not have a searcher and you have just applied a searcher to it (while the searcher will now be available), no results will be returned until you reindex JIRA. When you make changes to the search template, JIRA will alert you with a message that a reindex will be required.

> Prior to JIRA 5.2, reindex will make JIRA inaccessible until the process completes, and it can be time consuming for large instances. So, make sure you schedule a maintenance window to minimize the impact to your users. Starting with 5.2, JIRA lets you reindex in the background.

We will be discussing searching and indexing in more detail in *Chapter 9, Searching, Reporting, and Analysis*.

You can also delete the existing custom fields, as follows:

1.   Browse to the **Custom Fields** page.
2.   Select the **Delete** option by clicking on the tools icon for the custom field you wish to delete.
3.   Click on the **Delete** button to delete the custom field.

Once deleted, you cannot get the custom field back and you will not be able to retrieve and search the data held by those fields. If you try to create another custom field of the same type and name, it will not inherit the data from the previous custom field, as JIRA assigns unique identifiers to each of them. It is highly recommended to back up your production JIRA before you delete the field; we will discuss backup strategies in *Chapter 10, General Administration*.

Configuring a custom field

Now that we have seen how to create and manage custom fields, we can start looking at the more advanced configuration options. Different custom field types will have different configuration options available to them. For example, while all custom fields will have the option to specify one or more contexts, selecting list-based custom fields will also allow you to specify a list of options. We will look at each of the configuration options in the following sections.

To configure a custom field, you need to access the **Configure Custom Field** page, as follows:

1. Browse to the **Custom Fields** page.

2. Select the **Configure** option by clicking on the tools icon for the custom field you wish to configure from the list of custom fields. This will bring you to the **Configure Custom Field** page.

The following screenshot shows that the **Department** custom field has two available contexts, the default context (**Default Configuration Scheme** for **Department**), and **Support Context**, which is applied only to the **Support Desk** project:

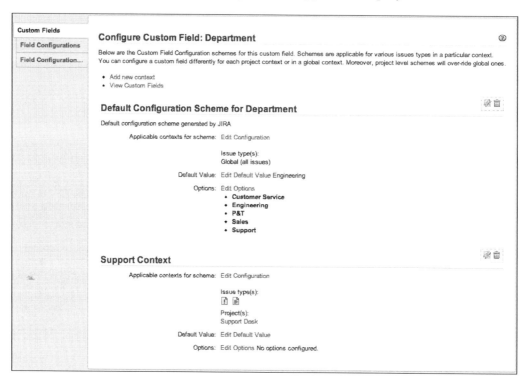

Adding custom field contexts

From time to time, you may need your custom fields to have different behaviors depending on what project the issue is in. For example, if we have a select list custom field called **Department**, we may want it to have a different set of options based on which project the issue is being created, or even a different default value.

To achieve this level of customization, JIRA allows you to create multiple custom field contexts for a custom field. As we have seen already, a custom field context is a combination of issue types and projects. So, in our example, we can create a context for issue type **Bug** and project **Support**, and set the default department to **Engineering**.

 JIRA allows you to configure custom fields based on issue types and projects through contexts. Each project can have only one configuration context per custom field.

Creating a new custom field context is simple. All you need to do is decide the issue type and project combination that will define the context:

1. Browse to the **Configure Custom Field** page for the custom field you wish to create a new context for.
2. Click on the **Add new context** link. This will take you to the **Add configuration scheme context** page.
3. Give a name to the new custom field context in the **Configuration scheme** label field.
4. Select the applicable issue types.
5. Select the applicable projects.
6. Click on the **Add** button to create the new custom field context.

Each project can only belong to one custom field context per custom field (global context is not counted for this). Once you have selected a project for a context, it will not be available the next time you create a new context. For example, if you have created a new context for **Project A**, it will not be listed as an option when you create another context for the same custom field. This is to prevent you from accidentally creating two contexts for the same project.

After a new custom field context has been created, it will not "inherit" any configuration values such as **Default Value** and **Select Options** from other contexts, such as the default context. You will need to repopulate and maintain the configuration options for each newly created context:

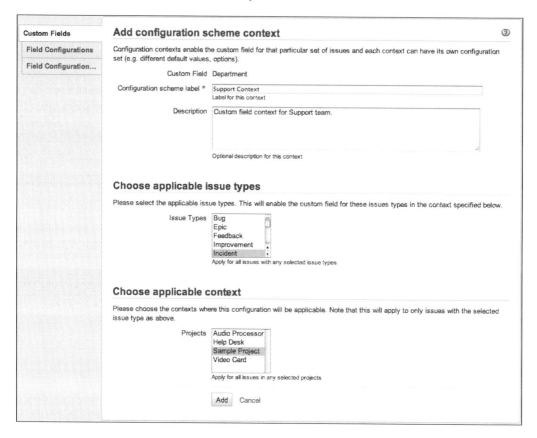

Configuring select options

For custom fields of types select list, checkboxes, radio buttons, and their multi versions, you need to configure their select options before they can become useful to the users. The select options are configured and set on a per custom field context basis. This provides the custom field with the flexibility to have a different set of options for a different context.

To configure the select options, you need to first select the custom field and then the context that the options will be applied to, as follows:

1. Browse to the **Custom Fields** page.

2. Click on the **Configure** option for the custom field you wish to configure select options for.

3. Click on the **Edit Options** link for the custom field context to apply the options for.

4. Fill in the option values in the **Add New Custom Field Option** section, and click on the **Add** button to add the value. The options will be added in the order they are entered into the system. You can manually move the option values up and down or click on **Sort options alphabetically** to let JIRA perform the sorting for you.

5. Click on the **Done** button once you have finished configuring the select options:

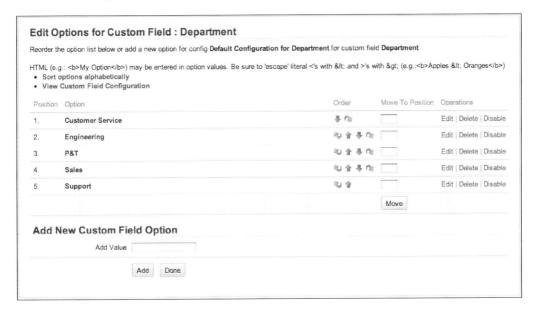

Setting default values

For most custom fields, you can set a default value so that your users will not need to fill them in unless they have special needs. For text-based custom fields, the default values will be displayed as text by default, when the users create or edit an issue. For selection-based custom fields, the default values will be options pre-selected for the users.

Just like setting selection options, default options are also set on a per-custom field context basis:

1. Browse to the **Custom Fields** page.
2. Click on the **Configure** option for the custom field you wish to configure select options for.
3. Click on the **Edit Default Value** link for the custom field context to apply the default values for.
4. Set the default value for the custom field.
5. Click on the **Set Default** button to set the default value.

The way to set the default value will be different for different custom field types. For text-based custom fields, you will be able to type any text string. For select-based custom fields, you will be able to select from the options you have added (if you have not set any options for the custom field, the only option available as a default value will be **None**). For picker-based custom fields, such as user picker, you will be able to select a user directly from the user base:

Field configuration

As you have already seen, fields are used to capture and display data in JIRA. Fields can also have behaviors, which are defined by field configuration. For each field in JIRA, you can configure its behaviors listed as follows:

*   **Field description**: This is the description text that appears under the field when an issue is edited.
*   **Visibility**: This determines if a field should be visible or hidden.
*   **Required**: This specifies if a field will be optional or required to have a value when an issue is being created/updated. When applied to a select, checkbox, and radio button custom fields, this will remove the **None** option from the list.
*   **Rendering**: This specifies how the content is to be rendered for text-based fields (for example, wiki renderer or simple text renderer for text fields).

A field configuration provides you with control over each individual field in your JIRA, including both built-in and custom fields. Since it is usually a good practice to re-use the same set of fields instead of creating new ones for every project need, JIRA allows us to create multiple field configurations, with which we can specify different behaviors on the same set of fields and apply them to different projects.

We will be looking at how to manage and apply multiple field configurations in the later sections in this chapter. But first, let's take a close look at how to create new field configurations and what we can do with these configurations.

You can access the field configuration management page through the JIRA Administration console:

1. Log in to JIRA as a JIRA Administrator.

2. Click on **Administration** at the top menu bar.

3. Select **Field Configurations** under the **Fields...** section. This will bring you to the **View Field Configurations** page:

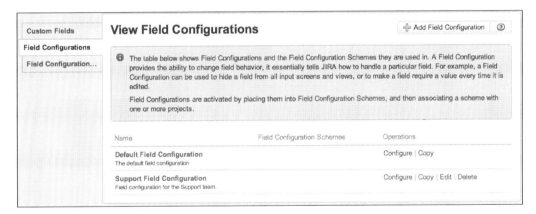

Adding a field configuration

Creating new field configurations is simple. All you need to do is specify the name and a short description for the new configuration:

1. Browse to the **View Field Configurations** page.

2. Specify the name for the new field configuration in the **Add Field Configuration** section.

3. Provide a short description for the field configuration.

4. Click on the **Add** button to create a field configuration.

As we will see later in the *Field Configuration Scheme* section, field configurations are linked to issue types, so it is recommended to name them based on the issue type they will be applied to and with a version number at the end; for example, `Bugs Field Configuration 1.0`. This way, when you need to make changes to the field configuration, you can increment the version number, leaving a history of changes that you can revert back to.

After a field configuration is created, it is put into what we call the inactive state. This means that the configuration is not being used anywhere in JIRA and you are free to edit and delete it. In order to activate the field configuration, we need to associate it with a field configuration scheme. We will look at how to do this in later sections.

Editing/deleting a field configuration

You can update existing field configuration details and delete them all together. The details you can edit are the configuration's name and description:

1. Browse to the **View Field Configurations** page.
2. Click on the **Edit** link for the field configuration you wish to edit. This will take you to the **Edit Field Configuration** page.
3. Update the **Name** and **Description** fields with new values.
4. Click on the **Update** button to apply the changes.

You will be able to edit field configuration details at anytime. However, for deletion, you can only delete the configuration when it is inactive. Once you have associated the configuration with a scheme, which will put the configuration into the active state, you cannot delete it until it is back in the inactive state. For you to put the field configuration back into the inactive state, you need to unassociate it from the field configuration scheme:

1. Browse to the **View Field Configurations** page.
2. Click on the **Delete** link for the field configuration you wish to delete. This will take you to the **Delete Field Configuration** page for confirmation.
3. Click on the **Delete** button to delete the field configuration.

Copying a field configuration

A field configuration contains configuration details for all fields in JIRA. For a moderately complicated instance, you are likely to have over 20 fields. It will be very unproductive if you have to reconfigure every single field again, whenever you need to create a new set of field configurations, usually with only minor differences for a few fields.

To simplify your task, JIRA allows you to copy an existing field configuration and use that as a base for you to make only the necessary changes. This greatly reduces the amount of effort required, as you will not have to reconfigure all the fields that are common across all the use cases:

1. Browse to the **View Field Configurations** page.
2. Click on the **Copy** link for the field configuration you wish to copy. This will take you to the **Copy Field Configuration** page.
3. Specify a new name for the field configuration.
4. Specify a description.
5. Click on the **Copy** button to copy the field configuration.

Managing field configurations

Now that we have seen how to create, edit, delete, and copy field configurations, it is time for us to take a closer look at the different configuration options. Just a quick recap—each field configuration includes all fields available in JIRA and their behaviors are defined specifically to each field configuration. We will then set a context for the field configurations through the use of the field configuration scheme, which will determine when a field configuration will become active for a given issue.

Perform the following steps to access the field configuration options:

1. Browse to the **View Field Configurations** page.
2. Click on the **Configure** link for the field configuration you wish to configure. This will take you to the **View Field Configuration** page (note singular).

On this page, all the fields and their current configuration options that are currently set for the selected field configuration are listed:

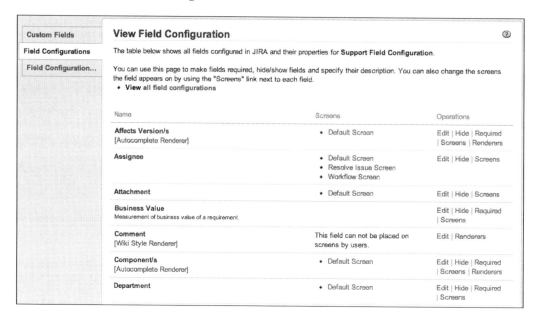

As you can see, there are several options you can configure for each field, and depending on the field type, the options may vary. While we will be looking at each of the options, it is important to note that some of the options will override each other. This is JIRA trying to protect you from accidentally creating a configuration combination that will break your JIRA. For example, if a field is set to both hidden and required, your users will not be able to create or edit issues, so JIRA will not allow you to set a field to required if you have already set it to hidden.

Field description

While having a meaningful name for your fields will help your users to understand what the fields are for, providing a short description will provide more context and meaning. Field descriptions are displayed under the fields when you create or edit an issue. To add a description for a field, do the following:

1. Browse to the **View Field Configuration** page for the field configuration you wish to use.

2. Click on the **Edit** link for the field you wish to set a description for.

3. Add the description for the field, and click on **Update**.

Field requirement

You can set certain fields as required or compulsory for issues. This is a very useful feature as it ensures that critical information can be captured when users create issues. For example, for our support system, it makes sense to have our users fill in the system that is misbehaving and make that field compulsory to help our support engineers.

You have already seen required fields in action. System fields, such as **Summary** and **Issue Type**, are compulsory in JIRA (and you cannot change that). When you do not specify a value for a required field, JIRA will highlight the field in red with an error message telling you that the field is required.

When you add a new field into JIRA, such as custom fields, they are optional by default; meaning users do not need to specify a value. You can then change the setting to make those fields required:

1. Browse to the **View Field Configuration** page for the field configuration you wish to use.

2. Click on the **Required/Optional** link for the field you wish to set its mandatory requirement.

You will notice that once a field is set to required, there will be a small text label **Required** in red next to the field name, and when you create or edit an issue, the field will have a red * character next to its name. This is JIRA's way to indicate that a field is required.

Field visibility

Most fields in JIRA can be hidden from users. When a field is set to hidden, users will not see the fields on any screens including issue create, update, and view. Perform the following steps to show or hide a field:

1. Browse to the **View Field Configuration** page for the field configuration you wish to use.

2. Click the **Show/Hide** link for the field you wish to show or hide respectively.

You will notice that when a field is set to hidden, its name gets grayed out. Once a field has been set to hidden, it will not appear on screen and you will not be able to search on it.

Not all fields can be hidden. Built-in fields, such as **Summary** and **Issue Type**, cannot be hidden. When you set a field to hidden, you will notice that you can no longer set the same field as required. As stated earlier, setting a field to be required will make JIRA enforce a value to be entered into the field when you create or edit an issue. If the field is hidden, there will be no way for you to set a value and you will be stuck. This is why JIRA will automatically disable the required option, if you have already hidden a field. On the other hand, if you have made a field required, when you hide the same field, you will notice that the field is no longer required. So the rule of thumb is that field visibility will override field requirement.

 A field cannot be both hidden and required.

Field rendering

Renderers control how a field will look when it is being viewed or edited. Some built-in and custom fields have more than one renderer, and for these fields, you can choose which one to use. For example, for text-based fields, such as **Description**, you can choose to use the default simple text renderer or the more sophisticated wiki style renderer that will allow you to use wiki markup to add more styling.

JIRA ships with four different renderers:

- **Default text renderer**: This is the default renderer for text-based fields. Contents are rendered as plain text. If the text resolves to a JIRA issue key, the renderer will automatically turn that into an HTML link.

- **Wiki style renderer**: This is an enhanced renderer for text-based fields. It allows you to use wiki markup to decorate your text content.

- **Select list renderer**: This is the default renderer for selection-based fields. It is rendered as standard HTML select lists.

- **Autocomplete renderer**: This is an enhanced renderer for selection-based fields and provides an autocomplete feature to assist users as they start typing into the fields.

The following table lists all the fields that can have special renders configured and their available options:

Field	Available renderers
Description	Wiki style renderer and default text renderer
Comment	Wiki style renderer and default text renderer
Environment	Wiki style renderer and default text renderer
Component	Autocomplete renderer and select list renderer
Affects version	Autocomplete renderer and select list renderer
Fix versions	Autocomplete renderer and select list renderer
Custom field of type "Free Text Field (unlimited text)"	Wiki style renderer and default text renderer
Custom field of type "Text Field"	Wiki style renderer and default text renderer
Custom field of type "Multi Select"	Autocomplete renderer and select list renderer
Custom field of type "Version Picker"	Autocomplete renderer and select list renderer

Perform the following steps to set the renderer for a field:

1. Browse to the **View Field Configuration** page for the field configuration you wish to use.

2. Click on the **Renderer** link for the field you wish to set a renderer for (if it is available). You will be taken to the **Edit Field Renderer** page.

3. Select the renderer from the available drop-down list.

4. Click on the **Update** button to set the renderer:

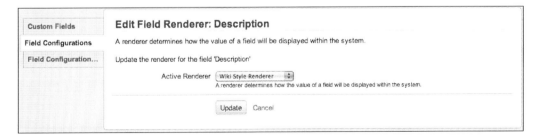

There are other custom renderers developed by third-party vendors. Just like custom fields, these are packaged as plugins that you can install in JIRA. Once installed, these custom renderers will be available for selection for the appropriate field types.

A good example is the **JEditor** plugin, which provides a rich text editor for all text-based fields such as **Description**.

Screens

In order for a field to appear, it needs to be placed onto a screen. You have already seen this when creating new custom fields. One of the steps in the creation process is to select what screens to add the custom field to. Screens will be discussed further in *Chapter 5, Screen Management*, so we will not spend too much time understanding it right now. What you need to know for now is, after a field has been added to a screen, you can add it to additional screens or take it off completely. If you are working with just one field, you can configure it here from the field configurations. If you have multiple fields to update, a better approach will be to work directly with screens, as we will see in *Chapter 5, Screen Management*.

Field configuration scheme

With multiple field configurations, JIRA determines when to apply each of the configurations through the field configuration scheme. A field configuration scheme maps field configurations to issue types. This scheme can then be associated with one or more projects.

This allows you to group multiple field configurations mapped to issue types, and apply them to a project in one go. The project will then be able to determine which field configuration to apply, based on the type of the issue. For example, for a given project, you can have different field configurations for bugs and tasks.

This grouping of configurations into schemes also provides you with the option to reuse existing configurations without duplicating work, as each scheme can be reused and associated to multiple projects.

Managing field configuration schemes

You can manage all your field configuration schemes from the **View Field Configuration Schemes** page. From there, you will be able to add, configure, edit, delete, and copy schemes:

1. Log in to JIRA as a JIRA administrator.

2. Click on **Administration** at the top menu bar.

3. Select **Field Configuration Schemes** at the left-hand side panel. This will bring you to the **View Field Configuration Schemes** page:

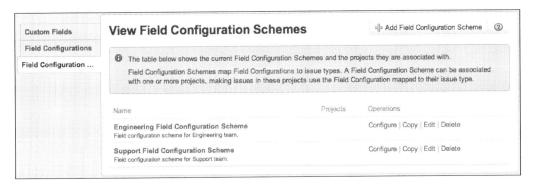

Adding a field configuration scheme

The first step to group your field configurations is to create a new field configuration scheme. By default, JIRA does not come with any field configuration schemes. All the projects will use the system default field configuration. The new field configuration scheme will hold all the mappings between our field configurations and issue types.

To create a new field configuration scheme, all you need to do is specify the name and an optional description for the scheme:

1. Browse to the **View Field Configuration Schemes** page.
2. Fill in a name for the new field configuration scheme in the **Add Field Configuration Scheme** section.
3. Optionally, provide a short description for the scheme.
4. Click on the **Add** button to create the scheme.

Since field configuration schemes are applied to projects, it is a good practice to name your them according to the projects. For example, the scheme for the Sales project can be named **Sales Field Configuration Scheme**. You can add a version number after the name to help you maintain changes.

Once the new field configuration scheme is created, it will be displayed in the table that lists all the existing schemes. At this time, the scheme is in the inactive state, as it does not contain any configuration mappings and is not yet active in JIRA.

Editing/deleting a field configuration scheme

You can update existing field configuration scheme details and delete them altogether. The details you can edit are the scheme's name and description. You can also update its field configurations mapping, which will be covered in later sections:

1. Browse to the **View Field Configuration Schemes** page.

2. Click on the **Edit** link for the field configuration scheme you wish to edit. This will take you to the **Edit Field Configuration Scheme** page.

3. Update the **Name** and **Description** fields with new values.

4. Click on the **Update** button to apply the changes.

Just like field configurations, you can only delete a field configuration scheme if it is in the inactive state. Once you have associated the scheme with a project, which will put the scheme into the active state, you cannot delete it until it is back in the inactive state. To inactivate a field configuration scheme, you will have to unassociate the scheme from all the projects you have applied it to:

1. Browse to the **View Field Configuration Schemes** page.

2. Click on the **Delete** link for the field configuration scheme you wish to delete. This will take you to the **Delete Field Configuration Scheme** page for confirmation.

3. Click on the **Delete** button to delete the scheme.

Copying a field configuration scheme

There will be times when you need a new field configuration scheme and the requirements are very similar to a scheme that you already have. So, instead of creating a new scheme from scratch, you can choose to copy the existing scheme as a base, and simply make some quick modifications. JIRA allows you to achieve this by letting you copy the existing schemes:

1. Browse to the **View Field Configuration Schemes** page.

2. Click on the **Copy** link for the field configuration scheme you wish to copy. This will take you to the **Copy Field Layout Configuration** page.

3. Specify the name and description of the new scheme.

4. Click on the **Copy** button to create a copy.

Once the new-copied scheme is created, you will be able to modify its field configuration and issue type mappings as per your requirements, which we will look at in the next section.

Configuring a field configuration scheme

Once you have a new field configuration scheme setup, you will be able to add mapping between field configurations and issue types. For each field configuration scheme, one issue type can be mapped to only one field configuration, while each field configuration can be mapped to multiple issue types. The following screenshot shows how **Development Field Configuration** is being applied to both the **Technical Task** and **Improvement** issue types, and **Bug Field Configuration** is applied to the **Bug** issue type.

> One issue type can only be mapped to one field configuration.

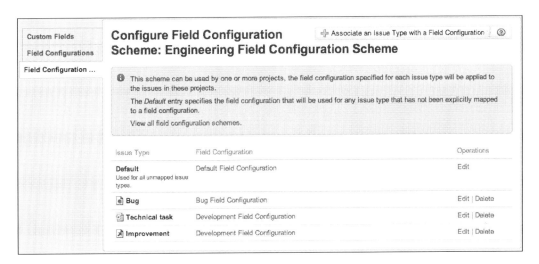

When a field configuration scheme is first created, JIRA creates a default mapping, which maps all unmapped issue types to the default field configuration. You cannot delete this default mapping as it acts as a "catch all" condition for mappings that you do not specify in your scheme. What you need to do is to add more specific mappings that will take precedence over this default mapping:

1. Browse to the **View Field Configuration Schemes** page.

2. Click on the **Configure** link for the field configuration scheme you wish to configure. This will take you to the **Configure Field Configuration Scheme** dialog.

3. Select the issue type and field configuration from the **Add Issue Type To Field Configuration Association** section to establish the mapping.

4. Click on the **Add** button to add the mapping.

You will notice that once you have added a mapping, the mapped issue type will disappear from the list of selectable issue types. This is JIRA preventing you from double mapping an issue type by accident. Once you have mapped all the available issue types, you will not be able to add any more mappings.

Associating a field configuration scheme with a project

After you have created a new field configuration scheme and established the mappings, the configurations will not take effect immediately. The scheme is still in the inactive state. In order to activate the scheme, you need to associate the scheme with a project for the configurations to take effect.

It is important to note that once you have associated the field configuration scheme with a project, you cannot delete it until you have removed all the associations so that the scheme becomes inactive again.

To activate a field configuration scheme, you need to establish the association on a per-project level. This means you need to go to each individual project and set the field configuration scheme option for them:

1. Log in to JIRA as a JIRA Administrator.

2. Click on **Administration** at the top menu bar.

3. Select the project you wish to associate the field configuration scheme to. This will bring up the **Project Administration** page.

4. Click on the **Fields** tab at the left-hand side panel.

5. Select **Use a different scheme** from the **Actions** menu. This will bring up the **Field Layout Configuration Association** page.

6. Select the new field configuration scheme and click on the **Associate** button:

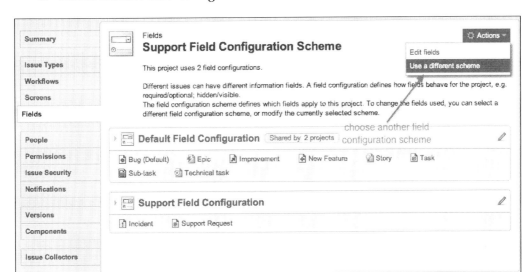

You can repeat steps 3 to 6 to associate the field configuration scheme with more projects.

The Help Desk project

Now that you have seen how to manage fields in JIRA, it is time to expand on your Help Desk project to include some customized fields and configurations to help your support staff.

What we will do this time is add a few new custom fields to help capture some additional useful data from the business users when they log an incident. We will also create a customized field configuration specially designed for our support team. Lastly, we will tie everything together by associating our fields, configurations, and projects through the field configuration schemes.

Setting up a custom field

Since you are implementing a support system, one common feature is to be able to escalate the incident, and for every escalation, a group of users will be notified automatically. The automatic escalation and notification aspects of this feature will be covered and implemented in later chapters, but what we do need right now is a way to capture the information, such as the following:

- Does the issue require escalation?
- What is the current escalation level?
- Who should be notified when the issue is escalated?

So, to address these requirements, we will be adding three custom fields, one per data requirement.

The first custom field we are going to add is Is Escalation Required. We want to have this option, so that not all tickets raised will require escalation. Some tickets may not be urgent or they are simply for investigation purposes. We will also make this field required, so the users will need to indicate if they require an escalation. To help our users, we will provide a default value of Yes, so tickets by default will require escalation. Since this is a single selection field, we will be using radio buttons:

1. Browse to the **View Custom Fields** page.
2. Click on the **Add Custom Field** link.
3. Select the **Radio Buttons** custom field type.
4. Give the custom field the name of Is Escalation Required.
5. Accept the default options and click on **Finish**.
6. Select **Default Screen** and click on **Update**.

The second custom field is a simple text-based field, which will indicate what level of escalation the ticket is currently at. We do not want users (support or business) to be able to change the values as this should be determined by the system automatically, so we will be using a read-only text field. We will make use of this field in later chapters.

1. Browse to the **View Custom Fields** page.
2. Click on the **Add Custom Field** link.
3. Select the **Read-only Text Field** custom field type.
4. Give the custom field the name of Escalation Level.

5. Accept the default options and click on **Finish**.
6. Select **Default Screen** and click on **Update**.

Finally, the third custom field will contain a list of users from JIRA's user base who will receive notifications when the ticket is being escalated:

1. Browse to the **View Custom Fields** page.
2. Click on the **Add Custom Field** link.
3. Select **Multi User Picker** custom field type.
4. Give the custom field the name `Escalation List`.
5. Accept the default options and click on **Finish**.
6. Select **Default Screen** and click on **Update**.

Now that we have created the necessary custom fields, the next step is to configure them. Remember our `Is Escalation Required` custom field will allow users to specify if the tickets they raised need escalation, so we need to add the options of `Yes` and `No` to the field. We also need to set the default `all tickets to require escalation`:

1. Browse to the **View Custom Fields** page.
2. Click on the **Configure** link for the **Is Escalation Required** custom field.
3. Click on **Edit Options**.
4. Add the options of `Yes` and `No`, click on the **Done** button when finished.
5. Click on the **Edit Default Value** link.
6. Select the **Yes** option for the default value.

Setting up the field configuration

Now that we have our custom fields, the next step is to create a new field configuration so that we can specify the behaviors of our custom fields. Previously, we had decided to make the **Is Escalation Required** field required, so there will be no ambiguity when it comes to determining if a ticket needs to be escalated. So, let's start with creating a new field configuration first.

1. Browse to the **View Field Configurations** page.
2. Name the new field configuration `Help Desk Field Configuration`.
3. Provide a helpful description **Field configuration** for the help desk team.
4. Click on the **Add** button to create a new field configuration.

Now that we have our new field configuration, we can start adding configurations to our new custom fields:

1. Click on the **Configure** link for **Help Desk Field Configuration**.

2. Click on the **Required** link for the **Is Escalation Required** custom field. (If you do not see the **Is Escalation Required** field in the list of fields, please go back to the **View Custom Fields** page to verify whether the field has been created successfully.)

Setting up a field configuration scheme

We have our custom fields, we have configured the relevant options, created a new field configuration, and set the behavior of our fields. It is time to add them to a scheme:

1. Browse to the **View Field Configuration Schemes** page.

2. Name the new field configuration scheme `Help Desk Field Configuration Scheme`, as we will be applying this to our Help Desk project.

3. Provide a helpful description Field configuration scheme for the help desk team.

4. Click on the **Add** button to create a new field configuration.

With the field configuration scheme in place, we can now activate our configurations. Since this is designed for our help desk team, we would want to apply the field configurations to the issue types that are applicable to the Help Desk project; that is, **Ticket** and **Incident**:

1. Click on the **Configure** link for **Help Desk Field Configuration Scheme**.

2. Select the issue type as **Ticket** and field configuration as **Help Desk Field Configuration**.

3. Click on the **Add** button to add the association.

4. Repeat steps 1 to 3 for the **Incident** issue type.

Putting it together

OK, we have done all the hard work. We have created new custom fields, a new field configuration, and a new field configuration scheme; the last step is to put everything together and see it in action:

1. Browse to the **Project Administration** page for our Help Desk project.

2. Click on the **Select** link for **Field Configuration Scheme**.

3. Select **Help Desk Field Configuration Scheme** and click on the **Associate** button.

Alright, we are all done! You can pat yourself on the back, sit back, and take a look at your hard work in action.

Create a new issue type **Incident** under the Help Desk project and you will see your new custom fields at the bottom of the page (you will not see **Escalation Level**, as it is read-only, so it does not appear on the **Create/Edit** screen).

Go ahead and create the incident by filling the fields. On the **View Issue** page, you will see your new custom fields displayed along with the values you have provided:

Summary

In this chapter, we have looked at fields in JIRA. We have looked at how JIRA is able to extend its ability to capture user data through custom fields. We have also explored how we can specify different behavior for fields under different contexts through the use of field configurations and schemes. In the next chapter, we will expand on what we have learned about fields by formally introducing you to screens, and how to combine fields and screens to provide your users with the most natural and logical forms, to assist them in creating and logging issues.

5
Screen Management

Fields collect data from users, and you have seen how to create your own custom fields from a wide range of field types, to address your different requirements. Indeed, data collection is at the center of any information system, but that is only half of the story. How data is captured is just as critical. Data input forms need to be organized, so that users do not feel overwhelmed, and the general flow of fields needs to be logically structured and grouped into sections, and this is where screens come in.

In this chapter, we will pick up where we left off from the last chapter and explore the relationship between fields and screens. We will further discuss how you can use screens to customize your JIRA to provide your users with a better user experience. By the end of the chapter, you will have learned the following:

- What screens are and how to create them
- How to add fields onto screens
- How to logically break down your screen into logical sections with tabs
- The relationship between screens and issue operations
- How to link screens with projects and issue types

JIRA and screens

Before you can start working with screens, you need to first understand what they are and how they are used in JIRA.

Compared to a normal paper-based form, fields in JIRA are like the checkboxes and spaces that you have to fill in, and screens are like the form documents themselves. When fields are created in JIRA, they need to be added to screens in order to be presented to users. So you can say that screens are like groupings or "containers" for fields.

In most cases, screens need to be associated with issue operations via what are known as screen schemes. **Screen schemes** map screens to operations such as creating, viewing, and editing issues, so you can have different screens for different operations. Screen schemes are then associated with issue type screen schemes, which when applied to projects will map screen schemes to issue types. This lets each issue type in a project to have its own set of screens. The only time when a screen will be used directly is when it is associated with a workflow transition, which we will cover in *Chapter 6, Workflows and Business Processes*.

To help you visualize how screens are used in JIRA, Atlassian has provided the following image that summarizes the relationship between fields, screens, and their respective schemes:

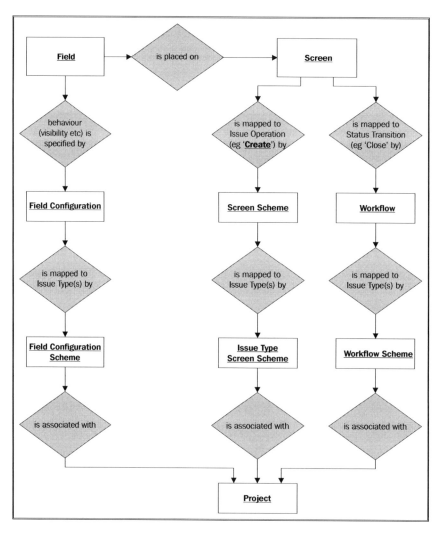

Working with screens

While many other software systems provide users with limited control over the presentation of screens, JIRA is very flexible when it comes to screen customizations. You can create your own screens and decide what fields are to be placed on them and their orders. You can also decide which screens are to be displayed for major issue operations. In JIRA, you can create and design customized screens for the following operations:

- Create an issue in the create issue dialog box.
- Edit an issue when an issue is being updated.
- View an issue after an issue is created and is being viewed by users.
- Manage workflows during workflow transitions (workflows will be covered in *Chapter 6, Workflows and Business Processes*).

Screens are maintained centrally from the administration console, which means you need to be a JIRA administrator to create and configure screens. Perform the following steps to access the screens page:

1. Log in to JIRA as a JIRA administrator.
2. Click on **Administration** at the top menu bar.
3. Click on **Screens** in the **Screens** section to bring up the **View Screens** page.

The **View Screens** page lists all the existing screens in your JIRA. From here, you can create new screens, configure what fields should be on these screens, and decide how you can divide a screen into various tabs.

For each of the screens listed here, JIRA will also tell you what screen scheme each of the screens are a part of and the workflows that are being used. You have probably noticed for screens that are either part of a screen scheme or workflow, there is no **Delete** option available, as you cannot delete screens that are in use. You need to unassociate the screen from screen schemes and/or workflows to delete them:

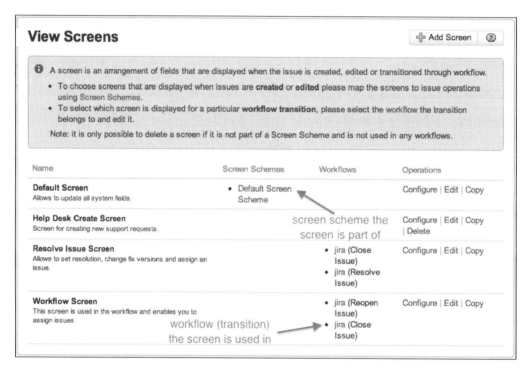

Adding a screen

JIRA comes with three screens by default. You have already seen them while creating a new issue, resolving an issue, and transitioning an issue through a workflow. As a matter of fact, if you have not made any customizations to screens, every issue screen you see will be one of the following:

- **Default Screen**: This screen is used for creating, editing, and viewing issues
- **Resolve Issue Screen**: This screen is used when resolving and closing issues
- **Workflow Screen**: This screen is screen used when transitioning issues through workflows (if configured to have a screen, such as **Reopen Issue**)

While these screens are able to cover the most basic requirements, you will soon find yourself outgrowing them, and adjustments will need to be made. For example, if you want keep certain fields, such as priority, read-only, so that they shouldn't be changed after issue creation, you can achieve this by setting up different screens for creating and editing issues. Another example will be to have different create and edit screens for different issue types, such as bug and task. In these cases, you will need to create your own screen in JIRA:

1. Browse to the **View Screens** page.
2. Click on the **Add Screen** button. This will bring up the **Add Screen** dialog box.
3. Provide a meaningful name for the new screen. It is a good idea to name your screen after its purpose, for example, `Bug Create Screen` to indicate that it is the screen for creating new bug issues.
4. Provide an optional short description for the screen.
5. Click on the **Add** button to create the screen.

At this point, your new screen is blank with no fields in it. You will see in later sections how to add fields onto screens and put them to use.

Editing/deleting a screen

You can edit existing screens to update their details to help keep your configurations up to date and consistent. Perform the following steps to edit a screen:

1. Browse to the **View Screens** page.
2. Click on the **Edit** link for the screen you wish to update. This will take you to the **Edit Screen** page.
3. Update the name and description of the screen.
4. Click on the **Update** button to apply your changes:

Edit Screen

Use the form below to change properties of the **Default Screen** screen.

Name *   Default Screen

Description   Allows to update all system fields.

[Update]   Cancel

To delete an existing screen, it must not be used by any screen schemes or workflows. If it is associated with a screen scheme or workflow, you will not be able to delete it. You will need to undo the association first. Perform the following steps to delete a screen:

1. Browse to the **View Screens** page.
2. Click on the **Delete** link for the screen you wish to remove. This will take you to the **Delete Screen** page for confirmation.
3. Click on the **Delete** button to remove the screen.

By deleting a screen, you do not delete the fields that are on the screen.

Copying a screen

Screens can be complicated with many of fields ordered logically, so creating a new screen from scratch may not be the most efficient method if there is already a similar one available. Just like with many other entities in JIRA, you can make a copy of an existing screen, thus cutting down the time that would otherwise take you to re-add all the fields:

1. Browse to the **View Screens** page.
2. Click on the **Copy** link for the screen you wish to copy. This will take you to the **Copy Screen** page.
3. Provide a new name and description for the screen.
4. Click on the **Copy** button to copy the screen:

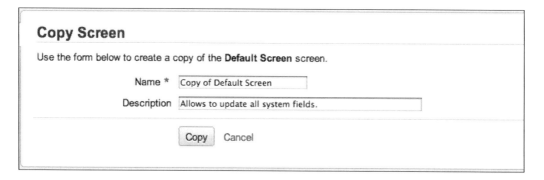

Configuring screens

Creating a new screen is like getting a blank piece of paper; the fun part is to add and arrange the fields on the screen. Fields in JIRA are arranged and displayed from top to bottom in a single column when you are on the create and edit screen, while for the view screen, fields are groups together by type. You have full control of what fields should be added and in what order they should be arranged. Furthermore, JIRA allows you to break your screens into tabs or "pages within a form", and you can do all of this within a single configuration page. It is this level of flexibility combined with its simplicity that makes JIRA a very powerful tool.

Perform the following steps to configure an existing screen:

1. Browse to the **View Screens** page.
2. Click on the **Configure** link for the screen you wish to configure:

On this page, you can do the following:

- Add/remove fields onto the screen
- Arrange the order of the fields
- Create/delete tabs on the screen
- Move fields from one tab to another

Adding a field to a screen

When you first create a screen, it is of little use. In order for screens to have items to present to the users, you must first add fields onto the screens:

1. Browse to the **Configure Screen** page for the screen you wish to configure.
2. Select the fields you would like to place on the screen in the **Add Field** section.
3. Optionally, specify the position where you would like to add those fields. If you do not specify a position, fields will be added at the bottom of the screen.
4. Click on the **Add** button to add fields to the screen.

 You can select more than one field by selecting multiple options while holding down the *Ctrl* key.

Deleting a field from a screen

Fields can be taken off from a screen completely. When a field is taken off, the field will not appear when the screen is presented to the users. There is a subtle difference between deleting a field from a screen and hiding it (discussed in the previous chapter). Although both the actions will prevent the field from showing up, by removing the field, issues will not receive a value for that field when they are created. This becomes important when a field is configured to have a default value. When the field is removed, the issue will not have the default value for the field, while if the field is simply hidden, the default value will apply.

You will also need to pay close attention to not delete the required fields, such as summary, from a screen used to create new issues. As seen in *Chapter 4, Field Management*, JIRA will prevent you from hiding fields that are marked as required, but JIRA does not prevent you from taking the required fields off the screen. So, it is possible for you to end up in a situation where JIRA requires a value for a field that does not exist on the screen. This can lead to very confusing error messages to the end users:

1. Browse to the **Configure Screen** page for the screen you wish to configure.
2. Select the checkbox for the fields you wish to delete from the screen under the **Remove** column.
3. Click on the **Remove** button to delete the selected fields from the screen.

Reordering fields on a screen

By default, fields are displayed from top to bottom, where new fields are added to the bottom. As your requirements for the screen design continue to evolve, the order of fields may need to be rearranged to flow more logically.

JIRA provides two methods for you to move fields around on a screen. You can move a field up and down one position at a time, or you can specify the position where you would like to place the field.

Perform the following steps to move a field up and down one position at a time:

1. Browse to the **Configure Screen** page for the screen you wish to configure.
2. Click on the up and down arrow icon for the field you wish to move.

You can also click on the **Move to First** and **Move to Last** arrows to move the field instantly to the top and bottom of the list respectively.

When your list of fields are long, instead of clicking multiple times to move your field to the desired position, you can specify where you would like it to go directly, as follows:

1. Browse to the **Configure Screen** page for the screen you wish to configure.
2. Specify the desired position in the **Move To Position** field for the field you would like to move (first field has a value of **1**).
3. Click on the **Move** button to move the field.

You can specify positions to move multiple fields at once, however, you cannot specify the same position value for more than one field.

Using screen tabs

For most cases, you will be sequentially adding fields to a screen, and users will fill them from top to bottom. However, there will be cases where your screen becomes over complicated and cluttered due to the sheer number of fields you need, or you simply want to have a way to logically group several fields together and separate them from the rest. This is where tabs come in.

If you think of screens as the entire form a user must fill in, then tabs will be individual pages or sections that make up the whole document. Tabs go from left to right, so it is a good practice to design your tabs to flow logically from left to right. For example, the first tab can gather general information, such as summary and description. Subsequent tabs will gather more domain-specific information:

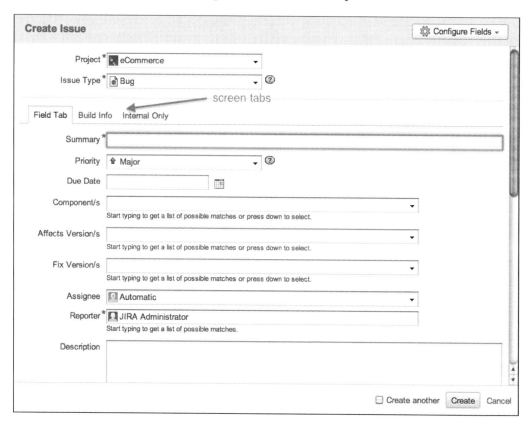

Adding a tab to a screen

You can add tabs to any screen in JIRA. In fact, by default, all screens have a default tab called **Field Tab** that is used to host all the fields. You can add new tabs to a screen to break down and better manage your screen presentation:

1. Browse to the **View Screens** page.
2. Click on the **Configure** link for the screen you wish to add a new tab for.
3. Provide a meaningful name for the new tab in the **Add New Tab** section at bottom of the page.
4. Click on the **Add** button to create the tab.

Once a tab is created, you will be able to add fields to it.

Editing/deleting a tab

Just like screens, you can maintain existing tabs by editing their names and/or removing them from the screen. Perform the following steps to edit a tab's name:

1. Browse to the **View Screens** page.
2. Click on the **Configure** link for the screen that has the tab you wish to edit.
3. Select the tab.
4. Provide a new name for the tab.
5. Click on the **OK** button to apply the change.

When you delete a tab, the fields that are on the tab will be taken off the screen. You will need to re-add or move them to a different tab if you still want those fields to appear on the screen. You cannot delete the last tab on the screen:

1. Browse to the **View Screens** page.
2. Click on the **Configure** link for the screen that has the tab you wish to edit.
3. Select the tab.
4. Click on the **Delete** link. This will take you to the **Delete Screen Tab** page for confirmation.

5. Click on the **Delete** button to remove the tab from the screen:

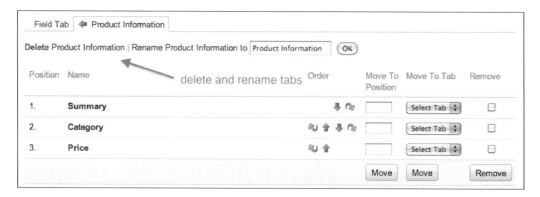

Reordering tabs

Tabs are organized horizontally from left to right. When you add a new tab to the screen, they are appended to the end of the list. So, there will be times when you will need to reshuffle them around, so that your screen flow makes more sense to the users. Perform the following steps to change the orders of your tabs:

1. Browse to the **View Screens** page.
2. Click on the **Configure** link for the screen with tabs you wish to reorder.
3. Select the tab you would like to move.
4. Click on either the left or right arrow to move the tab.

When you move tabs around, their fields will move along with the tabs.

Working with screen schemes

You have seen how we can create and manage screens and how to configure what fields to add to the screens. The next piece of the puzzle is letting JIRA know how to choose which screen to display for each operation.

Screens are displayed during issue operations and a screen scheme defines the mapping between screens and the operations. With a screen scheme, you can control the screen for displaying each of the issue operations, as follows:

*   **Create Issue**: This screen is shown when you create a new issue
*   **Edit Issue**: This screen is shown when you edit an existing issue
*   **View Issue**: This screen is shown when you view an issue

By default, all the three operations use the same screen, **Default Screen**. This is a sensible default as it displays the information to users consistently across all the three operations. However, there will be times when you would wish that certain fields should not available for editing once the issue is created, such as **Issue Type**. You may want to have finer control over the type of issues raised for reporting and statistical measurement reasons, so it is not a good idea to let the users freely change the issue type. Another example would be that certain fields are not required during the creation time, because the required information may not be available at the time. So, instead of confusing and/or overwhelm your users, you leave those fields out during issue creation and only ask for them to be filled in at a later time when the information becomes available.

As you can see, by dividing the screen into multiple issue operations rather than having the one screen fits all approach, JIRA provides you with a new level of flexibility to control and design your screens. As always, if there are no significant differences between the screens, for example create and edit, it is recommended that you create a base screen and use the **Copy Screen** feature to reduce your workload.

Just like screens, you need to be a JIRA administrator to manage screen schemes. Perform the following steps to manage screen schemes:

1. Log in to JIRA as a JIRA administrator.
2. Click on **Administration** at the top menu bar.
3. Select **Screen Schemes** from the left panel to bring up the **View Screen Schemes** page:

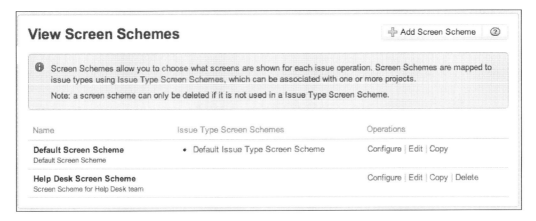

From the **View Screen Schemes** page, you will be able to see a list of all the existing screen schemes, create and delete screen schemes, and manage each scheme's configurations such as issue operation/screen associations.

Adding a screen scheme

JIRA ships with **Default Screen Scheme**, which uses **Default Screen** for viewing, creating, and editing issues. When you create a new project, by default, this is the screen scheme that will be used.

As your JIRA grows, different projects are created. It is a good practice to create separate, specialized screen schemes to better manage screen presentations. In this way, you will have a finer control over the screens used by the different issue operations and issue types. Perform the following steps to create a new screen scheme:

1. Browse to the **View Screen Schemes** page.
2. Click on the **Add Screen Scheme** button.
3. Provide a meaningful name for the new screen scheme.
4. Provide an optional short description for the screen scheme.
5. Select a default screen from the list of screens. This screen will be displayed when no specific issue operation is mapped.
6. Click on the **Add** button to create the screen scheme.

At this stage, the new screen scheme is not in use. This means that it is not yet associated with any issue type screen schemes yet (issue type screen schemes are covered in the later sections). You can tell whether a screen scheme is in use by checking if the **Delete** option is available. You cannot delete screen schemes that are in use.

After a screen scheme is created, it will apply the selected default screen to all the issue operations. We will look at how to associate screens to issue operations in later sections.

Editing/deleting a screen scheme

You can update the details of the existing screen schemes, such as its name and description. In order for you to make changes to the default screen selection, you need to configure the screen scheme, which will be covered in later sections. Perform the following steps to edit an existing screen scheme:

1. Browse to the **View Screen Schemes** page.
2. Click on the **Edit** link for the screen scheme you wish to edit. This will take you to the **Edit Screen Scheme** page.
3. Update the name and description with new values.
4. Click on the **Update** button to apply the changes.

Inactive screen schemes can also be deleted. If the screen scheme is active (that is, associated with an issue type screen scheme), then the delete option will not be present. Perform the following steps to delete a screen scheme:

1. Browse to the **View Screen Schemes** page.
2. Click on the **Delete** link for the screen scheme you wish to edit. This will take you to the **Delete Screen Scheme** page.
3. Click on the **Delete** button to confirm that you wish to delete the screen scheme.

Copying a screen scheme

While screen schemes are not as complicated as screens, there will still be times when you would like to copy an existing screen scheme rather than creating one from scratch. You might wish to copy the scheme's screens/issue operations associations, which we will cover in the next section, or make a quick backup copy before making any changes to the scheme.

Perform the following steps to copy an existing screen scheme:

1. Browse to the **View Screen Schemes** page.
2. Click on the **Copy** link for the screen scheme you wish to copy. This will take you to the **Copy Screen Scheme** page.
3. Provide a new name and description for the screen scheme.
4. Click on the **Copy** button to copy the selected screen scheme.

Just like creating a new screen scheme, copied screen schemes are inactive by default.

Configuring a screen scheme

As mentioned earlier, when you create a new screen scheme, it will use the same screen selected as your default screen for all issue operations. Now, if you want to use the same screen to create, edit, and view, then you are all set; there is no need to perform any further configuration to your screen scheme. However, if you need to have different screens displayed for different issue operations, then you will need to establish this association.

When an issue operation does not have an association with a screen, the selected default screen will be applied. If the issue operation is later given in a screen association, then the specific association will take precedence over the general fallback default screen.

The associations between screens and issue operations are managed on a per-screen scheme level. Perform the following steps to configure a screen scheme:

1. Browse to the **View Screen Schemes** page.

2. Click on the **Configure** link for the screen scheme you wish to configure. This will take you to the **Configure Screen Scheme** page:

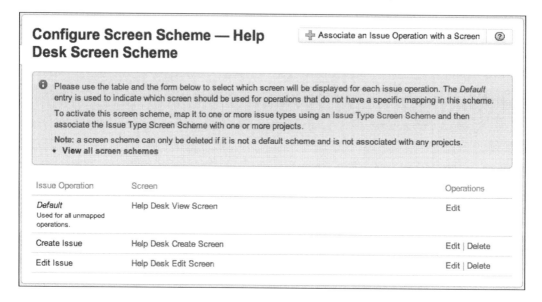

Adding an association

Each issue operation can be associated with one screen, and each screen can be associated with one or more issue operations. Perform the following steps to associate an issue operation with a screen:

1. Browse to the **Configure Screen Scheme** page for the screen scheme to be configured.

2. Click on the **Add an Issue Operation with a Screen** button.

3. Select an issue operation to be assigned to a screen.

4. Select the screen to be associated to the issue operation.

5. Click on the **Add** button to create the association.

As there are only three issue operations that can be associated, once you have configured all three, click on the **Add an Issue Operation with a Screen** button to prevent duplication.

Editing/deleting an association

After you create an association for an issue operation, JIRA prevents you from creating another association for the same issue operation by removing it from the list of available options. In order to change the association to a different screen, you need to edit the existing association, as follows:

1. Browse to the **Configure Screen Scheme** page for the screen scheme to be configured.

2. Click on the **Edit** link for the association you wish to edit. This will take you to the **Edit Screen Scheme Item** page.

3. Select a new screen to associate with the issue operation.

4. Click on the **Update** button to apply the change.

If you decide that one or more existing associations are no longer needed, then you can delete them from the screen scheme, by performing the following steps:

1. Browse to the **Configure Screen Scheme** page for the screen scheme to be configured.

2. Click on the **Delete** link for the association you wish to delete.

Please note that unlike other similar operations, deleting an issue operation association does not prompt you with a confirmation page. As soon as you click on the **Delete** link, your association will be deleted immediately.

An issue type screen scheme

Screen schemes group screens together and create associations with issue operations. The next piece of the puzzle is to tell JIRA to use our screen schemes when creating, viewing, and editing specific types of issues.

We do not directly associate screen schemes to JIRA. The reason for this is JIRA has the flexibility to allow you to define this on a per-issue type level. What this means is, instead of forcing all the issue types in a given project to use the same screen scheme, you can actually use different screen schemes for different issue types. This extremely flexible and powerful feature is provided through the issue type screen scheme.

Just like screens and screen schemes, you need to be a JIRA administrator to create and manage issue type screen schemes. Perform the following steps to manage issue type screen schemes:

1. Log in to JIRA as a JIRA administrator.

2. Click on **Administration** at the top menu bar.

3. Select **Issue Type Screen Schemes** in the left panel to bring up the **View Issue Type Screen Schemes** page:

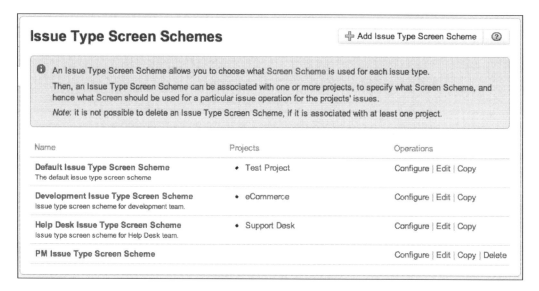

Adding an issue type screen scheme

You would have noticed by now that for any project, all of our issue types have the same screen layout. All projects, by default, use the default issue type screen scheme. But just like anything else in JIRA, you can create your own schemes and apply them to your projects.

Perform the following steps to create a new issue type screen scheme:

1. Browse to the **View Issue Type Screen Schemes** page.

2. Click on the **Add Issue Type Screen Scheme** button.

3. Provide a meaningful name for the new issue type screen scheme.

4. Provide an optional short description for the issue type screen scheme.

5. Select a default screen scheme from the list of screen schemes.

6. Click on the **Add** button to create the issue type screen scheme.

That's right, you guessed it! The new issue type screen scheme is "inactive" at this stage. It will only become active once it is applied to one or more projects, which we will look at shortly.

Editing/deleting an issue type screen scheme

You can make updates to an existing issue type screen scheme's name and descriptions. To change its screen scheme/issue type association details, you need to configure the issue type screen scheme, which will be covered in later sections. Perform the following steps to update an issue type screen scheme:

1. Browse to the **View Issue Type Screen Schemes** page.
2. Click on the **Edit** link for the issue type screen scheme you wish to edit. This will take you to the **Edit Issue Type Screen Scheme** page.
3. Update the name and description with new values.
4. Click on the **Update** button to apply the changes.

Just like all other schemes in JIRA, you cannot delete issue type screen schemes that are in use. You will have to make sure that no project uses it before JIRA allows you to delete the scheme:

1. Browse to the **View Issue Type Screen Schemes** page.
2. Click on the **Delete** link for the issue type screen scheme you wish to delete. This will take you to the **Delete Issue Type Screen Scheme** page.
3. Click on the **Delete** button to remove the issue type screen scheme.

Copying an issue type screen scheme

Issue type screen scheme cloning is also available in JIRA. You can easily make copies of the existing issue type screen schemes. One very useful application of this feature enables to you make backup copies before experimenting with new configurations. Note that copying the issue type screen scheme does not back up the screen schemes and screens that it contains.

Perform the following steps to copy an existing issue type screen scheme:

1. Browse to the **View Issue Type Screen Schemes** page.
2. Click on the **Copy** link for the issue type screen scheme you wish to copy. This will take you to the **Copy Issue Type Screen Scheme** page.
3. Provide a new name and description for the issue type screen scheme.
4. Click on the **Copy** button to copy the selected scheme.

Just like the newly created issue type screen schemes are inactive by default, cloned schemes only become active after being associated with projects.

Configuring an issue type screen scheme

By creating new issue type screen schemes, you create a mapping where you can establish associations between screen schemes and issue types. These associations are what tie the projects and issues types to the individual screens.

Each issue type screen scheme needs to be configured separately, and the associations created are specific to the configured scheme:

1. Browse to the **View Issue Type Screen Schemes** page.
2. Click on the **Configure** link for the issue type screen scheme you wish to configure. This will take you to the **Configure Issue Type Screen Scheme** page:

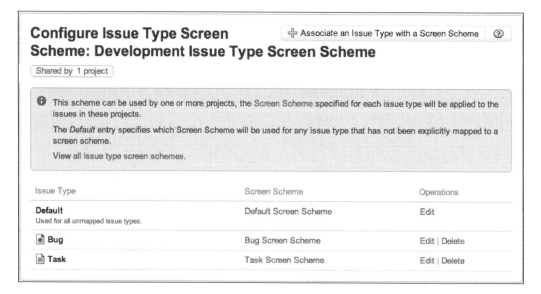

Associating issue types to screen schemes

JIRA determines which screen scheme to use for an issue type by establishing an association between screen schemes and issue types. Each issue type can have only one screen scheme associated with it. Each screen scheme however, can be associated with more than one issue types. Perform the following steps to add a new association:

1. Browse to the **Configure Issue Type Screen Scheme** page for the issue type screen scheme you wish to configure.

2. Click on the **Associate an Issue Type with a Screen Scheme** button.

3. Select the issue type to add an association for.

4. Select the screen scheme to be associated with the issue type.

5. Click on the **Add** button to create the association:

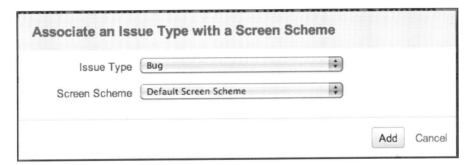

Since in an issue type screen scheme, each issue type can only be associated with one screen scheme, JIRA will not display the associated issue types in the available options.

Editing/deleting an association

You can update the existing associations such as the **Default** association, which is created automatically when you create a new issue type screen scheme:

1. Browse to the **Configure Screen Scheme** page for the screen scheme to be configured.
2. Click on the **Edit** link for the association you wish to edit. This will take you to **the Edit Screen Scheme Entry** page.
3. Select a new screen scheme to associate with the issue type.
4. Click the Update button to apply the change.

You can also delete the existing associations for issue types. This means that you cannot delete the **Default** association, since it is used as a catch for all the issue types that do not have an explicitly defined association. This is important because while you may have created associations for all the issue types right now, you might add new issue types down the track and forget to create associations for them:

1. Browse to the **Configure Issue Type Screen Scheme** page for the issue type screen scheme to be configured.
2. Click on the **Delete** link for the association you wish to delete.

Just like associations in screen schemes, you will not be taken to a confirmation page and the association will be deleted immediately.

Activating an issue type screen scheme

Perform the following steps in order to activate your new issue type screen scheme, which will display your new screens for the different issue operations:

1. Log in to JIRA as a JIRA administrator.
2. Click on **Administration** in the top menu bar.
3. Select the project you wish to associate the field configuration scheme with. This will bring up the **Project Administration** page.
4. Click on the **Screens** tab in the left panel.
5. Click on the **Actions** drop-down menu and select **Use a different scheme**:

6.   Select the issue type screen scheme from the **Scheme** select list.

7.   Click on the **Associate** button.

Compared to previous versions of JIRA, the project's screen page in JIRA 5 not only shows you which issue type screen scheme is being used, but it also lists its content, and you can drill down into the screen schemes to see what screens are being used.

So, unlike the old days where you had to go back and forth to see what screen and screen scheme is being used for each issue type, you get all this information on this one convenient page.

The Help Desk project

Armed with the new knowledge that you have gathered in this chapter, together with fields from the previous chapter, it is time for you to further customize your JIRA to provide a better user experience through presentation.

What we will do this time is create new screens and apply them to our Help Desk project. We want to separate the generic fields from our specialized custom fields designed for escalation. We also want to, at this time, apply the changes to the issues of type **Incident** only and not affect the other issue types. As with any changes to be done on a production system, it is critical that you have a backup of your current data before applying changes. Backup strategy is discussed in *Chapter 10, General Administration*.

Setting up screens

In *Chapter 4, Field Management*, you have created a few custom fields specifically designed for our support teams. As you have learned, those fields are added to the default screen. The first thing you need to do is to create a couple of screens for your Help Desk project only, to avoid affecting any other screens used by other projects and teams.

We will be creating three screens—one for creating and viewing issues, one for updating issues, and one to transition issues through the workflow. Since workflow is covered in the next chapter, we will just create the screen and come back to it when we discuss workflows:

1. Browse to the **View Screens** page and click on **Add Screen**.
2. Name the new screen `Help Desk Create/View Screen`.
3. Provide a helpful description as `Screen for create/view help desk issues`.
4. Click on the **Add** button to create the screen.

The next step is to set up the tabs for our new screen. We would like to have the default fields on the first screen to capture generic issue data, then we will place the new custom fields that were created in *Chapter 4, Field Management*, onto a new tab called **Escalation**, as follows:

1. Click on the **Configure** link for **Help Desk Create/View Screen**.
2. Rename the default tab to `General`.
3. Create a new tab called `Escalation`.

Now that you have your screen and tabs, it is time to place your fields onto them, using the following steps:

1. Move back to the **General** tab.
2. Add the fields from the **Default** screen onto the tab (see the next table for the complete list of fields to add).

3. Move to the **Escalation** tab.

4. Add the new escalation custom fields onto the tab:

Field	Tab
Summary	General
Issue Type	General
Security Level	General
Priority	General
Due Date	General
Component/s	General
Affects Version/s	General
Fix Version/s	General
Assignee	General
Reporter	General
Environment	General
Description	General
Time Tracking	General
Attachment	General
Escalation List	Escalation
Escalation Level	Escalation
Is Escalation Required	Escalation

Of course, you might be thinking that this can be done much faster if we just clone the default screen and move the escalation fields over to the new tab, and you are absolutely correct. However, we are just doing it manually this time to learn the process.

We have created and configured our first create/view screen. Our new edit screen is going to look very similar to this, with just a few modifications. We want to take the **Issue Type** field off since we do not want users to change the issue type all the time, and we are going to take the **Escalation Level** field off as it makes little sense to have a non-editable field on the edit screen. Since we are only taking off some fields from an existing screen, instead of going through the entire create and configure process, let's spare ourselves the tedious clicking, and copy the screen we just created, since we have already done it once:

1. Browse to the **View Screens** page.

2. Click on the **Copy** link for **Help Desk Create/View Screen**.

3. Name the new screen `Help Desk Edit Screen`.

4. Provide a helpful description as `Screen for edit help desk issues`.

5. Click on the **Copy** button to create the new screen.

Since we have copied the screen, we inherit all of the fields and tabs so there is no need to reconfigure them. All we need to do is to remove the fields we do not need:

1. Click on the **Configure** link for **Help Desk Edit Screen**.

2. Delete the **Issue Type** field in the **General** tab.

3. Delete the **Escalation Level** field in the **Escalation** tab.

The last step is to create your third screen, which we will use in the next chapter. This screen will be used during workflow transitions, and we would like to allow users to reassign the issue and also update the **Escalation List** field. Since this is going to be a fairly simple screen, we will create it from scratch:

1. Browse to the **View Screens** page.

2. Name the new screen as `Help Desk Workflow Screen`.

3. Provide a helpful description as `Screen for transition help desk issues`.

4. Click on the **Add** button to create the screen.

5. Click on the **Configure** link for **Help Desk Workflow Screen**.

6. Add the **Assignee** and **Escalation** fields to the screen.

You now have your fully configured screens set up, but they are not in use right now. The next step is to establish the associations with their respective issue operations.

Setting up screen schemes

With the screens created and configured, we now need to link them up with issue operations so that JIRA will know on which action the new screens should be displayed:

1. Browse to the **View Issue Type Screen Schemes** page and click on **Add Screen Scheme**.

2. Name the new screen scheme as `Help Desk Incident Screen Scheme`.

3. Provide a helpful description as `Screen scheme for Help Desk incidents`.

4. Select **Help Desk Create/View Screen** as the default screen.

5. Click on the **Add** button to create the screen scheme.

With our screen scheme in place, it is time to link up our screens with their respective issue operations:

1. Click on the **Configure** link for **Help Desk Screen Scheme**.
2. Select **Help Desk Edit Screen** for the **Edit Issue** operation.

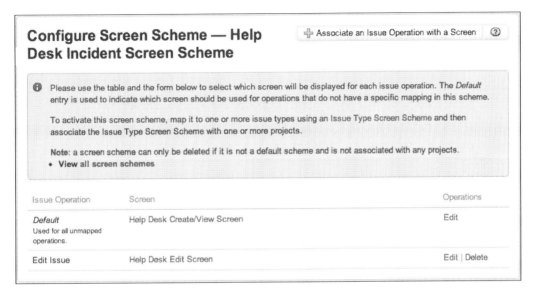

Since we have assigned **Help Desk Create/View Screen** to **Default**, this screen will be applied to the unmapped operations; that is, **Create Issue** and **View Issue**. There are no differences if you choose to explicitly set the mappings for the preceding two operations.

Setting up issue type screen schemes

Now, you need to tell JIRA which issue type to apply the screen scheme to that you just created. We will be applying our new screens to issues of type **Incident** initially, since those are usually the type of issues that require immediate attention and appropriate escalation. For future enhancements, you can further customize your design, so that each issue type will have its own screen design.

The first step is to create a new issue type screen scheme to be used specifically for our project:

1. Browse to the **View Issue Type Screen Schemes** page and click on the **Add Issue Type Screen Scheme** button.
2. Name the new screen scheme as Help Desk Issue Type Screen Scheme.

3. Provide a helpful description as **Issue type screen scheme for Help Desk team**.

4. Select **Default Screen Scheme** as the default screen scheme.

5. Click on the **Add** button to create the issue type screen scheme.

With the scheme created, you can establish the associations between screen schemes and issue types:

1. Click on the **Configure** link for **Help Desk Issue Type Screen Scheme**.

2. Select **Incident** for **Issue Type**.

3. Select **Help Desk Incident Screen Scheme** for the screen scheme to be associated.

4. Click on the **Add** button to create the association.

This will ensure that issues of type **Incident** will have your new screens applied while issues of other types will not be affected.

Putting it together

The last step is to activate all the screens and schemes you created so far in this chapter and see them in action. Remember that there is only one thing you need to do—choose your project and configure it to use your issue type screen scheme:

1. Browse to the **Project Administration** page for your Help Desk project.

2. Select the **Screens** tab on the left-hand side.

3. Click on the **Actions** drop-down menu and select **Use a different scheme**.

4. Select **Help Desk Issue Type Screen Scheme** and click on the **Associate** button.

If you are performing this on a live production system, it is recommended that you alert the users of the change and perform this when there are not many users on the system.

This is it; all done! You can now take a look at your hard work and see your custom screens, fields, and tabs, all working nicely together to present you with a custom form for collecting user data.

Let's go ahead and create a new incident and see what your newly customized **Create Issue** screen will look like:

As you can see, your new screen is nicely divided into two tabs with your new custom fields on the **Escalation** tab. If you create an issue of type **Ticket**, you will see that it will not have the tabbed screen design.

Summary

In this chapter, we have looked at how JIRA structures its presentation with screens. We looked at how screens are used in JIRA via screen schemes, which map screens to issue operations. We also looked at how issue type screen schemes are then used to map screen schemes to issue types. So for any given project, each issue type can have its own set of screens for create, edit, and view. We also discussed how screens could be broken down into tabs to provide a more logical grouping of fields, especially when your screens starts to have a lot of fields on it.

Together with custom fields that we saw in the previous chapter, we can now create effective screen designs to streamline our data collection. In the next chapter, we will delve into one of the most powerful features in JIRA, **workflows**.

6
Workflows and
Business Processes

In the previous chapters, we have learned some of the basics of JIRA and how to customize its look and feel for better data capture and presentation. In this chapter, we will dive in and take a look at workflows, one of the core and most powerful features in JIRA.

Workflow controls how issues in JIRA move from one stage to another, as they are being worked on, often passing from one assignee to another. Unlike many other systems, JIRA allows you to create your own workflows to resemble your processes.

By the end of this chapter, you will have learned:

- What a workflow is and what one consists of
- About the relationship between workflows and screens
- What are steps, transitions, conditions, validators, and post functions
- How to associate a workflow with projects

Mapping business processes

It is often said that a good software system is one that adapts to your business and not one that requires your business to adapt to the software. JIRA is an excellent example of the former. The power of JIRA is how easily you can configure it to model your existing business processes, through the use of workflows.

A business process flow can often be represented as a flow chart. For example, a typical document approval flow might include tasks such as document preparation, document review, and document submission, where the user needs to follow these tasks in a sequential order. You can easily implement this as a JIRA workflow. Each task will be represented as a workflow step, with transitions guiding you on how you can move from one step to the next. In fact, when working with workflows, it is often a good approach to first draft out the logical flow of the process as a flow chart, and then implement this as a workflow. As we will see, JIRA provides many tools to help you visualize your workflows.

Now that we have briefly seen how you can map a normal business process to a JIRA workflow, it is time to take a closer look at the components of a workflow and how you can create your own workflows.

Understanding workflows

Workflow is what JIRA uses to model business processes. It is a flow of states (**steps**) that issues go through one by one with paths between them (**transitions**). All issues in JIRA are based on their issue type and the project they are in, and they have a workflow applied. Issues move through workflows from one step (for example, Open) to another (for example, Closed). For this reason, it is sometimes referred to as the life cycle of issues. This life cycle is shown in the following diagram:

The preceding diagram shows a very simple workflow in JIRA. The rectangles represent the steps and the arrows represent transitions that link steps together. As you can see, this looks a lot like a normal flow chart depicting the flow of a process.

Issues in JIRA, starting from when they are created, go through a series of steps identified as **issue statuses**, such as **In Progress** and **Closed**. These movements are often triggered by user interactions. For example, when a user clicks on the **Start Progress** link, the issue is transitioned to the **In Progress** step as shown in the following screenshot:

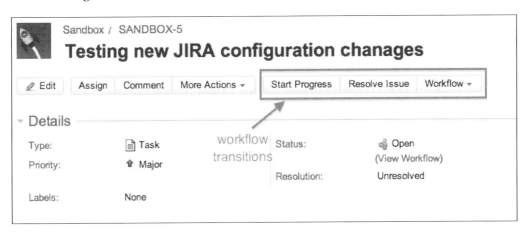

There is a definitive start of a workflow, which is when the issue is first created, but the end of a workflow can sometimes be ambiguous. For example, in the default workflow, issues can go from **Open** to **Closed**, and to **Reopened** and back to **Closed** again. By convention, when people talk about the end of a workflow, it usually refers to a step named **Closed** or the step where issues are given a **resolution**.

> When work for an issue is completed, it should be given a resolution.

Managing workflows

Workflows are controlled and managed centrally from the JIRA Administration console, so you need to be an administrator to create and configure workflows. To manage workflows you need to perform the following steps:

1. Log in to JIRA as a JIRA Administrator.
2. Click on **Administration** from the top menu bar.

3. Select **Workflows** under the **Workflows** section to bring up the **View Workflows** page.

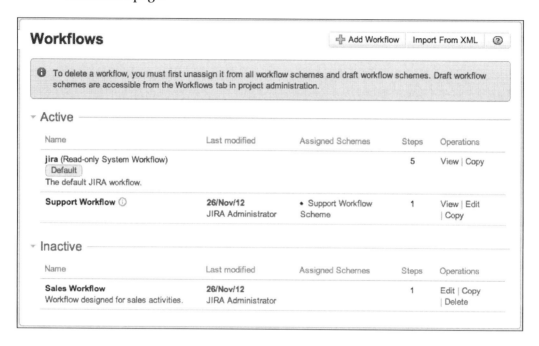

From the **View Workflows** page, you will be able to see a list of all the available workflows. You can also create new workflows, and manage existing workflows.

Workflows can have the following three statuses:

*   **Active** – this status means the workflow is currently being used by one or more projects. You cannot make changes directly to an active workflow.

*   **Inactive** – this status means the workflow is not being used by any project. You can update inactive workflows.

*   **Draft** – this status means the workflow is an inactive copy linked to the active workflow. You can think of this as an offline duplicate of an active workflow, which can be edited and published.

In JIRA 5, workflows will no longer be marked as **Draft**, and you cannot create multiple drafts for an active workflow. Instead, a workflow that has an unpublished draft will have an exclamation icon next to its name. For example, in the previous screenshot, **Support Workflow** has an unpublished draft.

Workflows can also be associated with one or more workflow schemes (discussed in later sections). When a workflow belongs to a workflow scheme, it cannot be deleted even if it is inactive.

JIRA comes with a default read-only workflow called **jira**. This workflow is applied to projects that do not have any specific workflow applied. For this reason, you cannot edit or delete this workflow.

JIRA 5 has made several key changes in the **Workflows** page to make it more intuitive. Firstly, all workflows are grouped into either the **Active** or **Inactive** section. By default, the **Inactive** section is collapsed to display only the active workflows. This may not seem like an important change at first, but when you have many workflows, this can save you a lot of time.

Creating a workflow

It is simple to create a new workflow in JIRA. All you need is a name and a description:

1. Browse to the **View Workflows** page.
2. Click on the **Add Workflow** button.
3. Provide a meaningful name for the new workflow in the **Add New Workflow** dialog.
4. Provide an optional short description for the workflow.
5. Click the **Add** button to create the workflow.

The newly created workflow will only contain the default create and open steps, and you will need to configure it by adding new steps and transitions to make it useful. One good practice to keep in mind is that it is often a good idea to not have a "dead end" state in your workflow, for example, allowing closed issues to be re-opened. This will prevent users from accidentally closing an issue and not being able to correct the mistake.

Editing a workflow

JIRA 5 has introduced a number of changes when it comes to editing workflows to make the workflow authoring experience as simple as possible.

The first change is that there is only one **Edit** link now, which will allow you to both edit the workflow's metadata such as its name, and also configure its steps and transitions at the same time.

The second change is that you will no longer need to manually create drafts for editing active workflows. If you want to edit a workflow, all you have to do is click on the **Edit** link and JIRA will automatically create a draft for you.

The third change is that JIRA now offers two modes for authoring workflows, namely the **Diagram** mode and the **Text** mode. The **Text** mode is the traditional workflow-authoring mode, where you use hyperlinks on the web page to make changes. The new **Diagram** mode provides a drag-and-drop interface where you can visually design your workflow. Both modes, when making changes to a draft workflow, will observe the same set of restrictions compared to editing an inactive workflow:

- Existing workflow steps cannot be deleted
- The associated status for an existing step cannot be edited
- If an existing step has no outgoing transitions, it cannot have any new outgoing transitions added
- Step IDs for the existing steps cannot be changed

If you need to make these changes, you will need to either deactivate the workflow by removing the associations of the workflow with all projects or create a copy of the workflow.

You can configure a workflow's content by performing the following steps:

1. Browse to the **View Workflows** page.
2. Click on the **Edit** link for the workflow you wish to configure. This will take you to the **Edit Workflow** page.

From this page, you get a one-page table view of all the steps and transitions in the current workflow. You can also add new steps and transitions, manage their properties and configurations. As stated earlier, the default **jira** workflow cannot be changed.

Publishing a draft

As we have mentioned, to edit an active workflow JIRA will automatically create a draft for you. However, you still have to publish the draft workflow yourself once you have completed making your changes. In fact, when you first edit an active workflow, JIRA will remind you with a message so that you do not forget, as shown in the preceding screenshot.

Publishing a draft is a very simple process, all you have to do is the following:

1. Click on the **Publish Draft** button. You will be prompted if you would like to first create a backup of the original workflow. It is recommended that you create a backup in case you need to undo your changes.

2. Select either **Yes** or **No** to create a backup of the current workflow before applying the changes. This is a handy way to quickly create a backup if you have not made a copy already. If you do choose to create a backup, it is a good idea to name your workflow with a consistent convention (for example, based on a version such as Sales Workflow 1.0) to keep track.

3. Click on the **Publish** button to publish the draft workflow and apply changes as shown in the following screenshot:

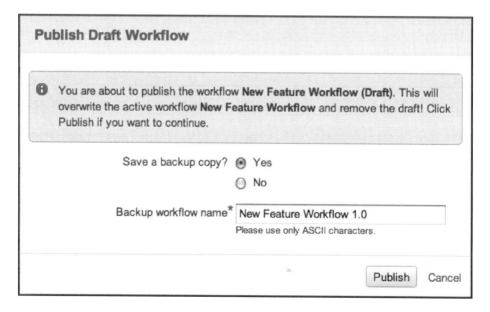

Steps and issue statuses

In a JIRA workflow, a **step** represents a state in the workflow for an issue. It describes the current status of the issue. If we look at a flow chart, the steps will be the rectangles and in the diagram they indicate the current status of the issue along the process. Just as a task can only be in one stage of a business process, an issue can be in only one step at any given time, for example, an issue cannot be both open *and* closed at the same time.

Status is what JIRA uses to show users where along the workflow an issue is. So, there is a one-to-one relationship between workflow steps and issue statuses. Each step is associated with an issue status, also known as **linked status**. In a JIRA workflow, when an issue has been transitioned into a specific step, JIRA updates the issue's status field.

Because you link a step to an issue status, when you view issues, JIRA will display the issue status rather than the step. When you search issues, you will not search by the workflow step the issue is in, but rather, you search by the status that is linked to the step.

Adding a step to a workflow

Each step is unique in a workflow. You can have two steps with exactly the same name in the same workflow, and JIRA will consider them to be different entities.

Steps and issue statuses have a one-to-one relationship. This means you can only have as many steps in a workflow as your issue statuses. In fact, if all your issue statuses are mapped in a given workflow, JIRA will kindly tell you this with a message at the bottom of the page:

1. Browse to the **Edit Workflow** page.
2. Provide a meaningful name for the new step in the **Add new Step** section. It is often a good idea to name the step after the issue status.
3. Select a linked status.
4. Click on the **Add** button to create the step.

Once the step is created, it will be added to the bottom of the table, and you will be able to use transitions to link existing steps to the new step.

Editing a step

You can edit a step to update its name and its associated linked status. However, as mentioned earlier, if you are configuring a draft workflow, you will not be able to change the step's linked status. Also, if all of your statuses are mapped, you will not be able to change the linked status, as the list will only contain free statuses. You will need to create a new status to act as an intermediate buffer. The following steps will help you do that:

1. Browse to the **Edit Workflow** page.
2. Click on the **Edit** link for the step you wish to update.
3. Provide a new name for the step.
4. Select a new linked status if available.
5. Click on the **Update** button to apply the changes.

Deleting a step

You can also delete redundant workflow steps if the workflow is not a draft. For you to delete a step, you have to first make sure that there are no incoming transitions. If there are transitions with a destination to the step you want to delete, JIRA will not display the delete option. To delete a step:

1. Browse to the **Edit Workflow** page.
2. Click on the **Delete Step** link for the step you wish to remove. This will take you to the **Delete Workflow Step** page.
3. Click on the **Delete** button to remove the step.

Transitions

Steps represent stages in a workflow, the **path** that takes an issue from one step to the next is known as a **transition**. A transition links two and only two steps together. A transition cannot exist on its own, meaning it must have a start and finish step, and can only have one of each. This means a transition cannot conditionally split off to different destination steps. Transitions are also one way only. This means if a transition takes an issue from step A to step B, you must create a new transition if you want to go back from step B to step A.

Step Name (id)	Linked Status	Transitions (id)	Operations
Open (1)	Open	*Start Progress* (4) >> In Progress *Resolve Issue* (5) >> Resolved *Close Issue* (2) >> Closed	Add Transition ⏐ Delete Transitions ⏐ Edit ⏐ View Properties
In Progress (3)	In Progress	Stop Progress (301) >> Open *Resolve Issue* (5) >> Resolved *Close Issue* (2) >> Closed	Add Transition ⏐ Delete Transitions ⏐ Edit ⏐ View Properties
Resolved (4)	Resolved	Close Issue (701) >> Closed *Reopen Issue* (3) >> Reopened	Add Transition ⏐ Delete Transitions ⏐ Edit ⏐ View Properties
Reopened (5)	Reopened	*Resolve Issue* (5) >> Resolved *Close Issue* (2) >> Closed *Start Progress* (4) >> In Progress	Add Transition ⏐ Delete Transitions ⏐ Edit ⏐ View Properties
Closed (6)	Closed	*Reopen Issue* (3) >> Reopened	Add Transition ⏐ Delete Transitions ⏐ Edit ⏐ View Properties

Adding a transition between steps

As we have seen, transitions provide the path between two steps. You can create any number of transitions for a step. You can even create multiple transitions between the same set of steps, although doing so is not encouraged.

When you create a new transition, you start with the originating step. This will be the step where you can execute your transition.

You then need to provide a name for your transition. This name will be what your users will see when they are presented with all available transitions. It is often a good idea to have your transitions' names start with a command. For example, "Submit Ticket" or "Provide Information", this way users will know that they are performing an action.

The next step is to determine the destination step. This is your issue's target state once the transition has been successfully executed. While transitions would have different originating and target steps, it is perfectly fine to have the same step for both. Although doing so is not common in a process flow scenario, it can be useful in some situations. For example, you have fields you do not want all users to be able to update via the edit issue operation. You can create a transition with an intermediate screen with those fields and restrict the users that can execute the transition.

The last piece to set is if the transition will have an intermediate screen. If you select a screen for Transition View, when the user clicks on the transition to execute it, the screen will be displayed before it is executed. This allows you to capture additional information that might be relevant for this transition. If you do not select a screen, the transition will be executed as soon as the user clicks on the transition:

1. Browse to the **Edit Workflow** page.
2. Click on the **Add Transition** link for the step that will be the start of the transition.
3. Provide a meaningful name for the new transition. It is often a good idea to have the name start with a verb.
4. Provide an optional description.
5. Select the destination step for the transition.
6. Select a screen if the transition will have an intermediate screen when being executed.
7. Click on the **Add** button to create the transition.

This screenshot provides you with a view of what you will be looking at:

Once you have created the transition, it will be listed under the `Transitions` column for the step it is created under. You will also see next to its name, there is a number in bracket. That is the unique ID for the transition in the workflow. This can be very useful when you have multiple transitions with the same name (for example, a `Go Back` transition).

Editing a transition

After a transition has been created, you can update its details at any time. Most commonly, you will need to change its destination step and transition screen:

1. Browse to the **Edit Workflow** page.
2. Click on the transition you wish to edit. This will take you to the **Transition** page.
3. Click on the **Edit** link. This will take you to the **Update Workflow Transition** page.
4. Provide new values for the name and description for the transition.
5. Select a new **Destination Step**.
6. Select a new **Transition View**.
7. Click on the **Update** button to apply the changes.

Deleting a transition

You can also delete transitions from a workflow step. When a transition is deleted, users will no longer see the transition link when viewing issues.

There are two ways of deleting transitions. You can delete a specific transition by going to the **Transition** page and perform the following steps:

1. Browse to the **Transition** page for the transition you wish to remove.
2. Click on the **Delete** link. This will take you to the **Delete Workflow Transitions** page.
3. Click on the **Delete** button to remove the transition.

You can also delete multiple transitions that belong to a step:

1. Browse to the **View Workflow Steps** page.
2. Click on the **Delete Transitions** link for the step you wish to delete transitions from. This will bring you to **the Delete Workflow Transitions** page, listing all the transitions belonging to the step.
3. Select the transitions you wish to remove.
4. Click on the **Delete** button to remove all the selected transitions.

Configuring a transition

Transitions are actions in a workflow, so they are more complex than steps. With transitions, you can add three additional components—**Conditions**, **Validators**, and **Post Functions**.

Each of the three components defines the behavior of the transitions, allowing you to perform pre and post validations on the transition execution, and also perform post execution processing. We will discuss these three components in depth in the next sections.

A screenshot illustrating the components is shown as follows:

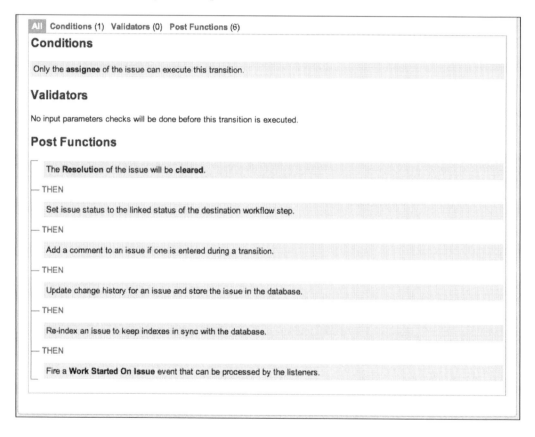

Conditions

Sometimes you might want to have control over who can execute a transition or when a transition can be executed. For example, an authorization transition can only be executed by users in the managers group so normal employees will not be able to authorize their own requests. This is where conditions come in.

Conditions are criteria that must be fulfilled before the user is allowed to execute the transition. If the conditions on transitions are not met, the transition will not be available to the user when viewing the issue. The following table shows a list of conditions that are shipped with JIRA:

Condition	Description
Code Committed Condition	Allows transition to execute only if code has/have not (depending on configuration) been committed against this issue
No Open Reviews Condition	Allows transition to execute only if there are no related open Crucible reviews
Only Assignee Condition	Only allows the issue's current assignee to execute the transition
Only Reporter Condition	Only allows the issue's reporter to execute the transition
Permission Condition	Only allows users with the given permission to execute the transition
Sub-Task Blocking Condition	Blocks the parent issue transition depending on all its sub-tasks' statuses
Unreviewed Code Condition	Allows transition to execute only if there are no unreviewed change sets related to this issue
User Is In Group	Only allows users in a given group to execute the transition
User Is In Group Custom Field	Only allows users in a given group custom field to execute a transition
User Is In Project Role	Only allows users in a given project role to execute a transition

Adding a condition to transition

New transitions do not have any conditions by default. This means anyone that has access to the issue will be able to execute the transition. JIRA allows you to add any number of conditions to the transition:

1. Browse to the **Manage Transition** page for the transition you wish to add a condition for.
2. Click on the **Conditions** tab.
3. Click on the **Add** link. This will bring you to the **Add Condition To Transition** page, which lists all the available conditions you can add.
4. Select the condition you wish to add.
5. Click on the **Add** button to add the condition.

6. Depending on the condition, you may be presented with the **Add Parameters To Condition** page where you can specify configuration options for the condition:

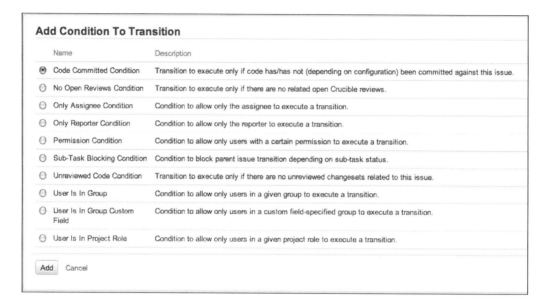

Newly added conditions are appended to the end of the existing list of conditions, creating a **condition group**. By default, when there is more than one condition, logical AND is used to group the conditions. This means that all conditions must pass for the entire condition group to pass. If one condition fails, the entire group fails, and the user will not be able to execute the transition. You can switch to use logical OR, which means only one of the conditions in the group needs to pass for the entire group to pass. This is a very useful feature as it allows you to combine multiple conditions to form a more complex logical unit.

For example, the **User Is In Group** condition lets you specify a single group, but with the AND operator, you can add multiple **User Is In Group** conditions to ensure the user must exist in all the specific groups to be able to execute the transition. If you use the OR operator, then the user will only need to belong to one of the listed groups. There is one restriction to this however; you cannot use both operators for the same condition group.

 One transition can only have one condition group, and each conditional group can only have one logical operator.

Validators

Validators are similar to conditions in nature. Conditions check for criteria *before* a transition is performed; validators check criteria *after* a user has executed a transition. If one of the validators fails, the transition fails and will be rolled back to its original state. The following table shows a list of validators that come shipped with JIRA:

Validator	Description
Permission Validator	Validates that the user has permission. This is useful when checking the person who has executed the transition has the required permissions.
User Permission Validator	Validates that the user has permission, where the OSWorkflow variable holding the username is configurable. This is obsolete.

Adding a validator to transition

Like conditions, transitions by default do not have any validators associated. This means transitions are completed as soon as they are executed. You can add validators to transitions to make sure executions are only allowed to complete when certain criteria are met. Use the following steps to add a validator to a transition:

1. Browse to the **Manage Transition** page for the transition you wish to add a condition for.

2. Click on the **Validators** tab.

3. Click on the **Add** link. This will bring you to the **Add Validator To Transition** page, which lists all the available validators you can add.

4. Select the validator you wish to add.

5. Click on the **Add** button to add the validator.

6. Depending on the validator, you may be presented with the **Add Parameters To Validator** page where you can specify configuration options for the validator.

Similar to conditions, when there are multiple validators added to a transition, they form a **validator group**. But unlike conditions, you can only use logical AND for the group. This means in order for a transition to complete, every validator added to the transition must pass its validation criteria. Transitions cannot selectively pass validations by using logical OR.

Post functions

As the name suggests, post functions are functions that occur after (post) a transition has been executed. This allows you to perform additional processes once you have executed a transition. JIRA heavily uses post functions internally to perform a lot of its functions. For example, when you transition an issue, JIRA uses post functions to update its search indexes so your search results will reflect the change in issue status.

If a transition has failed to execute (for example, failing validation from validators), post functions attached to the transition will not be triggered. The following table shows a list of post functions that come shipped with JIRA:

Post function	Description
Assign to Current User	Assigns the issue to the current user if the current user has the "Assignable User" permission
Assign to Lead Developer	Assigns the issue to the project/component lead developer
Assign to Reporter	Assigns the issue to the reporter
Create Perforce Job Function	Creates a Perforce Job (if required) after completing the workflow transition
Notify HipChat	Sends a notification to one or more HipChat rooms
Trigger a Webhook	If this post function is executed, JIRA will post the issue content in JSON format to the URL specified
Update Issue Field	Updates a simple issue field to a given value

Adding a post function to transition

Transitions by default are created with several post functions. These post functions provide key services to JIRA's internal operations, so they cannot be deleted from the transition. These post functions perform the following:

- Set issue status to the linked status of the destination workflow step
- Add a comment to an issue if one has entered during a transition
- Update change history for an issue and store the issue in the database
- Re-index an issue to keep indexes in sync with the database
- Fire an event that can be processed by the listeners

As you can see, these post functions provide some of the basic functions such as updating a search index and setting an issue's status after transition execution, which are essential in JIRA. So instead of letting users having to manually add them in and risk the possibility of leaving one or more out, JIRA adds them for you automatically when you create a new transition:

1. Browse to the **Manage Transition** page for the transition you wish to add a post function for.

2. Click on the **Post Functions** tab.

3. Click on the **Add** link. This will bring you to the **Add Post Function To Transition** page, which lists all the available post functions you can add.

4. Select the post function you wish to add.

5. Click on the **Add** button to add the post function.

6. Depending on the post function, you may be presented with the **Add Parameters To Function** page where you can specify configuration options for the post function.

Just like conditions and validators, multiple post functions form a post function group in a transition. After a transition is executed, each post function in the group is executed sequentially as it appears in the list, from top to bottom. If any post function in the group encounters an error during processing, you will receive an error.

Because post functions are executed sequentially and some of them have the abilities to modify values and perform other tasks, often, their sequence of execution becomes very important. For example, if you have a post function that changes the issue's assignee to the current user and another post function that updates an issue field's value with the issue's assignee, obviously the update assignee post function needs to occur first, so you need to make sure it is above the other post function.

You can move the positions of post functions up and down along the list, by clicking on the **Move Up** and **Move Down** links. Note that not all post functions can be repositioned.

Using the workflow designer

We have seen how to configure workflows the old-fashioned way via the traditional text mode; it is time to take a look at the alternative. In JIRA 5, there is a new a drag-and-drop tool called the **workflow designer**, to help you create and configure workflows. If you are familiar with diagramming tools such as Microsoft Visio, you will feel right at home.

You have probably already seen this since in JIRA 5, it is the default workflow-authoring tool. When you are on the **Edit Workflow** page, you can toggle between the **Diagram** and **Text** options to choose how you would like to configure your workflow:

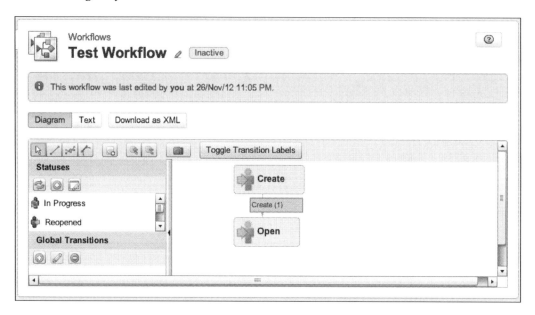

The workflow designer panel is divided into three sections. On the right-hand side, you have your main section, where you can get a visual representation of your workflow. From there, you can move the steps within the workflow around so they will appear more logically, and create new transitions between them. You can click on the existing steps and transitions to edit their properties, and for transitions, you can also add conditions, validators, and post functions.

On the left-hand side, you have your statuses and transitions, which you can simply drag over to the right and drop them where you want them to be. You can create new statuses and drag them in to be part of your workflow.

One of the big advantages of using the designer is that you can do everything right in this one place, without having to move back and forth between different parts of the JIRA administration.

One thing to note is that the workflow designer is a Flash-based tool, so you will need to have Flash installed and enabled for your browser.

Deleting a workflow

It is usually a good practice to review unused workflows and delete them from JIRA, especially when your JIRA starts to grow with old, redundant workflows building up. One thing you will notice is that only workflows under the **Inactive** heading will have the delete option, this is because you cannot delete active workflows:

1. Browse to the **View Workflows** page.
2. Select the **Delete** link for the workflow you wish to remove.
3. Click on the **Delete** button when prompted to remove the workflow permanently.

Copying a workflow

Workflows are often very complex and creating a new workflow can sometimes be time consuming and may not always be the most efficient option, especially if you already have one that is very similar to your requirements. JIRA allows you to copy existing workflows. Once a workflow has been copied, both workflows will exist as separate entities and you can edit them without affecting the other as shown in the following steps:

1. Browse to the **View Workflows** page.
2. Click on the **Copy** link for the workflow you wish to copy.
3. Provide a new name and description for the workflow.
4. Click on the **Copy** button to copy the workflow.

As with creating a new workflow, the newly copied workflow is inactive until it has been associated.

Importing/exporting a workflow

JIRA allows you to export existing workflows into an XML file, which can be imported into a different JIRA. This is a useful feature as it allows you to quickly replicate complex workflows across different instances of JIRA. This is often an ideal solution when workflows developed in a test environment need to be deployed onto a production environment where a full system restore will be inappropriate. There are however, caveats that one will need to look out for while performing workflow imports, which we will discuss later. But first, let's take a look at how to export workflows in JIRA.

To export a workflow, perform the following steps:

1. Browse to the **View Workflows** page.
2. Click on the **Edit** link for the workflow you wish to export.
3. Click on the **Download as XML** button to export. Depending on your browser setup, you may or may not get a save file dialog prompt.
4. Select the location where you would like to save the exported workflow XML file if you are prompted with the save file dialog.

You can open the exported XML file and edit the workflow directly. A detailed explanation on the contents of the workflow XML file is beyond the scope of this book. JIRA uses the OSWorkflow engine from OpenSymphony. You will be able to find more information online about how you can tweak the XML content at `https://confluence.atlassian.com/x/9UkC`. However, this is only recommended for advanced users.

As we can see, exporting a workflow is quite simple and straightforward. Importing, however, takes a bit of planning. When you export a workflow, what you are exporting is not only the workflow entities such as steps and transitions, but also references to other related entities such as statuses linked to the steps, and fields used by post functions and validators. These entities are not exported along with the workflow; if they do not exist in the target system, the import will not work. References that are most likely to be different between systems include:

- Steps and their linked statuses, as it is important to note that the statuses need to have the same ID across both systems, not just the names
- Custom screens referenced by workflow transitions
- Custom fields referenced by post functions, validators, and conditions
- Field values such as `Priority` being referenced

For this reason, it is only recommended to import workflows into a system with an identical setup (such as production and staging). However, often you will need to copy workflows between two JIRAs that have different setups. For example, when you need to promote a new workflow from the test environment into the production environment, or between two JIRAs used by different departments.

In cases like these, where the causes of differences between systems are due to the introduction of new custom fields or statuses as part of a new workflow, it is recommended to follow these steps:

1. Create the new entities (custom fields, statuses, and so on) in the target JIRA system.

2. Export the workflow from the base system.

3. Edit the exported XML file and update the referenced IDs with the actual IDs in the target system.

4. Import the workflow into the target system.

Once you have made sure that all the external entities have been created in the target system, you can start importing the workflow using the following steps:

1. Browse to the **View Workflows** page.

2. Click on the **Import From XML** button. This will take you to the **Import Workflow** dialog.

3. Provide a name for the workflow to be imported. The name must be unique so it cannot be the same as an existing workflow.

4. Provide an optional description for the workflow.

5. Select the **Workflow Definition** option to either import from an existing XML file or paste in the file content directly.

6. Click on the **Import** button to import the workflow.

These steps are illustrated in the following screenshot:

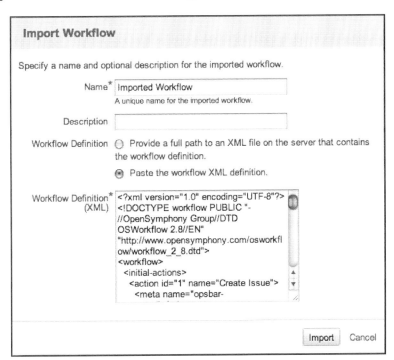

Using the JIRA workflow sharing plugin

As we have seen, JIRA's built-in workflow import/export tool has many limitations. Administrators often find it challenging to keep multiple JIRA instances in-sync in order to take advantage of this feature. Some of the challenges faced by administrators include the following:

- Making sure all third-party plugins that are used as part of the workflow will be available in the target JIRA

- Making sure the target JIRA has the necessary custom fields and screens configured

Recognizing this, Atlassian has released a more advanced tool called the **JIRA Workflow Sharing Plugin** to provide a solution for the aforementioned problems. Currently, this is a separate add-on that can be installed free of charge. In the future, Atlassian may bundle this along with JIRA, but for now, you will have to manually get it from the Atlassian Marketplace, using the following link:

```
https://marketplace.atlassian.com/plugins/com.atlassian.jira.plugins.
jira-workflow-sharing-plugin
```

With the JIRA Workflow Sharing Plugin, a new concept called the **workflow bundle** is introduced. A workflow bundle is a ZIP file (the bundle) that contains everything about a workflow, including the XML file representation of the workflow, any custom fields and screens, and all the plugins that are being used.

Exporting a workflow bundle

The JIRA Workflow Sharing Plugin adds a new **Export** option to all workflows except the default **jira** workflow. This allows you to export your workflow as a workflow bundle, which can be imported later via the plugin's import tool.

The workflow bundle export tool has a wizard-driven interface to help guide you along the process. The first step is to identify all the third-party plugins that are part of the workflow. The export tool is smart enough to automatically detect this and provide you with a summary list for review as shown in the following screenshot:

After you have reviewed the list of plugins, you can move onto the second step, which allows you to provide any additional notes on how to import the workflow bundle.

Once you have documented all the necessary information, you then move onto the last step of the process, where a .jwb file (**JIRA Workflow Bundle**) will be generated and you can download it directly.

Importing a workflow bundle

To import a workflow bundle, the JIRA Workflow Sharing Plugin provides an import wizard that will guide you through the import process. The import wizard will walk through the following steps:

1. Select the workflow bundle to import.
2. Specify the new workflow's name.
3. Map statuses from the workflow bundle to existing statuses in JIRA, or create new statuses.
4. List all required plugins and their compatibility. If a plugin cannot be installed due to an error, all references to the plugin in the workflow will be removed. You can also choose to not install certain plugins on the list. This step may be skipped if the workflow bundle contains no plugins.
5. You are presented with the import summary before the actual import.
6. Run the import process.
7. The screen presents you with the final report on the import process.

These steps are illustrated in the following screenshot:

Note that while the JIRA Workflow Sharing Plugin is a very useful tool, it is still in its early development stage, so there might be small glitches with some of its functions. Atlassian has built a feature into the plugin to collect some anonymous information on its usage to help them make it better. You can choose to disable this, but it will be helpful if you leave this on to assist Atlassian to continue improving this plugin.

Using other workflow plugins

Other than the JIRA Workflow Sharing Plugin, there are a number of other very useful plugins, which will provide additional components such as conditions, validators, and post functions. The following list presents some of the most popular workflow-related plugins. In *Chapter 10, General Administration*, we will talk about plugins in more details and also how you can look for plugins yourself.

JIRA Suite Utilities

```
https://marketplace.atlassian.com/plugins/com.googlecode.jira-suite-
utilities
```

This contains a number of very useful conditions, validators, and post functions. For example, the **Update Issue Field** post function that ships with JIRA allows you to update any issue fields such as priority and assignee when a workflow transition completes. The JIRA Suite Utilities plugin complements this by providing a very similar **Update Issue Custom Field** post function, which handles custom fields. There are many other useful components such as the **Copy Value From Other Field** post function, which will allow you to implement some amazing logics with your workflow. A true must-have for any JIRA.

JIRA Workflow Toolbox

`https://marketplace.atlassian.com/plugins/com.fca.jira.plugins.`
`workflowToolbox.workflow-toolbox`

As the name suggests, a workflow toolbox with a rich set of workflow conditions, validators, and post functions intended to fill many gaps when developing complex workflows. For example, it provides a condition and validator that allows you to specify the checking rules with regular expressions.

JIRA Misc Workflow Extensions

`https://marketplace.atlassian.com/plugins/com.innovalog.jmwe.jira-`
`misc-workflow-extensions`

This is another plugin with an assortment of conditions, validators, and post functions. Normal post functions let you alter the current issue's field values. This plugin provides post functions that will allow you to set a parent issue's field values from subtasks, along with many other features.

JIRA Workflow Enhancer

`https://marketplace.atlassian.com/plugins/com.tng.jira.plugins.`
`workflowenhancer`

This contains a variety of validators and conditions around comparisons of the value of a field with another field, and lets you set up validation logic to comparing dates, numeric, and Boolean value.

Workflow schemes

While workflows define and model business processes, there still needs to be a way to tell JIRA the situations in which to apply the workflows. As with other configurations in JIRA, this is achieved through the use of schemes. As we have seen in the previous chapters, schemes act as self-contained, re-usable configuration units that associate specific configuration options with projects and optionally issue types.

A workflow scheme establishes the association between workflows and issue types. The scheme can then be applied to multiple projects. Once applied, the workflows within the scheme become active.

To view and manage workflow schemes, perform the following steps:

1. Log in JIRA as a JIRA Administrator.

2. Click on **Administration** from the top menu bar.

3. Select **Workflow Schemes** under the **Workflows** section to bring up the **Workflow Schemes** page as shown in the following screenshot:

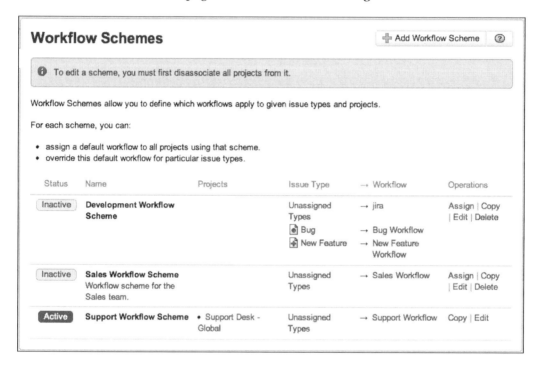

The **Workflow Schemes** page shows each scheme's workflow association. For example, in the previous screenshot, we can see that for **Development Workflow Scheme**, the issue type **Bug** is assigned with **Bug Workflow**, while the issue type **New Feature** is assigned **New Feature Workflow**. It also shows if the workflow scheme is active, that is, if it is being used by a project.

Creating a workflow scheme

JIRA allows you to create new workflow schemes to associate workflows to issue types. This allows you to group all your associations into a single re-usable unit (a scheme) that can be applied to multiple projects:

1. Browse to the **Workflow Schemes** page.

2. Click on the **Add workflow scheme** button. This will take you to the **Add Workflow Scheme** dialog.

3. Provide a meaningful name for the new workflow scheme. For example, you can choose to name your workflow after the project/issue type it will be applied to.

4. Provide an optional description.

5. Click on the **Add** button to create the workflow scheme.

You will be taken back to the **Workflow Schemes** page once the new scheme has been created, and it will be listed in the table of available workflow schemes.

When you first create a new workflow scheme, the scheme is empty. This means it contains no associations of workflows and issue types. What you need to do next is to configure the associations by assigning workflows to issue types.

Configuring a workflow scheme

Workflow schemes contain associations between issue types and workflows. After you have created a workflow scheme, you need to configure and maintain the associations as your requirements change. For example, when a new issue type is added to the projects using the workflow scheme, you may need to add an explicit association for the new issue type.

To configure a workflow scheme, perform the following steps:

1. Browse to the **Workflow Schemes** page.

2. Click on the **Assign** link for the workflow scheme you wish to configure. This will take you to the **Assign Workflows & Issue Types** page as shown in the following screenshot:

From this page, you will be able to see a list of existing associations, create new associations for issue types, and delete associations that are no longer relevant.

Assigning a workflow to an issue type

Issue type and workflow have a many-to-one relationship. This means each issue type can be associated with one, and only one workflow. One workflow can be associated with multiple issue types. This rule is applied on a per workflow scheme basis, so you can have a different association of the same issue type in a different workflow scheme.

When you add a new association, JIRA will present you with a list of issue types that have no associations and a list of all available workflows. Once you have assigned a workflow to the issue type, it will not appear in the list again until you remove the original association.

Among the list of issue types, there is an option called **All Unassigned Issue Types**. This option acts as a catch-all option for issue types that do not have an explicit association. This is a very handy feature if all issue types in your project are to have the same workflow; instead of mapping them out manually one by one, you can simply assign the workflow to all with this option. This option is also important as new issue types are added and assigned to a project; they will automatically be assigned to the catch all workflow. If you do not have an **All Unassigned Issue Types** association, new or unassigned issue types will be assigned to use the default basic **jira** workflow. As with normal issue types, you can have only one catch-all association.

> If all issues types will be using the same workflow, use the **All Unassigned Issue Types** option.

To associate an issue type to a workflow, perform the following steps:

1. Browse to the **Assign Workflow & Issue Type** page for the workflow you wish to configure.

2. Click on the **Associate an Issue Type with a Workflow** button. This will bring up the **Assign Workflow to Scheme** dialog.

3. Select the issue type to add an association for.

4. Select the workflow to associate to the issue type.

5. Click on the **Assign** button to create the association as shown in the following screenshot:

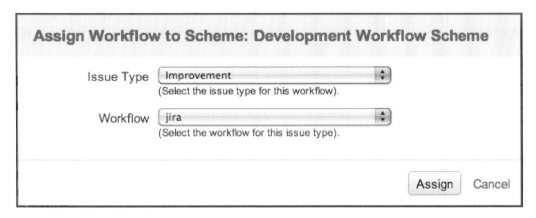

Once an association has been added, you will be taken back to the **Configure Workflows for Scheme** page, and the new association will be listed in the table of associations.

Editing/deleting an association

Once you have associated an issue type to a workflow in a scheme, you cannot add a new association for the same issue type. There is also no edit option to change the association. What you need to do is to delete the existing association and create a new one using the following steps:

1. Browse to the **Assign Workflow & Issue Type** page for the workflow you wish to configure.
2. Click on the **Delete** link for the association you wish to remove. You will be prompted if you want to delete the association.
3. Click on the **Delete** button to confirm the removal.

Once an association is deleted, you will be able to create a new one for the issue type. If you do not assign a new workflow to the issue type, it will be given either the catch-all workflow (if present), or use the default **jira** workflow.

Editing a workflow scheme

You can maintain your workflow scheme's details by updating its name and description. Often a name that makes sense at one time may not a few months later:

1. Browse to the **Workflow Schemes** page.

2. Click on the **Edit** link for the workflow scheme you wish to update. This will take you to the **Edit Workflow Scheme** dialog.

3. Update the name and description with new values.

4. Click on the **Update** button to apply the changes.

Deleting a workflow scheme

Unused workflows schemes can be deleted from JIRA. Workflow schemes can only be deleted if they are not being used by projects. You cannot delete workflow schemes if they are being used by one or more projects:

1. Browse to the **Workflow Schemes** page.

2. Click on the **Delete** link for the workflow scheme you wish to update. You will be prompted to confirm.

3. Click on the **Delete** button to remove the workflow scheme.

When you delete a workflow scheme, you are removing the associations from the system. The issue types and workflows are not affected.

Copying a workflow scheme

You can also make copies of existing workflow schemes. When you make a copy, all of the original scheme's associations will be copied over. Once copied, both copies exist as separate entities:

1. Browse to the **Workflow Schemes** page.

2. Click on the **Copy** link for the workflow scheme you wish to copy.

Unlike most other copy operations in JIRA, you will not be prompted with a copy page asking for a new name and description of the new workflow scheme. Instead, JIRA will create a copy of the workflow scheme immediately, with a predefined name. For example, if you copied the workflow named "jira", the copy would be called "Copy of jira".

Copying workflow schemes can become really handy when you need to make configuration changes. As we have seen, you cannot configure or edit existing workflow schemes if they are active. Normally, this means you have to remove all the associations between projects and the workflow scheme one by one, before you can make your changes. As we will see later in the chapter, changing workflow associations can sometimes be rather disruptive.

So a better approach is to first make a copy of the workflow scheme you wish to change, and apply your changes to the copy first. You then update the projects to use the new workflow scheme. This approach still requires you to update the projects one by one, but it offers the following advantages:

- Less disruption to the users as the projects are not modified until the workflow scheme changes are ready

- An easier transition when updating projects to the new workflow scheme (as we will see later in this chapter)

- It provides you with a sandbox to experiment without the risk of breaking the existing configurations

- It allows you to have a versioning system with the old and new workflow scheme (for example, the copied scheme can be named as `Development Workflow Scheme 2.0`), letting you easily find and roll back to the old scheme

Activating a workflow scheme

Workflow schemes are inactive by default, after they are created. This means there are no projects in JIRA using the workflow scheme. To activate a workflow scheme, you need to select the scheme and apply it to the project.

When assigning a workflow scheme to a project, you need to follow the three basic steps:

1. Select the project that will be using the workflow scheme.

2. Select the workflow scheme to apply

3. Map any differences between the old and new workflow, and apply the change.

When associating workflow schemes to projects, you have to do it at the project level, from the **Workflows** tab of the project's administration page. JIRA 5 has made many changes to this page. They are as follows:

- The first change is you will be able to see, both in the diagram mode and the text mode, each workflow and the issue type association of the currently applied workflow scheme.

- The second change is you will be able to work with the workflows and the workflow scheme directly. For example, you will be able to edit the workflow directly by clicking on the **Edit** button, or add a new workflow issue type association by clicking on the **Add Workflow** button. Note that you are not actually creating a new workflow, but rather, just associating issue types to an existing workflow.

These changes make it so much easier for administrators to quickly work out how everything is being tied together without having to go back and forth between different configuration pages:

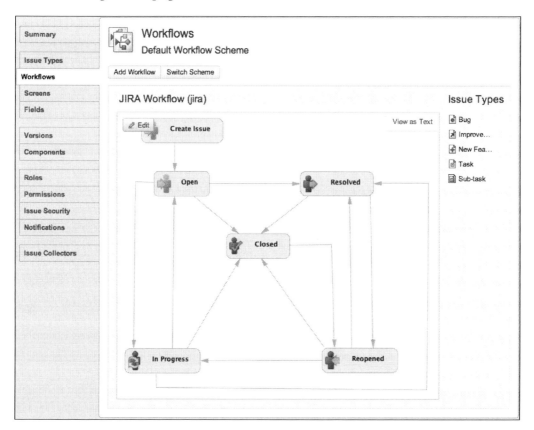

After you have reviewed and decided that you need to apply a new workflow scheme, you should:

1. Click on the **Switch Scheme** button.

2. Select the workflow scheme to use.

On the confirmation page, depending on the differences between the current and new workflow, you will be prompted to make migration decisions for existing issues. For example, if the current workflow has a step called **Reopened** and the new workflow does not (or it has something equivalent but with a different ID), you need to specify the new step to place the issues that are currently in the **Reopened** step. Once mapped, JIRA will start migrating existing issues to the new step using the following steps:

1. Select new workflow steps for the existing issues that are in steps that do not exist in the new workflow.

2. Click on the **Associate** button to start the migration as shown in the following screenshot:

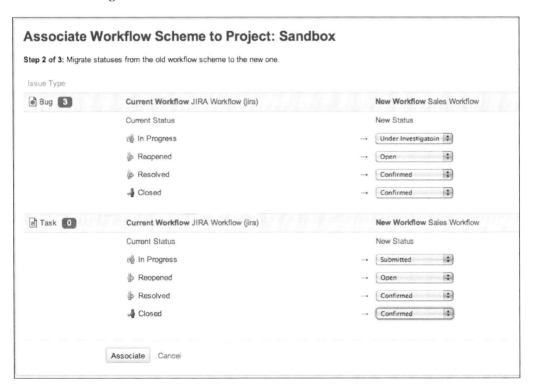

Once the migration starts, JIRA will display a progress bar showing you the progress. Depending on the number of issues that need to be migrated, this process may take some time. It is recommended to allocate a time frame to perform this task as it can be quite resource intensive for large instances.

The Help Desk project

We have seen the power of workflows and how we can enhance the usefulness of JIRA by adapting to everyday business processes. With our help desk project, as with most support-oriented systems, it is often the case that our help desk staff will require more information from the business user who has submitted the support ticket to help further diagnose and solve the problem. Our requirements for the business process would then include the following:

- Ability for support staff to request more information from the business user
- Allowing business users to reassign the ticket back after the requested information is supplied

Furthermore as a bonus, it will be ideal to automate certain aspects of this process. For example, whenever our help desk staff requests information, he/she will not need to decide who to assign the ticket to, but rather, let the system work it out. The same can be applied to the business user so when he/she resubmits the ticket, it will be reassigned accordingly. As we will see in the next chapter, this level of automation not only enhances the user experience, it is also very useful when facilitating communication between parties involved.

Setting up an issue status

The first task when setting up our workflow is to make sure we have the issue statuses prepared so we can map them to steps. From our requirements, we need to create a new step, which represents waiting for additional information from the business users, so we will need to create the issue status for this.

We have seen how to manage issue statuses from *Chapter 2, Project Management*, so if you have skipped or forgotten some of the steps, now will be a good time for a refresh:

1. Browse to the JIRA Administration console.
2. Select **Statuses** under the **Issue Attributes** section.
3. Name our new status, `Waiting for Info`.

4. Provide a helpful description such as `The issue is waiting for additional information from users.`

5. Choose **/images/icons/status_needinfo.gif** for **Icon URL**.

6. Click on the **Add** button to create the new status.

Now that we have our status, we can use that as the linked status for our workflow step.

Setting up workflows

Now it is time to create our new workflow. Since our requirements state that we need to have an extra step that will allow our help desk team to reassign the issue back to the business user (reporter), instead of creating a workflow from scratch, we will make a copy of the existing workflow as a template, and modify its configurations. This is usually the preferred approach as it saves you time to set up some of the common transitions.

The first step is to create a workflow for the help desk team by performing the following steps:

1. Browse to the JIRA Administration console.

2. Select **Workflows** under the **Workflows** section.

3. Click on the **Copy** link for the **jira** workflow.

4. Name the new workflow, `Help Desk Workflow`.

5. Provide a helpful description such as `Workflow for the help desk team`.

6. Click on the **Copy** button to create our workflow.

The next step is to add in the extra steps we have:

1. Click on the **Edit** link for **Support Workflow**.

2. Name our new step, `Waiting for Info`.

3. Select **Waiting for Info** for **Linked Status**.

4. Click on the **Add** button to create the workflow step.

Now that we have our step added to our workflow, we need a way for our help desk team to get there, and the answer is to add a new transition. What we need is to be able to go after users for more information once our team has started working on the issue, and once the business users provide the information, the issue can then be handed back to the help desk team. So what we need to do is to add a new transition to the **In Progress** step that will link to the new **Waiting for Info** step:

1. Click on the **Add Transition** link for **In Progress** step. This will bring up the **Add Workflow Transition** page.

2. Name the new transition, `Request for Info`.

3. Provide a helpful description such as `Request the business user for additional information`.

4. Select **Waiting for Info** for **Destination Step**.

5. Select **No view for transition**.

6. Click on the **Add** button to create the transition.

We will also need to add another transition that will link the issue back to **In Progress** when the business users have provided the requested information:

1. Click on the **Add Transition** link for the **Waiting for Info** step.

2. Name the new transition, `Re-submit`.

3. Provide a helpful description such as `Resubmitting the ticket back to support`.

4. Select **In Progress** for **Destination Step**.

5. Select **No view for transition**.

6. Click on the **Add** button to create the transition.

With this setup, our team can continue requesting information if required. Now, we would want to make sure that only the currently assigned help desk team member can ask business users for more information, and to automatically reassign the issue back to the business user (reporter) so he/she will be notified. This means we need to add a condition and a post function to our transition:

1. Click on the **Request for Info** transition link for the **In Progress** step.

2. Click on the **Conditions** tab.

3. Click on the **Add** link to bring up the **Add Condition To Transition** page.

4. Select **Only Assignee Condition**.

5. Click on the **Add** button to add the condition.

6. Click on the **Post Functions** tab.

7. Click on the **Add** link.

8. Select **Assign to Reporter**.

9. Click on **Add** to add the post function to the transition.

Now, only the team member who is the currently assigned the ticket will be able to request the business users for information, and when he/she does, the ticket will be automatically reassigned back to the business user. We will also need to do the same for the resubmit transition, so when the business user provides the requested information, the issue will be reassigned back to the help desk team:

1. Click on the **Re-submit** transition link for the **In Progress** step.

2. Click on the **Post Functions** tab.

3. Click on the **Add** link to bring up the **Add Post Function To Transition** page.

4. Select **Assign to Lead Developer**.

5. Click on **Add** to add the post function to the transition.

Setting up workflow schemes

With our workflow in place and set up, we need to let JIRA know which issue types will be using our new workflow, so we need to create a new workflow scheme:

1. Browse to the **Workflow Schemes** page.

2. Click on the **Add Workflow Scheme** button.

3. Name the new workflow scheme, Help Desk Workflow Scheme.

4. Provide a helpful description such as Workflow Scheme for the help desk team.

5. Click on the **Add** button to create the workflow scheme.

We now need to associate our new support workflow with the appropriate issue types:

1. Click on the **Assign** link for **Support Workflow Scheme**.

2. Click on the **Assign an Issue Type with a Workflow** button to bring up the **Add Workflow to Scheme** dialog.

3. Select **Incident** for **Issue Type**.

4. Select **Help Desk Workflow** for **Workflow**.

5. Click on **Add** to create the association.

6. Repeat this for the **Ticket** issue type.

7. Create another association for **All Unassigned Issue Types**; this time, select **jira** as the workflow.

This associates our new workflow with the issue types specifically for our help desk team project and uses the default workflow for the others.

Putting it together

We have created a status, workflow, and workflow scheme; all we have to do now is tell our project to use them all, and this is the easiest part:

1. Browse to the **Project Administration** page for our **Help Desk** project.
2. Select the **Workflows** tab.
3. Click on the **Switch Scheme** button.
4. Select **Help Desk Workflow Scheme** and click on the **Associate** button.
5. Click on the **Associate** button again in the next screen for JIRA to migrate all existing issues to use the new workflow.

Wait for JIRA to finish migrating the existing issue and that's it, all done! We can now create a new ticket, and start testing our implementation. Since we need to simulate a scenario where a business user submits a ticket to the help desk team, we need to create a new business user and add him/her to the **jira-developers** group. We will look at user management and security in *Chapter 8, Securing JIRA*. For now, we will simply add a new user to our system:

1. Browse to the JIRA Administration console.
2. Select **Users** under the **Users** section.
3. Click on the **Create User** button to bring up the **Create New User** dialog.
4. Name the new user john.doe (John Doe).
5. Set the password and e-mail address for this new user.
6. Unselect the **Send Notification Email** option.
7. Click on the **Create** button to create the user.
8. Click on the **Edit Groups** link.
9. Select **jira-developers** from the **Available Groups** list.
10. Click on the **Join** button.

Now log in to JIRA as a new business user **john.doe** and create a new incident. After you have created the incident issue, you will notice that you cannot execute any transitions. This is because the issue is not currently assigned to you. You need to be the assignee of the issue (member of the help desk team) to start working on the issue. So let's log out and log back in as a member of the team (**admin**).

Once logged in, you will see familiar transitions such as **Start Progress** and **Resolve Issue** are once more available. If you click on the **Workflow** drop-down box, you will also see that our new **Request for Info** transition is listed as shown in the following screenshot:

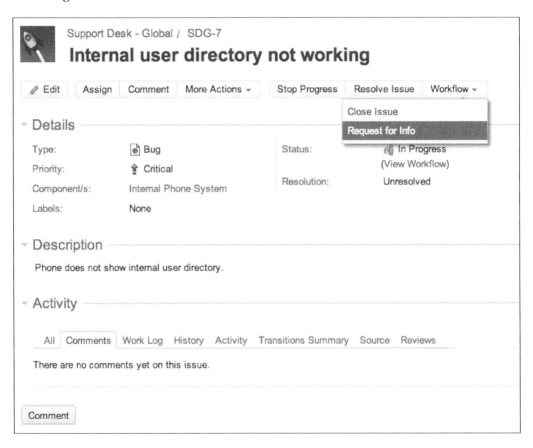

Executing that transition will place the issue in the **Waiting for Info** status and the **Assignee** field automatically changed to **John Doe**, the reporter of the issue, as shown in the following screenshot:

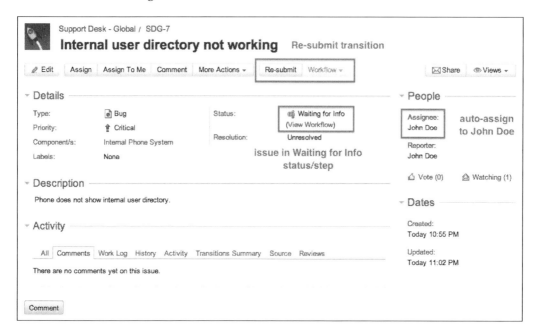

Try resubmitting the issue as the business user and you will see that the issue will be reassigned back to **Administrator**.

You will notice right now, even as a member of the help desk team, you are able to resubmit the issue, which is not ideal. As an exercise, you need to add a validation rule so that only the business user will be able to resubmit the issue back.

Summary

In this chapter, we have looked at how JIRA can be customized to adapt to your organization. In the heart of this powerful feature is a robust workflow system that allows you to model JIRA workflows based on existing business processes. We have also looked at the various components within a workflow and how to perform validations and post processing provides a level of process automation.

In the next chapter, we will look at how we can combine the power of workflow and its event-driven system to facilitate communication through JIRA notifications and the e-mail system.

7
E-mails and Notifications

So far, we have learned how to use and interact with JIRA directly from its web interface through a browser. However, you are not restricted only to a web browser; you can also communicate with JIRA through e-mails.

One powerful feature of JIRA is its ability to update the users of their issue's progress automatically through e-mails, and also to create and comment on issues based on e-mails sent from the user. This provides you with a whole new option of how you and your users can interact with JIRA. By the end of the chapter, you will have learned the following:

- How to set up a mail server in JIRA
- What a mail handler is
- How to create issues and comments by sending e-mails to JIRA
- Events and how they are related to notifications
- How to configure JIRA to send out notifications based on events

JIRA and e-mail

E-mails have become one of the most important communication tools in today's world. Businesses and individuals rely on e-mails to send and receive information around the world almost instantly. So, it should come as no surprise that JIRA comes fully equipped and integrated with e-mail support.

JIRA's e-mail support comes in several flavors. First, JIRA can send out e-mails to users to notify them about actions being performed on their issues, to keep them updated with their issues' progress. Second, JIRA can also poll mailboxes for e-mails and create issues and comments based on its content. The third feature is the ability for users to create and subscribe to filters to set up feeds in JIRA (we will discuss filters in *Chapter 9, Searching, Reporting, and Analysis*). These features open up a whole new dimension on how users can interact with JIRA.

In the following sections, we will look at what you need to do to enable JIRA's powerful e-mail support and also explore the tools and options at your disposal to configure JIRA to "e-mail it" your way. The following diagram shows how JIRA interacts with various mail servers:

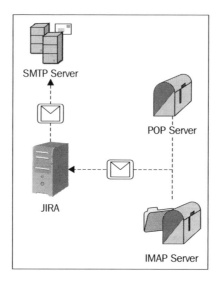

Mail servers

In order for JIRA to communicate with e-mails, you need to configure or register your mail servers in JIRA. There are two types of mail servers you need to configure:

- **Outgoing**: This mail server is used to send e-mails with an SMTP server
- **Incoming**: This mail server is used by JIRA to retrieve e-mails from a POP or an IMAP server

Working with outgoing mails

JIRA will only let you set up one outgoing mail server that will be used as the primary mail server to send out e-mails.

Unlike many settings in JIRA, you need to be a JIRA system administrator (the user created during the initial setup is a system administrator) to configure mail server details. Perform the following steps to manage the outgoing mail server:

1. Log in to JIRA as a JIRA administrator.

2. Click on **Administration** in the top menu bar.

3. Select **Outgoing Mail** under the **Mail** section:

Adding an outgoing mail server

There are two ways of adding an outgoing mail server in JIRA, but before you get to that, regardless of which option you take, there are some common configuration parameters that you will need to fill in. The following table shows those parameters:

Field	Description
Name	This specifies a name for the mail server.
Description	This specifies a brief description for the mail server.
From address	This specifies an e-mail address that outgoing e-mails will appear to have come from.
Email prefix	This specifies a prefix that will appear with all the e-mails sent from JIRA. This allows your users to set up filter rules in their mail clients. The prefix will be added to the beginning of the e-mail subject.
Host Name	This specifies the host name of your mail server (for example, smtp.example.com).
SMTP Port	This specifies the port number your mail server will be running on. This is optional; if left blank, the default port number 25 will be used.
Username	This is used to authenticate against the mail server if required. Note that mail servers may require authentication to relay e-mails to non-local users.

Field	Description
Password	This is used to authenticate the user against the mail server, if required.
JNDI Location	This is the JNDI lookup name if you already have a mail server configured for your application server. Please refer to the following section for details.

For the rest of the parameters, depending on which option you take to set up your mail server, you only need to fill in the ones that are appropriate.

The first option is to specify the mail server's details, such as its host name and port number directly in JIRA. This is the approach that most people will use, as it is simple and straightforward. With this approach, the administrator fills in the mail server's host information, such as the host name and port number:

1. Browse to the **Mail** section and select the **Outgoing Mail** tab.
2. Click on the **Configure new SMTP mail server** button. This will bring you to the **Add SMTP Mail Server** page.
3. Fill in the details of your mail server, including the host name, port number, username, and password.
4. Click on the **Add** button to register to the mail server:

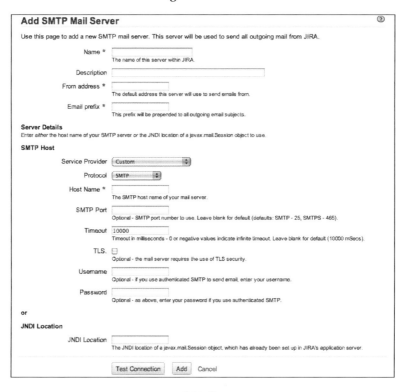

The second option is to use JNDI. This approach is slightly more complicated as it requires configuration on the application server itself (which is different per-application server), and sometimes requires a restart of the application server.

If you are using the standalone distribution, which uses Tomcat, the JNDI location will be `java:comp/env/mail/JiraMailServer`. You will also need to specify the mail server details as a JNDI resource in the `server.xml` file in the `JIRA_INSTALL/conf` directory.

A sample declaration for Apache Tomcat is shown in the following code snippet. You will need to substitute in your mail server's details:

```
<Resource name="mail/JiraMailServer"
  auth="Container"
  type="javax.mail.Session"
  mail.smtp.host="mail.server.host"
  mail.smtp.port="25"
  mail.transport.protocol="smtp"
  mail.smtp.auth="true"
  mail.smtp.user="username"
  password="password"
/>
```

You will need to restart JIRA after you have saved your changes.

Disabling the outgoing mail

In the older versions of JIRA, there is no easy way of disabling outgoing e-mails from JIRA. Administrators often had to delete the SMTP server and add it back again. In JIRA 5, you can disable all outgoing e-mails by just clicking on the **Disable Outgoing Mail** button in the **Outgoing Mail** page.

Enabling SSL over SMTP

To increase security, you can encrypt the communication between JIRA and your mail server, if your mail server supports SSL. There are two steps involved in enabling SMTP over SSL in JIRA.

The first step is to import your mail server's SSL certificate into Java's trust store. You can do this with Java's `keytool` utility. On a Windows machine, run the following command in a command prompt:

```
Keytool -import -alias mail.yourcompany.com -keystore $JAVA_HOME/jre/lib/
security/cacerts -file yourcertificate
```

The second step is to configure your application server to use SSL for mail communication. The following declaration is for Apache Tomcat that is used by JIRA Standalone. We use the same configuration file and only need to add two additional parameters:

```
<Resource name="mail/JiraMailServer"
  auth="Container"
  type="javax.mail.Session"
  mail.smtp.host="mail.server.host"
  mail.smtp.port="25"
  mail.transport.protocol="smtp"
  mail.smtp.auth="true"
  mail.smtp.user="username"
  password="password"
  mail.smtp.atarttls.enabled="true"
  mail.smtp.socketFactory.class="javax.net.ssl.SSLSocketFactory"
/>
```

Once you have imported your certificate and configured your mail server, you will have to restart JIRA.

Sending a test mail

It is always a good idea to send a test e-mail after you have configured your SMTP mail server, to make sure the server is running and you have set it correctly in JIRA:

1. Browse to the **Outgoing Mail** page.
2. Click on the **Send a Test Email** link for your SMTP mail server. This will take you to the **Send Mail** page.
3. Click on the **Send** button to send the e-mail. JIRA should auto-fill the **To** address based on your user profile.

If everything is correct, you should see a confirmation message in the **Mail log** section and receive the e-mail in your inbox. If there are errors, such as mail server connection, then the **Mail log** section will display the problems. This is very useful to troubleshoot any problems with JIRA's connectivity with the SMTP server:

Send Email

You can send a test email here.

To `admin@example.com`

Subject `Test Message From JIRA`

Message Type `Text ▾`

Body

```
This is a test message from JIRA.
Server: Default SMTP Server
SMTP Port: 25
Description: Local SMTP mail server.
From: support@company.com
Host User Name: null
```

SMTP logging ☐
Log SMTP-level details

[Send]   Cancel

Mail log

Log

```
An error has occurred with sending the test email:
com.atlassian.mail.MailException: javax.mail.MessagingException: Could not
connect to SMTP host: localhost, port: 25;
   nested exception is:
       java.net.ConnectException: Connection refused
       at
com.atlassian.mail.server.impl.SMTPMailServerImpl.sendWithMessageId(SMTPMa
ilServerImpl.java:201)
       at
com.atlassian.mail.server.impl.SMTPMailServerImpl.send(SMTPMailServerImpl.jav
a:149)
       at
com.atlassian.jira.plugins.mail.webwork.SendTestMail.doExecute(SendTestMail.jav
a:107)
       at webwork.action.ActionSupport.execute(ActionSupport.java:165)
```

Log of the events for sending mail.

In the preceding screenshot, you can see that the test e-mail delivery has failed and the error is because JIRA was unable to connect to the configured SMTP server.

Mail queues

E-mails in JIRA are not sent immediately when an operation is performed. Instead, they are placed in a mail queue, which JIRA empties periodically (every minute). This is very similar to the real-life scenario, where e-mails are placed in post boxes and picked up everyday.

Viewing the mail queue

Normally, you do not need to manage the mail queue. JIRA automatically places e-mails into the queue and flushes them periodically. However, as an administrator, there may be times when you wish to inspect the current queue and check if there are e-mails that are "stuck" and cannot be sent. E-mails can be stuck for a number of reasons. For example, if configured, SMTP mail server is not accessible. JIRA will automatically re-try.

Perform the following steps to view the mail queue and the mails it contains:

1. Browse to the **Mail** section.
2. Click on the **Mail Queue** tab to bring up the **Mail Queue** page:

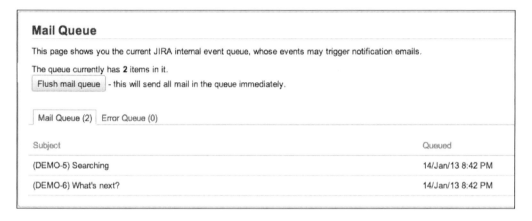

This page provides you with a one-page view of the current e-mails in the queue waiting to be delivered. There are two queues, the main mail queue and the error queue.

The **main mail queue** contains all the e-mails that are pending to be delivered. If JIRA is able to successfully deliver the e-mails, they will be removed from the queue. Items listed in red indicate that JIRA has unsuccessfully attempted to send those e-mails. JIRA will re-try ten times, and if still unsuccessful, these items will be moved to the error queue.

The **error queue** contains e-mails that cannot be delivered by JIRA. You can choose to resend all the failed items in the error queue, or delete all of them.

Flushing the mail queue

While JIRA automatically flushes the mail queue, you can also manually flush the queue if the queue gets stuck or send out e-mails immediately. When you manually flush the queue, JIRA will try to send all the e-mails that are currently in the queue.

Perform the following steps to manually flush the mail queue:

1. Browse to the **Mail Queue** page.
2. Click on the **Flush mail queue** button.

If JIRA is successful in sending the e-mails, you will see the queue shrink and the items disappear. If some e-mails fail to be delivered, those items will be highlighted in red.

Manually sending e-mails

Sometimes, you as the administrator may need to send out e-mails to a wide audience for important messages. For example, if you are planning for some maintenance work that will take JIRA offline for an extended period of time, then you may want to send out e-mails to all JIRA users to let them know of the outage.

JIRA has a built-in facility, where you can manually send out e-mails to specific groups of users. There are two options when manually sending e-mails—you can either send based on groups or by projects.

When sending by groups, all you have to do is select one or more groups in JIRA, and all users that belong to the selected groups will receive the e-mail. Users belonging to more than one group will not get duplicated e-mails.

When sending by projects, you have to first select one or more projects, and then the project roles. We will discuss project roles in more detail in the next chapter; for now, you can think of them as groups of users within projects. So, for example, you can send e-mails to all users that are a part of the demonstration project rather than all the users in JIRA.

The following screenshot shows an example of sending e-mails by group, where you send an outage notification to all members of the jira-user group, which is the default group for all JIRA users:

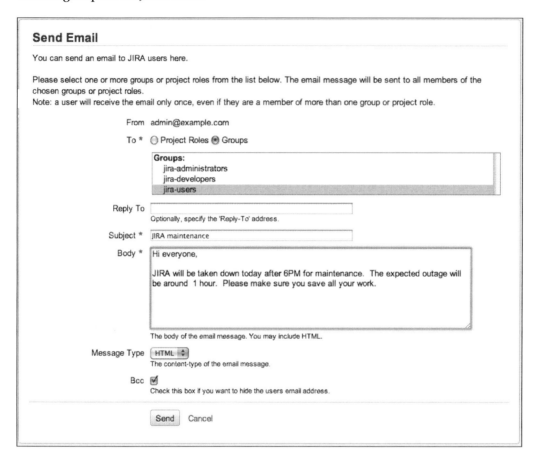

Since JIRA does not provide a WYSISYG editor for composing e-mails, you might want to draft an e-mail and send it to yourself first before sending it out to everyone.

Events

JIRA is an event driven system. This means that usually when an action occurs (for example, when an issue is created), JIRA fires off a corresponding event. This event is then picked up by components that are designed to listen to the event. Not surprisingly, they are called **listeners**. When a listener picks up an event, it will perform its duty such as keeping issues up to date with changes or send an e-mail to users watching the issue.

This mechanism allows JIRA to process operations asynchronously. The advantage of this model is operations, such as sending e-mails, are separated from JIRA's core functions like issue creation. If there is a problem with the mail server, for example, then you will not want this problem to prevent your users from creating issues.

There are two types of events in JIRA:

- **System events**: These are internal events used by JIRA, and they usually represent the main functionalities in JIRA. They cannot be added, edited, or deleted.
- **Custom events**: These events are created by users. They can be added and deleted and are fired via workflow post functions.

The following table lists all the system events in JIRA and what they are used for:

Event	Description
Issue Created	An issue has been created in JIRA.
Issue Updated	An issue has been updated (for example, changes to its fields).
Issue Assigned	An issue has been assigned to a user.
Issue Resolved	An issue has been resolved (usually applied to the resolve workflow transition).
Issue Closed	An issue has been closed (usually applied to the closed workflow transition).
Issue Commented	A comment has been added to an issue.
Issue Comment Edited	A comment has been updated.
Issue Reopened	An issue has been reopened (usually applied to the reopen workflow transition).
Issue Deleted	An issue has been deleted from JIRA.
Issue Moved	An issue has been moved (to a different or the same project).
Work Logged On Issue	Time has been logged on this issue (if time tracking has been enabled).

Event	Description
Work Started On Issue	The assignee has started working on this issue (usually applied to the start progress workflow transition).
Work Stopped On Issue	The assignee has stopped working on this issue (usually applied to the stop progress workflow transition).
Issue Worklog Updated	Worklog has been updated (if time tracking has been enabled).
Issue Worklog Deleted	Worklog has been deleted (if time tracking has been enabled).
Generic Event	A generic event that can be used by any workflow post function.
Custom Event	Events created by user to represent arbitrary events generated by business processes.

As an administrator, you will be able to get a one-page view of all the events in JIRA. You just need to do the following:

1. Log in to JIRA as a JIRA administrator.
2. Click on **Administration** in the top menu bar.
3. Select **Events** under the **Advanced** section. This will bring up the **View Events** page.

Like most other entities in JIRA, such as screens, events can be either active or inactive. New events are inactive by default, and they need to be associated with a notification scheme or workflow post function to become active. While you cannot edit or delete system events, you can deactivate them by removing their association with notification schemes and workflow post functions.

Each event is associated with a template, often referred to as **mail template**. These templates contain the base e-mail contents when notifications are sent. For system events, you cannot change their templates (you can change the template files, however). For custom events, you can choose to use one of the existing templates or create your own mail template.

Adding a mail template

Mail templates are physical files that you create and edit directly via a text editor. Each mail template is made up of three files:

- **Subject**: This file contains the template used to generate the e-mail's subject.

- **Text template**: This file contains the template used by JIRA when the e-mail is sent as plain text.

- **HTML template**: This file contains the template used by JIRA when the e-mail is sent as HTML.

Mail templates are stored in the `<JIRA_INSTALL>/atlassian-jira/WEB-INF/classes/templates/email` directory. Each of the three files listed are placed in their respective directories called `subject`, `text`, and `html`.

While creating new mail templates, it is a good practice to name your template files after the issue event. This will help future users understand the purpose of the templates.

Mail templates use Apache's Velocity template language (`http://velocity.apache.org`). For this reason, creating new mail templates will require some understanding of HTML and template programming.

If your templates only contain static text, you can simply use standard HTML tags for your template. However, if you need to have dynamic data rendered as part of your templates, such as the issue key or summary, you will need to use the **Velocity syntax**. A full explanation of Velocity is beyond the scope of this book. The following section provides a quick introduction to creating simple mail templates for JIRA. You can find more information on Velocity and its usage in JIRA mail templates at `https://confluence.atlassian.com/x/dQISCw`.

In a Velocity template, all the text will be treated as normal. Anything that starts with a dollar sign (`$`) such as `$issue` is a Velocity statement. The `$` sign tells Velocity to reference the item after the sign, and when combined with the period (`.`), you are able to retrieve the value specified. For example, the following command will get the issue key and summary from the current issue, separated by a – character:

```
$issue.key - $issue.summary
```

JIRA provides a range of Velocity references that you can use for creating mail templates. You can find a comprehensive list at `https://developer.atlassian.com/display/JIRADEV/Velocity%20Context%20for%20Email%20Templates`.

Now that you have a brief understanding of how Velocity works, you first need to create a template for the mail subject. The following command shows a typical subject template:

```
$eventTypeName: ($issue.key) $issue.summary
```

When the template is processed, JIRA will substitute in the actual values for event type (for example, Issue Created), issue key, and issue summary (for example, Issue Escalated: HD-11 – Database server is running at very slow).

You then need to create a template for the actual e-mail content. You need to create a text and HTML version. The following code shows a simple example of a text-based template, which displays the key for the escalated issue:

```
Hello,

The ticket $issue.key has been escalated and is currently being worked
on.  We will contact you if we require more information.

Regards
Support team.
```

Before JIRA sends out the e-mail, the preceding text will be processed, where all Velocity references, such as `$issue.key`, will be converted into proper values, for example, `DEMO-1`.

After creating your mail templates, register them with JIRA. To register your new templates, locate and open the `email-templates-id-mappings.xml` file in the `<JIRA_INSTALL>/atlassian-jira/WEB-INF/classes` directory in a text editor. Add a new entry to the end of the file before the closing the `</templatemappings>` tag, as follows:

```
<templatemapping id="10001">
  <name>Example Custom Event</name>
  <template>examplecustomevent.vm</template>
  <templatetype>issueevent</templatetype>
</templatemapping>
```

Here, we have registered a new custom mail template entry:

Parameter	Description
id	The unique ID for the template.
name	A human-readable name for JIRA to display.
template	The mail template file names for `subject`, `text`, and `html`. All three template files must be named as specified here.
type	Template type. For events generated from an issue, the value will be `issueevent`.

After creating your templates and registering them in the mapping file, you will have to restart JIRA for the changes to be picked up.

Adding a custom event

JIRA comes with a comprehensive list of system events focused around issue-related operations. However, there will be times when you will need to create custom-designed events representing specialized business operations, or you simply need to use a custom e-mail template.

Perform the following steps to add a new custom event:

1. Browse to the **View Events** page.
2. Provide a meaningful name for the new event in the **Add New Event** section.
3. Provide an optional description.
4. Select the mail template for the new event.
5. Click on the **Add** button to create the new event:

New events are inactive by default. Associating them with a notification scheme or workflow post function will activate them.

Firing a custom event

Unlike system events, with custom events, you need to tell JIRA when it should fire a custom event.

Custom events are mostly fired by workflow transitions. If you recall from *Chapter 6, Workflows and Business Processes*, you can add post functions to workflow transitions. Almost all JIRA's transitions will have a post function that fires an appropriate event. It is important to understand that just because an event is fired, it does not mean that there needs to be something to listen to it.

If you have skipped *Chapter 6, Workflows and Business Processes*, or still do not have a good understanding on workflows, now will be a good time to go back and revisit the chapter.

Perform the following steps to fire a custom event from a workflow post function:

1. Browse to the **View Workflows** page.
2. Create a draft of the workflow if it is active or click on the **Steps** link if the workflow is inactive.
3. Click on the transition that will fire the event when executed.
4. Click on the **Post Functions** tab.
5. Click on the **Edit** link for the post function that reads **Fire a <event name> event that can be processed by the listeners**:

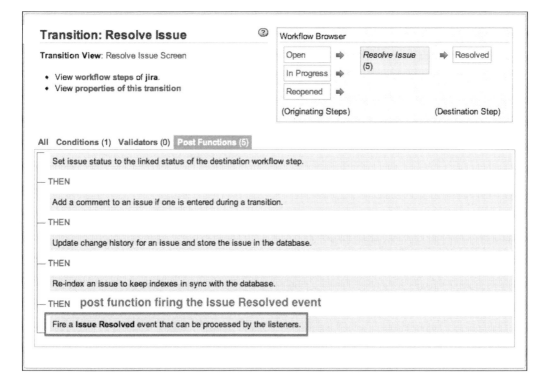

6. Select the custom event from the drop-down list.
7. Click on the **Update** button to apply the changes to the post function.
8. Publish the workflow.

Now, whenever the workflow transition is executed, the `post` function will run and fire the selected event. Each transition can fire only one event, so you cannot have **both Issue Created** and **Issue Updated** events being fired from the one transition.

Notifications

Notifications associate events (both system and custom) to e-mail recipients. When an event is fired and picked up, e-mails will be sent out. Notification recipients are defined by notification types. For example, you can set it to only send e-mails to a specific user or all members from a given user group. You can add multiple notifications to a given event.

JIRA ships with a comprehensive list of notification types that will cover many of your needs. The following table lists all the notification types available and how they work:

Notification type	Description
Current Assignee	The current assignee of the issue.
Reporter	The reporter of the issue (usually the person who originally created the issue).
Current User	The user who fired the event.
Project Lead	Lead of the project that the issue belongs to.
Component Lead	Lead of the component the issue belongs to.
Single User	Any user that exists in JIRA.
Group	All users that belong to the specified group.
Project Role	All users that belong to the specified project role.
Single Email Address	Any e-mail address.
All Watchers	All users that are watching this issue.
User Custom Field Value	The users specified in the user type custom field. For example, if you have a **User Picker** custom field called **Recipient**, the user selected in the custom field will receive notifications if he/she has access to the issue.
Group Custom Field Value	All users that belong to the group in the group type custom field. For example, if you have a **Group Picker** custom field called **Approvers**, all users from the group (with access to the issue) selected in the custom field will receive notifications.

As you can see, the list includes a wide range of options from issue reporters to values contained in custom fields. Basically, anything that can be represented as a user in JIRA can have notifications set up.

If a user belongs to more than one notification for a single event, JIRA will make sure that only one e-mail will be sent so the user does not receive duplicates. In order for a user to receive notifications, the user must have permission to view the issue. The only exception to this is when using the **Single Email Address** option (we will discuss security in *Chapter 8, Securing JIRA*). If the user does not have the permission to view the issue, JIRA will not send a notification e-mail.

We will look at how you can add notifications to events, so that users can start receiving e-mails, but before that, you need to first take a look at the notification scheme.

The notification scheme

The notification scheme is a reusable entity that links events with notifications. In other words, it contains the associations between events and their respective e-mail recipients:

1. Log in to JIRA as a JIRA administrator.

2. Click on **Administration** in the top menu bar.

3. Select **Notification Schemes** at the bottom to bring up the **Notification Schemes** page:

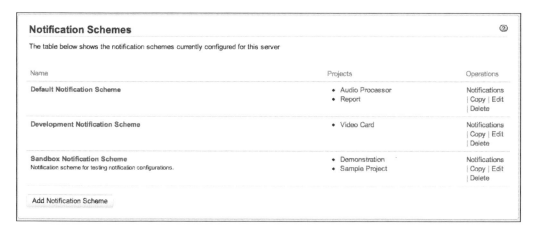

From this screen, you can see a list of all the notification schemes and what projects are currently using them.

JIRA comes with a generic default notification scheme. The default scheme is set up with notifications set for all the system events. This allows you to quickly enable notification in JIRA. The default setup has the following notifications:

- **Current Assignee**
- **Reporter**
- **All Watchers**

You can modify the default notification scheme to add your own notification rules, but it is a better idea to create a new scheme from scratch or copy the default scheme and make your modifications.

Adding a notification scheme

As with all other aspects in JIRA, you are not forced to use the default configurations provided. JIRA allows you to create your own custom notification schemes to set up customized notification rules that can be applied to your projects.

Perform the following steps to create a new notification scheme:

1. Browse to the **Notification Schemes** page.
2. Click on the **Add Notification Scheme** link. This will bring you to the **Add Notification Scheme** page.
3. Provide a meaningful name for the new notification scheme.
4. Provide an optional description that will help explain the purpose and usage of the new scheme.
5. Click on the **Add** button to create the notification scheme.

When you create a new notification scheme, you create a blank scheme that can be configured later to add your own notification rules in. It is important that after you have created a new notification scheme, you configure its notification rules before applying the scheme to projects, otherwise no notifications will be sent out. You will look at how to configure notification rules later in this chapter.

Editing a notification scheme

You can keep your notification scheme's name and description up to date editing it. Do not confuse this with updating the scheme's configuration. Just like other schemes, a notification scheme's name and description details are kept and managed separately from its configuration contents.

Perform the following steps to edit a notification scheme:

1. Browse to the **Notification Schemes** page.
2. Click on the **Edit** link for the notification scheme you wish to update. This will bring up the **Edit Notification Scheme** page.
3. Provide a new name and description.
4. Click on the **Update** button to apply the changes.

You can make updates to the notification scheme at any time, regardless of whether it is being used by projects.

Deleting a notification scheme

Unlike most other schemes, such as workflow, JIRA allows you to delete notifications schemes even when they are being used by projects. However, JIRA does prompt you with a warning when you attempt to delete a notification scheme that is in use.

Perform the following steps to delete a notification scheme:

1. Browse to the **Notification Schemes** page.
2. Click on the **Delete** link for the notification scheme you wish to remove. This will bring up **the Delete Notification Scheme** page.
3. Click on the **Delete** button to remove the notification scheme.

Once you have deleted a notification scheme, the projects that were previously using the scheme will have no notification schemes, so you will have to reapply schemes individually.

When you delete a notification scheme, you remove all the notifications you set up in the scheme.

Copying a notification scheme

It is always a good idea to make a backup copy of your notification schemes before making changes or deleting them. This allows you to quickly roll back your changes if problems are detected. Another benefit of copying an existing notification scheme is the amount of time it can save. As you have seen, when you create a new notification scheme from scratch, it will contain no notifications. Most of the time, it will be more efficient to use the default notification scheme provided by JIRA as a base and modify the notification rules accordingly.

Whatever the reason may be, you will find the ability to make copies of existing notification schemes to be handy from time to time. Perform the following steps to copy a notification scheme:

1. Browse to the **Notification Schemes** page.
2. Click on the **Copy** link for the notification scheme you wish to copy. A copy of the notification scheme will be made immediately with the name **Copy of** appended to the original notification scheme.

Once you have copied a notification scheme, you can edit its name and description to better describe its purpose, and configure its notifications as explained in the next sections.

Managing a notification scheme

Notification schemes contain notifications that are set on events in JIRA.

Perform the following steps to configure a notification scheme:

1. Browse to the **Notification Schemes** page.
2. Click on the **Notifications** link for the notification scheme you wish to configure. This will bring you to the **Edit Notifications** page.

This page lists all the existing events in JIRA and their corresponding notification recipients. If you configure a new notification scheme, there will be no notifications set for the events.

Adding a notification

There are two ways you can add a new notification. You can add a notification for a specific event, or you can add a notification for multiple events.

Perform the following steps to add a new notification:

1. Browse to the **Edit Notifications** page for the notification scheme you wish to configure.
2. Click on the **Add notification** link or the **Add** link for the event you wish to add a notification for. This will bring you to the **Add Notification** page. If you click on the **Add** link, the **Events selection** list will preselect the event for you.
3. Select the notification type from the available options.

4. Click on the **Add** button:

Once added, the notification will be listed against the events selected. You can continue adding notifications for the events by repeating the same steps.

Deleting a notification

When notifications are no longer required for certain events, you can also have them removed. To remove notifications, you will need to do it one by one, per event:

1. Browse to the **Edit Notifications** page for the notification scheme you wish to configure.

2. Click on the **Delete** link for the notification you wish to remove. This will bring you to the **Delete Notification** page.

3. Click on the **Delete** button to remove the notification for the event.

After you have removed a notification, users affected by that notification will stop receiving e-mails from JIRA. However, you need to pay attention to your configurations, as there might be other notifications for the same event that will continue to send e-mails to the same user. For example, if you have created two notifications for the event **Issue Created**—one set to the **Single User** admin (who belongs to the `jira-administrator` group), and another set to **Group** (`jira-administrator`). If your goal to is prevent e-mails being sent to the user admin, you will need to remove both the notifications from the event instead of simply the **Single User** option.

Assigning a notification scheme

When new projects are created, they are automatically assigned to use the default notification scheme. If you want your project to use a different scheme, you will need to go to the **Notifications** section of your project's administration console:

1. Go to the target project's administration console.

2. Select the **Notifications** tab. In the **Notifications** section, you will be able to see the current notification scheme and its configurations.

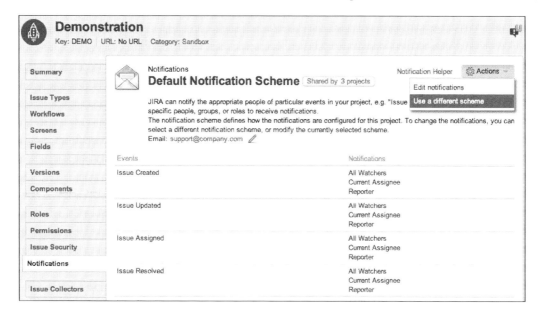

3. Select **Use a different scheme** in the **Actions** menu. This will bring up the **Associate Notification Scheme to Project** page.

4. Select the notification scheme to use.

5. Click on the **Associate** button.

As soon as a notification scheme is applied to the project, it will take effect immediately and you will see e-mails being sent out for the events that have been configured in the scheme. Like any other schemes in JIRA, notification schemes can be assigned to multiple projects to share the same notification behavior.

Troubleshooting notifications

Often, when people do not receive notifications from JIRA, it can be difficult and frustrating to find the cause. The two most common causes for notification-related problems are either outgoing mail server connectivity or misconfiguration of the notification scheme.

Troubleshooting outgoing mail server problems is quite simple. All you have to do is try to send out a test e-mails as described in the earlier section. If you receive your test e-mail, then there should be no problems with your outgoing mail server configuration, and you can focus on your notification configurations.

Troubleshooting notifications is not as straightforward, since there are a number of things that you will need to consider. To help with this challenge, JIRA 5 has introduced a new feature called the **Notification Helper**. The notification helper can save the JIRA administrators' time by helping them to pinpoint why a given user does or does not receive notifications. All the administrator has to do is to tell the helper who the user is, which issue (or an example issue from a project) the user should or should not be receiving notifications for, and the event that is triggering the notification:

1. Log in to JIRA as a JIRA administrator.
2. Click on **Administration** in the top menu bar.
3. Select **Notification Helper** under **Admin Helper** section.
4. Specify the user that is or is not receiving notifications in the **User** field.
5. Specify the issue to test with.
6. Select the type of notification event.
7. Click on **Submit**.

Notification Helper will then process the input and report back if the user should be receiving notifications and why, based on notification scheme settings:

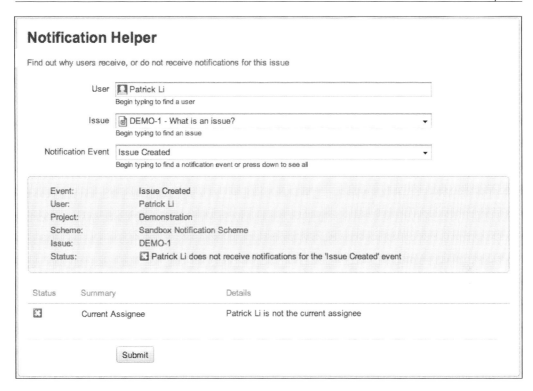

As you can see from the preceding screenshot, the user **Patrick Li** is currently not receiving notifications for **DEMO-1** issue, because the notification is set up to have only the **Current Assignee** receive e-mails, and **Patrick Li** is not the assignee.

Incoming e-mails

We have seen how you can configure JIRA to send e-mails to notify users of updates on their issues. But this is only half of the story when it comes to JIRA's e-mail support.

You can also set up JIRA for it to periodically poll mailboxes for e-mails and create issues based on the e-mails' subject and content. This is a very powerful feature with the following benefits:

- Hides the complexity of JIRA from business users, so that they can log issues more efficiently and leave the complexity to your IT team.

- Allows users to create issues even if JIRA can only be accessed within the internal network. Users can send e-mails to a dedicated mailbox for JIRA to poll.

Adding an incoming mail server

For JIRA to retrieve e-mails and create issues from them, you need to add the POP/IMAP mail server configurations to JIRA. **POP** and **IMAP** are mail protocols used to retrieve e-mails from the server. E-mail clients, such as Microsoft Outlook and Mozilla Thunderbird, can use one of these protocols to retrieve your e-mails.

Unlike outgoing mail servers, JIRA allows you to add multiple incoming mail servers. This is because while you only need one mail server to send e-mails, you might have multiple mail servers or multiple mail accounts (on the same server) that people will use to send e-mails to. For example, you might have one dedicated to support and another one for sales. It is usually a good idea to create separate mail accounts to make it easier when trying to work out which e-mail should go into which project. For this reason, adding POP/IMAP mail servers can be thought of as adding multiple mail accounts in JIRA:

Perform the following steps to add an incoming mail server:

1. Browse to the **Incoming Mail** page.
2. Click on the **Configure POP/IMAP mail server** button. This will bring you to the **Add POP/IMAP Mail Server** page.
3. Provide a meaningful name for the mail server.
4. Provide an optional description.
5. Select the type of mail service provider. For example, if you are using your own hosted mail service, or one of the recognized Cloud provider such as Google.
6. Specify the host name of the POP/IMAP server if you are using your own (custom provider).
7. Enter the username/password credentials for the mail account.
8. Click on the **Add** button to create the POP/IMAP mail server:

Add POP / IMAP Mail Server

Use this page to add a new POP / IMAP server for JIRA to retrieve mail from.

Name *

The name of this server within JIRA.

Description

Service Provider `Custom`

Protocol `POP`

Host Name *

The host name of your POP / IMAP server.

POP / IMAP Port

Optional - The port to use to retrieve mail from your POP / IMAP account. Leave blank for default. (defaults: POP - 110, SECURE_POP - 995, IMAP - 143, SECURE_IMAP - 993)

Timeout `10000`

Timeout in milliseconds - 0 or negative values indicate infinite timeout. Leave blank for default (10000 mSecs).

Username *

The username used to authenticate your POP / IMAP account.

Password *

The password for your POP / IMAP account.

Test Connection | Add | Cancel

You can repeat this and add additional POP/IMAP mail servers.

Mail handlers

Mail handlers are what JIRA uses to process retrieved e-mails. Each mail handler is able to process e-mails from one incoming mail server, and periodically scan for new e-mails.

JIRA ships with a number of mail handlers, each with their own features. In the following sections, we will discuss each of the handlers in detail.

Creating a new issue or adding a comment to an existing issue

Creating a new issue or adding a comment to an existing issue mail handler (also known as the Create or Comment Handler in previous version of JIRA), is the most used mail handler. It will create new issues from the received e-mails and also add comments to existing issues if the incoming e-mail's subject contains a matching issue key. If the subject does not contain a matching issue key, a new issue is created:

Parameter	Description
Project	The project in which issues will be created. This is not used for commenting where the e-mail subject will contain the issue key.
Issue Type	The issue type for newly created issues.
Strip Quotes	If present in the parameters, quoted text from the e-mail will not be added as a part of the comment.
Catch Email Address	Specifies if JIRA is to only handle e-mails that are sent to the specified address.
Bulk	This specifies how to handle auto-generated e-mails, such as those generated by JIRA. It is possible to create a loop, if JIRA sends e-mails to the same mailbox where it also picks up e-mails. In order to prevent this, you can specify to either of the following: • `ignore`: Ignore these e-mails • `forward`: Forward these e-mails to another address • `delete`: Delete these e-mails altogether Generally, you should set it to `forward`.
Forward Email	If specified, then if the mail handler is unable to process an e-mail message it receives, an e-mail message indicating this problem will be forwarded to the e-mail address specified in this field.
Create Users	If the e-mail is sent from an unknown address, JIRA will create a new user based on the e-mail "from" address and randomly generate a password. An e-mail will be sent to the "from" address informing the new JIRA account.
Default Reporter	Specifies the username of a default reporter, which will be used if the e-mail address in the **From:** field of any received messages does not match the address associated with that of an existing JIRA user.

Parameter	Description
Notify Users	Uncheck this option if you do not want JIRA to notify new users created as per the **Create Users** parameter.
CC Assignee	JIRA will assign the issue to the user specified in the **To** field first. If no user can be matched from the **To** field, JIRA will then try the users in the **CC** and then **BCC** list.
CC Watchers	JIRA will add users in the **CC** list (if they exist) as watchers of the issue.

Adding a comment with the entire e-mail body

This mail handler extracts text from an e-mail's content and adds it to the issue with a matching issue key in the subject. The author of the comment is taken from the **From** field.

It has a similar set of parameters to the Create and Comment handler.

Adding a comment from the non-quoted e-mail body

Adding a comment from the non-quoted e-mail body is very similar to the Full Comment Handler, but only extracts non-quoted texts and adds them as comments. Texts that start with ">" or "|" are considered to be quoted.

It has a similar set of parameters to the Create and Comment handler.

Creating a new issue from each e-mail message

Creating a new issue from each e-mail message is very similar to the Create and Comment handler except this will always create a new issue for every received e-mail.

It has a similar set of parameters to the Create and Comment handler.

Adding a comment before a specified marker or separator in the e-mail body

Adding a comment before a specified marker or separator in the e-mail body is a more powerful version of the comment handlers. It uses regular expressions to extract texts from e-mail contents and add them to the issue:

Parameter	Description
Split Regex	The regex expression to use to extract contents. There are two rules for the regex expression:

- It must start and end with a delimiter character, usually /

- It cannot contain commas. For example, /-{}{}
  {}{}{}\s*Original Message\s*{}-/ or
  /_____*/

Adding a mail handler

You can set up as many mail handlers as you want. It is recommended that you create dedicated mailboxes for each project you wish to allow JIRA to create issues from e-mails. For each account, you will then need to create a mail handler. The mailbox you set up needs to be accessible via POP or IMAP.

Perform the following steps to add a mail handler:

1. Browse to the **Incoming Mail** page.
2. Click on the **Add** incoming mail handler button. This will bring up the **Mail Handler** dialog box.
3. Provide a meaningful name to the new mail handler.
4. Select an incoming mail server or **Local Files**.
5. Specify how long JIRA should wait to poll the mailbox for new e-mails (in minutes). You will want to keep this long enough to allow enough time for JIRA to process all the e-mails, but not too long so you end up having to wait for a long time to see your e-mails converted into issues in JIRA.
6. Select the type of handler you want to add.
7. Click on the **Next** button:

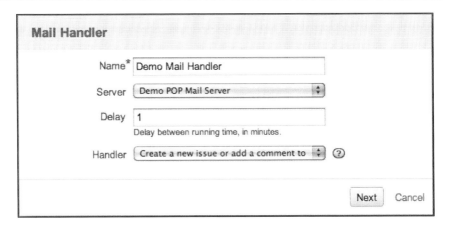

Depending on the handler type you have selected, the next screen will vary. On the next screen, you will need to provide the required parameters for the mail handler, as described in the preceding section. The following screenshot shows an example configuration dialog box, where new issues will be created in the **Demonstration** project as **Bugs**:

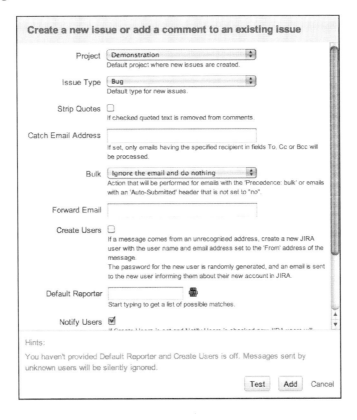

Editing and deleting a mail handler

You can update the details of your mail handlers at any time. You would often need to tune your handler parameters a few times until you get your desired results. Perform the following steps to update a mail handler:

1. Browse to the **Incoming Mail** page.

2. Click on the **Edit** link for the mail handler you wish to update.

3. Update the configure options.

Once updated, the changes will be applied immediately and JIRA will use the new handler parameters for the next polling run.

You can also delete mail handlers that are no longer required at any time.

1. Browse to the **Incoming Mail** page.

2. Click on the **Delete** link for the mail handler you wish to remove.

> You will not be prompted with a confirmation page. The mail handler will be removed immediately, so think carefully before you delete it.

The Help Desk project

Users will often want to get progress updates on their issues after they have logged them. So, instead of business users having to ask for updates, we will proactively update them through our newly acquired knowledge; that is JIRA notifications.

In *Chapter 4, Field Management*, we added a custom field called **Escalation List**, which allows users to add who else will receive notifications along with the issue's reporter and assignee.

Another customization we have made is to the workflows in *Chapter 6, Workflows and Business Processes*, with new transitions. We need to make sure those transitions fire appropriate events and also send out notifications. In summary, we need to do the following:

- Send out notifications for the new custom events fired by our custom workflow transitions

- Send out notifications to users specified in our **Escalation List** custom field

While you can achieve both by using other JIRA features, such as adding users as watchers to the issue and reusing existing JIRA system events, this exercise will explore the options available to you, and as you will see in later chapters, there are other criteria to consider while deciding on the best approach.

Setting up mail servers

The first step to enable e-mail communication, as you will have guessed, is to register mail servers in JIRA. If you are using the standalone distribution of JIRA, it is recommended that you add your mail server by entering the host information:

1. Log in to JIRA as a JIRA administrator.
2. Click on **Administration** in the top menu bar.
3. Select **Outgoing Mail** from the **Mail** section.
4. Click on the **Configure new SMTP mail server** button.
5. Fill in your mail server information.

After adding your mail server, you can try sending yourself a quick test mail to see if JIRA is able to access your server successfully.

Setting up custom events

In *Chapter 6, Workflows and Business Processes*, we created two new workflow transitions. One is for the help desk staff to request additional information from the business user, and another for the business user to supply the requested information. What you need to do now is create custom events for the transitions when they are executed:

1. Log in to JIRA as a JIRA administrator.
2. Click on **Administration** in the top menu bar.
3. Select **Events** at bottom of the page..
4. Name the new event `Info Requested`.
5. Provide a description for the event—`This is the request information event`.
6. Select the **Issue Updated** template.
7. Click on the **Add** button to create the new event.

With your event created, you now need to update your workflow so that your transitions can fire the correct event:

1. Browse to the **View Workflows** page.
2. Create a draft of **Help Desk Workflow**.
3. Click on the **Request for Info** transition.
4. Update the post function to fire our **Info Requested** event rather then the **Generic Event**.

In this case, you can reuse the **Issue Updated** event and it will work just as fine. However, there are advantages to having your own custom events as it helps to distinguish exactly what is the nature of the update. When you have the listeners' components in JIRA, having specialized events helps to distinguish the origin and act accordingly.

Setting up a notification scheme

Now you need to have your own notification scheme, so you can start adding notifications to your events. We will be basing our notification scheme on the default scheme to help us get things set up quickly:

1. Log in to JIRA as a JIRA Administrator.
2. Click on **Administration** in the top menu bar.
3. Select **Notification Schemes** under the **Issues** section.
4. Click on the **Copy** link for **Default Notification Scheme**. A new notification scheme named **Copy of Default Notification Scheme** will be created.
5. Click on the **Edit** link of **Copy of Default Notification Scheme**.
6. Rename it to Help Desk Notification Scheme.

This will create a new notification scheme with the basic notifications prepopulated. All you need to do now is modify the events and add your own notification needs.

Setting up notifications

There are two rules you need to follow to add our notifications. First, you need to add notifications for your custom events, so that e-mails will be sent out when they are fired. Second, you will want users specified in the **CC** list custom field to also receive e-mails along with the assignee and reporter of the issue:

1. Click on the **Notifications** link for **Help Desk Notification Scheme**.
2. Click on the **Add notification** link.
3. Select all the event types.
4. Select **User Custom Field Value** for notification type and select **CC List** from the drop-down list.
5. Click on the **Add** button.

Nice and easy. With just a few clicks, JIRA has allowed us to add a new notification to not only all the system events, but also our new custom events.

Putting it together

The last step, as always, is to associate your scheme with projects for activation:

1. Browse to the **Project Administration** page for your Help Desk project.
2. Click on the **Notifications** tab.
3. Select **Use a different scheme** in the **Actions** menu.
4. Select **Help Desk Notification Scheme**.
5. Click on the **Associate** button.

With just a few clicks, you have enabled your JIRA to automatically send out e-mails to update users with their issue's progress. Not only this, you have tied in the custom fields you created from earlier chapters to manage who, along with the issue assignee and reporter, will also get the notifications. So let's put this to test!

1. Create a new issue in the Help Desk project.
2. Select one or more users for the **Escalation List** custom field. It is a good idea not to select yourself since the reporter will get notifications by default. Also make sure that the user selected has a valid e-mail address.
3. Execute the **Request for Info** transition on the new issue.
4. You should receive e-mails from JIRA within minutes.

If you do not receive e-mails from JIRA, check your mail queue and see if the mail is getting generated, and follow the steps from the *Troubleshooting Notifications* section.

Summary

In this chapter, we have looked at how JIRA can stay in touch with your users with the use of e-mails. Indeed, with today's new gadgets, such as smart phones and tablets, being able to keep users up to date with e-mails is a very powerful feature, and JIRA has a very flexible structure in place to define the rules on who will receive notifications.

We have also very briefly mentioned some of the security rules about who can receive notifications. JIRA performs security checks prior to sending out notifications for two very good reasons — one, there is no point sending out an e-mail to a user who cannot view the issue; two, you will not want unauthorized users to view the issue to receive updates that they should not know about.

In the next chapter, we will look into the security aspects of JIRA and how you can secure your data to prevent unauthorized access.

8
Securing JIRA

In the previous chapters, you have learned how to store data in JIRA by creating issues. As you can see, as an information system, JIRA is all about data. So, it should come as no surprise to you that security plays a big role in JIRA to not only ensure only the right people will get access to our data, but also maintain data integrity by preventing accidental changes.

Starting with JIRA 4.4, there have been many significant improvements in the user management area, including simplifying the LDAP integration and adding the ability to have multiple user repositories with the user directory feature. JIRA 5 has continued on this path and kept on improving these features.

By the end of the chapter, you will have learned the following:

- User directories and how to connect JIRA to LDAP
- General access control in JIRA
- Managing fine-grained permission settings
- How to troubleshoot permission problems

Before we delve into the deep end of how JIRA handles security, let's first take a look at how JIRA maintains user and group memberships.

User directories

User directories are what JIRA uses to store information about users and groups. A user directory is backed by a user repository system, such as LDAP, a database, or a remote user management system, such as Atlassian Crowd.

You can have multiple user directories in JIRA. This allows you to connect your JIRA to multiple user repositories. For example, you can have an LDAP directory for your internal users and a database directory (for example, JIRA internal directory) for external users. For example, in the following screenshot, we have two user directories configured. The first user directory is connected to **Microsoft Active Directory (Read Only)**, while the second one is a built-in JIRA **Internal** directory running on a database:

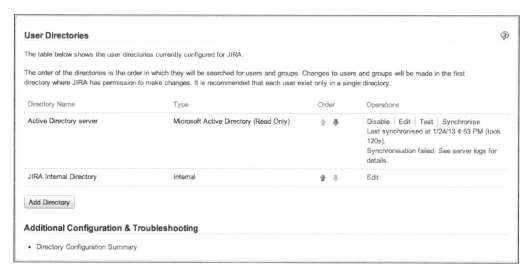

Perform the following steps to access the user directories interface:

1. Browse to the JIRA administration console.

2. Select **User Directories** from the **Users** section.

While adding a new user directory, you need to first decide on the directory type. There are several different user directory types within JIRA:

- **JIRA internal directory**: This is the built-in default user directory when you first install JIRA. With this directory, all the user and group information is stored in the JIRA database.

- **Active directory/LDAP**: This is used when you want to connect JIRA to an LDAP server. With this directory, JIRA will use the backend LDAP to query user information and group membership. This is also known as **LDAP Connector**, and should not be confused with Internal and LDAP Authentication directories.

JIRA supports a wide range of LDAP servers including Microsoft Active Directory, OpenLDAP, and Novell eDirectory server. If a particular LDAP is not listed as one of the options, then there is also a **Generic Directory Server** option.

When using the AD/LDAP connector directory type, you can choose to connect with one of the permission options:

- **Read only**: JIRA cannot make any modifications to the LDAP server.

- **Read only, with local groups**: Information retrieved from LDAP will be read only, but you can also add users to groups created within JIRA. These changes will not be reflected in LDAP.

- **Read/Write**: JIRA will be able to retrieve and make changes to the LDAP server.

- **Internal with LDAP authentication**: Also known as **Delegated LDAP**, with this directory type, JIRA will only use LDAP for authentication, and will keep all user information internally in the database. This approach can have better performance. Since LDAP is only used for authentication, this avoids the need to download larger numbers of groups from LDAP.

- **Atlassian Crowd**: If you are also using Atlassian Crowd (a user management and SSO solution), you can use this directory type to connect to your Crowd instance. With this option, you can also configure your JIRA to participate in the SSO session.

- Atlassian JIRA: JIRA is capable of acting as a user repository for other compatible applications. If you have another JIRA instance running, you can use this directory type to connect to the other JIRA and for user information.

Managing user directories

When you have multiple user directories configured for JIRA, there are a few important points to keep in mind.

The order of the user directories is important, as it will directly affect the order JIRA will use to search users, and apply changes made to users and groups. For example, if you have two user directories, both have a user called **admin** with different passwords, this will have the following effects:

- When you log in to JIRA with the user admin, you will be logged in as the admin user from the first user directory that is able to validate the password, in the order of listed directories.

- After logging in, you will be granted with group membership from the directory that has validated your password. Any other directories will be skipped.

- If you make a change to the admin user, such as the full name, then the changes will only be applied to the first directory JIRA has write access to.

Another important point to remember when working with user directories is that you cannot make changes to the user directory when you are logged in with a user account that belongs to the said directory. For example, if you are logged in with an LDAP account, then you will not be able to make changes to JIRA's LDAP settings, since there is a potential where the new change may actually lock you out of JIRA.

> Always have an active administrator user account ready in the default JIRA Internal directory; for example, the account created during initial setup. This will provide you with an administrator account that can help you fix user directory problems such as the preceding scenario.

Connecting to LDAP

In the days prior to user directories, connecting to LDAP was a tedious process of manually editing configuration files and restarting the system. With user directories, it is much easier to connect JIRA to an LDAP server for user management.

To connect your JIRA to LDAP, all you have to do is to add a new user directory:

1. Browse to the **User Directories** page.
2. Click on on the **Add Directory** button and select the either **Microsoft Active Directory** or **LDAP**.
3. Provide your LDAP server information.

Since every LDAP is different, the exact parameters that are required will vary. At a minimum, you need to provide the following information:

Parameter	Description
Name	This is the name of the user directory.
Directory Type	Select the flavor of your LDAP. This will help JIRA to prefill some of the parameters for you.
Hostname	This is the hostname of your LDAP server.
Port	This is the port number of your LDAP server. JIRA will prefill this based on your directory type selection.

Parameter	Description
Base DN	This is the root node for JIRA to search for users and groups.
LDAP Permissions	This helps choose whether JIRA should be able to make changes to LDAP.
Username	This is the username JIRA should use to connect to LDAP for user and group information.
Password	This is the password for JIRA to use to connect to LDAP.

You can see these sections filled in the following screenshot:

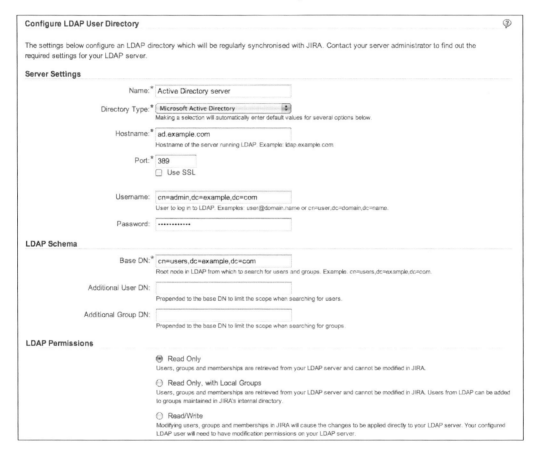

Apart from the preceding parameters are additional advanced settings such as **User configuration** and **Group schema configuration**. After filling in the form, you can click on on the **Quick Test** button to verify if JIRA is able to connect to your LDAP server and authenticate with the username and password provided. Note that this does not test for things such as the user look up. If the initial quick test is successful, then you can go ahead and click on the **Save and Test** button. This will add the user directory and take you to the test page where you can test the settings with a proper user credential (this should be different than the one used by JIRA to connect to LDAP):

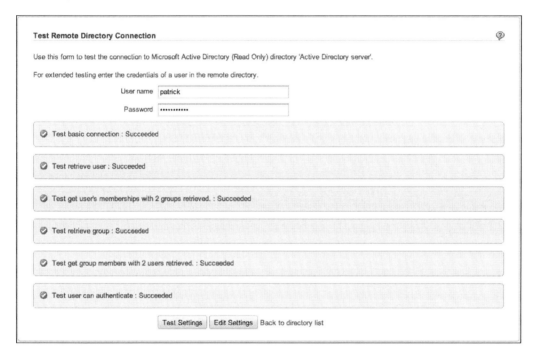

After the new user directory is added, JIRA will automatically synchronize with the LDAP server and pull in users and groups. Depending upon the size of your LDAP, this may take some time to complete. After the initial synchronization, JIRA will periodically synchronize with LDAP for any changes.

Users

In any information system, for users to access the system, they need to have an account. In JIRA, each user needs to have his/her own user account for him/her to access JIRA, unless JIRA is configured to allow anonymous access. Each user is identified by his/her username, which cannot be changed after account creation.

User Browser

User Browser is where you will be able to see a list of all the users in JIRA, including their usernames, e-mail addresses, last login attempt, and which user directory they belong to. **User Browser** also provides you with search capabilities. You will be able to search for users that fit the criteria such as username, full name, e-mail address, and group association. Perform the following steps to access the user browser:

1. Browse to the JIRA administration console.
2. Select **Users** under the **Users** section to bring up the **User Browser** page.

By default, the results will be paginated to show twenty users per page, but you can change this setting to show up to a hundred users per page. When dealing with large deployments having hundreds of users, these options will become very useful to quickly find the users you need to manage.

Other than the ability for you to effectively search for users, **User Browser** also serves as the portal for you to add new users to JIRA and manage a user's group/role associations:

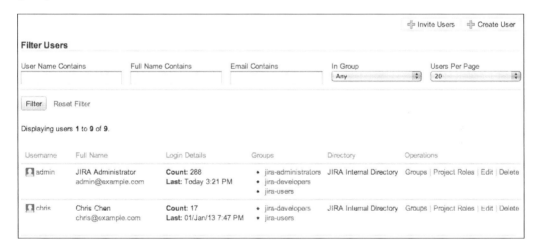

Adding a user

User accounts can be created directly from JIRA in two ways, and if you are using an external user directory, such as LDAP, then you can also create accounts in LDAP and JIRA will automatically synchronize the new users. The first option is to have centralized management, where only the JIRA administrators can create and maintain user accounts. This option is applicable to the most private JIRA instances designed to be used by an organization's internal users.

The second option is to allow users to sign up for accounts by themselves, and this is most useful when you run a public JIRA instance, where manually creating user accounts is not scalable enough to handle the volume. We will be looking at how to enable public signup options in the later sections. For now, we will first examine how administrators can create user accounts manually:

1. Browse to the **User Browser** page.

2. Click on on the **Create User** button. This will bring you to the **Create New User** dialog box.

3. Provide a unique username for the new user. The username cannot be changed once it is set.

4. Specify the password, full name, and e-mail address for the user.

5. Optionally, select the **Send Notification Email** option if you have an outgoing mail server configured for JIRA (see *Chapter 7*,). If checked, JIRA will send an e-mail to the user with a link for them to reset their password.

6. Click on the **Create** button to create the new user:

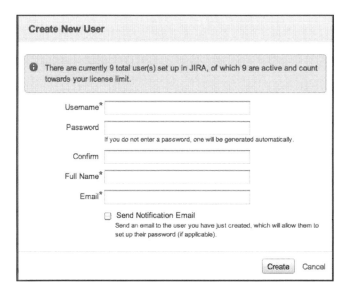

Alternatively, the administrator can also choose to invite users, so that they can create their accounts by themselves. This is different than the public signup option, since only recipients of the invitations will be able to create accounts. For this feature to work, you will need to have an outgoing mail server configured, as the invitations will be sent as e-mails. Perform the following steps to invite users to sign up:

1. Browse to the **User Browser** page.

2. Click on on the **Invite Users** button. This will bring you to the **Invite Users** dialog box.

3. Specify the e-mail addresses for the people you wish to invite. You can invite multiple people at once.

4. Click on the **Send** button to send out the invitations:

Enabling public signup

If your JIRA is public (for example, as a public support system) then creating user accounts individually as explained earlier will become a very demanding job for your administrator. For this type of JIRA setup, you can enable public signup to allow users to create accounts by themselves. Perform the following steps to enable public signup in JIRA:

1. Browse to the JIRA administration console.

2. Select **General Configuration** under the **System** section.

3. Click on the **Edit Configuration** button at bottom of the page.

4. Select **Public** for the **Mode** field.

5. Click on the **Update** button to apply the setting.

Once you have set JIRA to run in the **Public** mode, users will be able to sign up and create their own accounts from the login page:

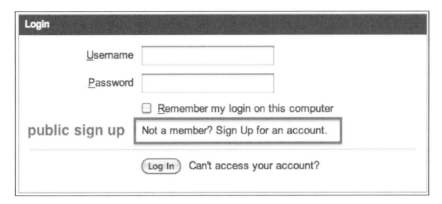

As you will see in the later section *Global permissions*, once a user signs up for a new account, he/she will automatically join groups with JIRA users global permission. If you have set JIRA to run in the **Private** mode, then only the administrator will be able to create new accounts.

Enabling CAPTCHA

If running JIRA in the **Public** mode, you run the risk of having automated spam bots creating user accounts on your system. To counter this, JIRA provides the CAPTCHA service, where potential users will be required to type in a word represented in an image into a text field. Perform the following steps to enable the CAPTCHA service:

1. Browse to the JIRA administration console.
2. Select **General Configuration** under the **System** section.
3. Click on the **Edit Configuration** button at the bottom of the page.
4. Select **On** for the **CAPTCHA on sign up** field.
5. Click on the **Update** button to apply the setting.

Now, when someone tries to sign up for an account, JIRA will present him/her with a CAPTCHA challenge that must be verified before the account is created:

Groups

Groups are a common way of managing users in any information system. A group often represents a collection of users, usually based on their positions and responsibilities within the organization. In JIRA, groups provide an effective way to apply configuration settings to users, such as permissions and notifications.

Groups are global in JIRA, which is something that should not be confused with project roles (discussed later). This means if you belong to the `jira-administrators` group, then you will always be in that group regardless of which project you are accessing. You will see in later sections how this is different from project roles and their significance.

One important point to keep in mind is that group association does not cascade in JIRA. For example, just because a user is in the `jira-developers` group, it does not mean he/she will have the privileges of the `jira-users` group.

Group Browser

Similar to User Browser, **Group Browser** allows you to search, add, and configure groups within JIRA:

1. Browse to the JIRA administration console
2. Select **Groups** under the **Users** section to bring up the **Group Browser** page:

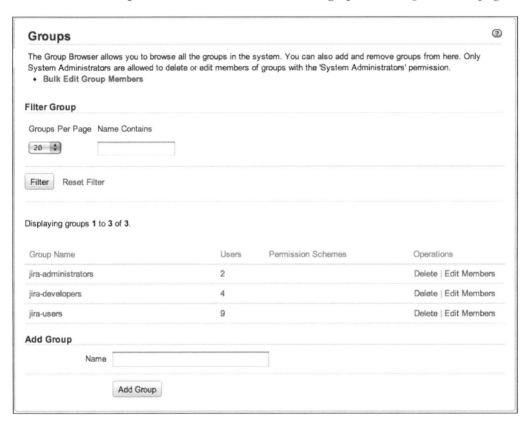

JIRA comes with three default groups. These groups are created automatically when you install JIRA:

Group	Description
jira-administrators	Administrators of JIRA
jira-developers	Usually developers or people that will work on issues
jira-users	Normal users in JIRA

Out of the three groups, jira-administrators and jira-users are of most significance. As you will see later in this chapter, by default, users of jira-administrators are given the global permission to administer JIRA while users of jira-users are given permission to access JIRA. You can, as we will learn, change this default behavior to have your custom groups have the same permissions.

Adding a group

Other than the three groups that come by default with JIRA, you can create your own groups. It is important to note that once you have created a group, you cannot change its name. So, make sure you think about the name of the group carefully before you create it:

1. Browse to the **Group Browser** page.
2. Specify a unique name of the new group in the **Add Group** section.
3. Click on the **Add Group** button to create the new group.

After a group has been created, it will be empty and have no members. It will also have no configuration settings, such as the permissions applied.

Editing group membership

Often, people move around within an organization, and your JIRA needs to be kept up to date with the movement.

In **Group Browser**, there are two ways to manage group membership. The first option is to manage the membership on a per-group level, and the second option is to manage several groups at the same time. Both the options are actually very similar, so we will be covering both at the same time.

Perform the following steps to manage individual groups:

1. Browse to the **Group Browser** page.
2. Click on the **Edit Members** link for the group you wish to manage the member for. This will bring you to the **Bulk Edit Group Members** page.

Perform the following steps to manage multiple groups:

1. Browse to the **Group Browser** page.
2. Click on the **Bulk Edit Group Member** link. This will bring you to the **Bulk Edit Group Members** page.

You will notice that both options will take you to the same page. The difference is if you have chosen the individual group option, JIRA will auto select the group to update, and if you have chosen the bulk edit option, then no groups will be selected. However, regardless of which option you choose, you can still select one or all of the groups to apply your changes to.

Perform the following steps to update the membership in one or more groups:

1. Browse to the **Bulk Edit Group Members** page.
2. Select one or more groups to update.
3. Select users from the middle box and click on the **Leave** button to take users out of the groups.
4. Specify users (by typing usernames) in the right-hand box and click on the **Join** button to add users to the groups.

Deleting a group

If a group has become redundant, you can remove it from JIRA:

1. Browse to the **Group Browser** page.
2. Click on the **Delete** link for the group you wish to remove. This will take you to the **Delete Group** page.
3. Click on the **Delete** button to permanently remove the group.

Once you remove the group, all the users who previously belonged to it will have their group associations updated to reflect the change.

Project roles

As you have seen, groups are collections of users and are applied globally. JIRA offers another way of grouping users, which is applied on the project level only:

Project role	Description
Administrators	This project role represents the administrator of the project (for example, project manager).
Developers	This project role represents the developer of the project.
Users	This project role represents the user of the project (for example, tester).

Project Role Browser

Similar to users and groups, project roles are maintained by the JIRA administrator through the Project Role Browser. There is a slight difference, however, since project roles are specific to projects, JIRA administrators only define what roles are available in JIRA and their default members. Each project's administrators (discussed in later sections) can further define each role's membership for their own projects, overriding the default assignment. We will first look at what JIRA administrators can control through the Project Role Browser and then look at how project administrators can fine-tune the membership assignment later. Perform the following steps to access the Project Role Browser:

1. Click on **Administration** in the top menu bar.
2. Select **Roles** in the **Users** section to bring up the **Project Role Browser** page.

Adding a project role type

As an administrator, you can create new role types, which can then be used by project administrators for their projects. Perform the following steps to create a new project role type:

1. Browse to the **Project Role Browser** page.
2. Specify a unique name for the new project role in the **Add Project Role** section.
3. Specify an optional description.
4. Click on the **Add Project Role** button to create the project role.

Once you have added a new project role, it will appear for all the projects.

Editing a project role

You can update a project role's name and description, as follows:

1. Browse to the **Project Role Browser** page.
2. Click on the **Edit** link for the project role you wish to update. This will take you to the **Edit Project Role** page.
3. Specify a new name and description.
4. Click on the **Update** button to apply the changes.

Deleting a project role

Existing project roles can be deleted if they are no longer used, as follows:

1. Browse to the **Project Role Browser** page.
2. Click on the **Delete** link for the project role you wish to remove. This will bring up the **Delete Project Role** page.
3. Click on the **Delete** button to remove the project role.

Managing default members

As new projects are created in JIRA, it will often happen that those projects will share a similar security requirement. So, it becomes desirable to have default members assigned to the project roles when new projects are created.

Default members are an efficient way for JIRA administrators to assign project role members automatically, without having to manually manage each new project as they come in.

For example, by default, users in the `jira-administrators` group will have the **Administrators** project role. This increases the efficiency of the security setup by creating a baseline for new projects, but also offers the flexibility to allow modifications to the default setup to cater for unique requirements.

Perform the following steps to set default members for a project role:

1. Browse to the **Project Role Browser** page.
2. Click on the **Manage Default Members** link for the project role you wish to remove. This will take you to the **Edit Default Members for Project Role: Administrators** page.

In this page, you will see all the default members assigned to the selected project role. Default members can be logically assigned project roles based on the group setup. Users can be useful when you have exceptional cases, such as a lead developer that should have the **Developers** role in all software development projects.

Perform the following steps to add a default user/group for the project role:

1. Click on the **Edit** link for the default member option (either user or group).
2. Use the user picker/group picker function to select the users/groups you wish to assign to the project role.

3.   Click on the **Add** button to assign the role:

Assign Default Groups to Project Role: Administrators

You can add and remove default groups from the project role **Administrators** by using the 'Join' and 'Leave' buttons below.

- << Return to viewing project role Administrators

Add group(s) to project role:

☐ Groups in Project Role

☐ jira-administrators

Remove

Add

Once added, any new projects created will have the specified users/groups assigned to the project role. It is important to note that after you have set default members, only new projects will have the settings applied. Existing projects will not retrospectively have the default members applied.

Assigning project role members

As you have seen, JIRA allows you to assign default members to projects when they are created. This might be sufficient for most projects when they start. Changes will often need to be made due to staff movements throughout the project life cycle. While it is possible for the JIRA administrator to continue maintaining each project's membership, it can easily become an overwhelming task, and in most cases, since project roles are specific to each project, it makes sense to delegate this responsibility to the owner of each project.

In JIRA, an owner of a project is someone with the **Administer Projects** permission. By default, members of the Administrators' project role will have this permission. We will see in a later section how to manage permissions in JIRA.

As a project administrator, you will be able to assign members to the various project roles for your project. You can assign roles from the project administration page, as follows:

1.   Browse to the **Project Administration** page for the project you want to assign project roles for.

2.   Select the **Roles** tab.

3.   Click directly on either the **Users** or **Groups** column for the role you want to update in the assignment

4. Use the user/group picker to search and select users/groups to assign to the project role.

5. Click on the **Update** button.

The users and groups assigned to the project role will be for the current project only. You will have to reconfigure the members again for other projects. In this way, project role members are maintained separately for each project:

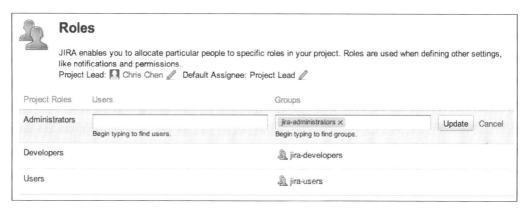

JIRA permissions hierarchy

JIRA manages its permissions in a hierarchical manner. Each level is more fine-grained than the one above it. For a user to gain access to a resource, for example to view an issue, he/she needs to satisfy all three levels of permission (if they are all set on the issue in question):

- **JIRA global permission**: This permission controls the overall access rights to JIRA. For example, who can access JIRA.

- **Project-level permission**: This permission controls the project-level permissions.

- **Issue-level security**: This permission controls the view access on a per-issue level.

You will look at each of the permission levels and how you can configure them to suit your requirements, starting from the most coarse-grained permission level – global permissions.

Global permissions

Global permissions, as the name suggests, is the highest permission level in JIRA. These are coarse-grained permissions applied globally across JIRA, controlling broad security levels such as the ability to access JIRA and administer configurations.

Because they are not fine-grained security, global permissions are applied to user groups rather than users. The following table lists all the permissions and what they control in JIRA:

Global permission level	Description
JIRA System Administrators	Permission to perform all JIRA administration functions. This is akin to the `root` or `god` mode in other systems.
JIRA Administrators	Permission to perform most JIRA administration functions that are not related to system-wide changes. (for example, configure SMTP server, export/restore JIRA data).
JIRA Users	Permission to log in to JIRA. Newly created users will automatically join the groups with this permission.
Browse Users	Permission to view the list of JIRA users and groups. This permission is required if the user needs to use the user/group picker function.
Create Shared Object	Permission to share filters and dashboards with other users.
Manage Group Filter Subscriptions	Permission to manage group filter subscriptions. Filters will be discussed in *Chapter 9*.
Bulk Change	Permission to perform bulk operations including the following: • Bulk edit • Bulk move • Bulk delete • Bulk workflow transition

JIRA system administrator versus JIRA administrator

For people who are new to JIRA, it is often confusing when it comes to distinguishing between the JIRA system administrator and JIRA Administrator. For the most part, both are identical, in that they can carry out most of the administrative functions in JIRA.

The difference is JIRA administrators cannot access functions that can affect the application environment or network while the JIRA system administrator has access to everything.

Although it is not necessary to have a separate role for both, it is sometimes useful to have one person overlook general JIRA administrative tasks while have another with the ability to configure system-wide settings such as the SMTP mail service, which is a system resource outside of the JIRA application. By default, the `jira-administrators` group has both JIRA system administrators' and JIRA administrators permission.

The following list shows system operations that are only available to people with JIRA system administrators' permission:

- Configure SMTP server details
- Configure CVS source code repository
- Configure listeners
- Configure services
- Configure where JIRA stores index files
- Import data into JIRA from an XML backup
- Export data from JIRA to an XML backup
- Configure where attachment settings
- Access JIRA license details
- Grant/revoke JIRA system administrators' global permission
- Delete users with JIRA system administrators' global permission

Configuring global permissions

Global permissions are configured and maintained by JIRA administrators and JIRA system administrators (to grant JIRA system administrator global permission), as follows:

1.   Browse to the JIRA administration console.

2.   Select **Global Permissions** to bring up the **Global Permissions** page:

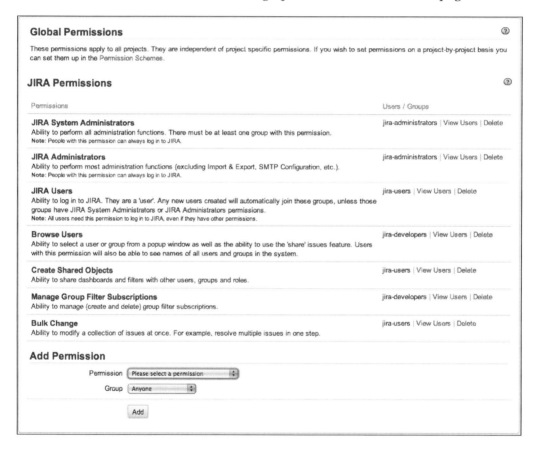

Granting global permissions

Global permissions can only be granted to groups. For this reason, you will need to organize your users into logical groups for global permissions to take effect. For example, you will want to have all your users belong to a single group such as the `jira-users` group, so you can grant them the permission to access JIRA:

1. Browse to the **Global Permissions** page.
2. Select the permission you wish to assign from the **Add Permission** section.
3. Choose the group to be given the permission.
4. Click on the **Add** button to add the assignment.

The **Group** drop-down list will list all the groups in JIRA. It will also have an extra option called **Anyone**. This option includes users that are not logged in. You cannot select this option when granting the **JIRA Users** permission, as **JIRA Users** is required to log in and **Anyone** refers to a non-logged-in user. For a production system, it is recommended to take care when granting any global permission to **Anyone** (non-logged-in users) as this can lead to security and privacy concerns. For example, by granting **Anyone** as the global permission for **Browse Users**, anyone with access to your JIRA instance will be able to get your registered users' information.

Revoking global permissions

Global permissions can also be revoked. There are, however, a few rules and restrictions you need to be aware of:

- Both JIRA system administrators and JIRA administrators can revoke global permissions, but JIRA administrators cannot revoke the JIRA system administrator global permission.
- If you revoke JIRA users' permission, you are effectively disallowing the affected users from accessing JIRA (they will not be able to log in to JIRA).
- You will not be able to grant additional JIRA users permission if you have exceeded the number of users permitted by your license.

Perform the following steps to delete a global permission from a group:

1. Browse to the **Global Permissions** page.
2. Click on the **Delete** link for the group you wish to remove from the global permission. This will take you to the **Delete Global Permission** page.
3. Click on the **Delete** button to remove the global permission.

JIRA has built-in validation rules to prevent you from accidentally locking yourself out by accidentally removing the wrong permissions. For example, JIRA will not let you delete the last group from JIRA system administrators' global permission, as doing so will effectively prevent you from adding yourself back (as only JIRA system administrators can assign/revoke global permissions).

Project permissions

As you have seen, global permissions are rather coarse in what they control and are applied globally. Since they can only be applied to groups, they are rather inflexible when it comes to decide whom to grant the permissions to.

To provide a more flexible way of managing and designing permissions, JIRA allows you to manage permissions on the project level, which allows each project to have its own distinctive permission settings. Furthermore, JIRA allows you to grant permissions to users through a range of options including the following:

- **Reporter**: This is the user who submitted the issue
- **Group**: These are all users that belong to the specified group
- **Single user**: This is any user in JIRA
- **Project lead**: This is the lead of the project
- **Current assignee**: This is the user currently assigned to the issue
- **User custom field Value**: This user is specified in a custom field of type User Custom Field.
- **Project role**: These are all users that belong to the specified role.
- **Group custom field Value**: These are users within the specified group in a Group Custom Field.

The list of permissions is also more fine-grained and designed more around controlling permissions on a project level. The only catch to this is that the list is final, and you cannot add new permission types.

Permission	Description
Administer Project	Permission to administer a project. Users with this permission are referred to as **project administrators**. Users with this permission are able to edit project role membership, components, versions, and general project details such as name and description.
Browse Project	Permission for users to browse and view the project and its issues. If a user does not have the browse project permission for a given project, the project will be hidden from him/her, and notifications will not be sent.

Permission	Description
View Version Control	Permission to view version control system configured for this project (usually for software development projects).
Create Issues	Permission for users to create issues.
Edit Issues	Permission for users to edit issues
Schedule Issues	Permission for users to set and update due dates for issues.
Move Issues	Permission for users to move issues.
Assign Issues	Permission for users to assign issues to different users.
Assignable User	Users that can be assigned to issues.
Resolve Issues	Permission for users to resolve an issue and set values for the **Fix For Version** field.
Close issues	Permission for users to close an issue.
Modify Reporter	Permission for users to change the value of the **Reporter** field.
Delete issues	Permission for users to delete an issue.
Link Issues	Permission for users to link issues together (if issue linking is enabled).
Set Issue Security	Permission for users to set issue security levels to enable issue-level security. Please go through the next sections to know more about Issue Security.
View Voters and Watchers	Permission to view the voters and watchers' list of issues.
Manage Watchers	Permission to manage the watchers' list of issues (add/remove watchers).
Add Comments	Permission for users to add comments to issues.
Edit All Comments	Permission for users to edit comments made by all users.
Edit Own Comments	Permission to edit own comments.
Delete All Comments	Permission to delete all comments.
Delete Own Comments	Permission to delete own comments.
Create Attachments	Permission to add attachments to issues (if attachment is enabled).
Delete All Attachments	Permission to delete all attachments on issues.
Delete Own Attachments	Permission to delete attachments on issues added by yourself.
Work On Issues	Permission to log work done on issues (if time tracking is enabled).
Edit Own Worklogs	Permission to edit worklogs made by yourself.
Edit All Worklogs	Permission to edit all worklogs.

Permission	Description
Delete Own Worklogs	Permission to delete worklogs made by yourself.
Delete All Worklogs	Permission to delete all worklogs.

As you can see, even though the list cannot be modified, JIRA provides you with a very comprehensive list of permissions that will cover almost all of your permission needs.

As you would have guessed, with this many permissions, it will be highly inefficient if you have to create them individually for each project you have. JIRA lets you define your permissions once and apply them to multiple projects, with permission schemes.

Permission schemes

Permission schemes, like other schemes such as notification schemes, are collections of associations between permissions and users or a collection of users. Each permission scheme is a reusable, self-contained entity that can be applied to one or more projects.

Like most schemes, permission schemes are applied at the project level. This allows you to apply fine-grained permissions for each project. Just like project roles, JIRA administrators oversee the creation and configuration of permission schemes, and it is up to each project's administrator to choose and decide which permission scheme to use. This way, it encourages administrators to design their permissions that can be reused based on the common needs of an organization, and with meaningful scheme names and descriptions, project administrators will be able to choose the scheme that will fit their needs the best, instead of requesting a new set of permissions to be set up for each project.

We will first look at how JIRA administrators manage and configure permission schemes and then how project administrators can apply them in their projects.

Perform the following steps to start managing permission schemes:

1. Browse to the JIRA administration console.
2. Select **Permission Schemes** to bring up the **Permission Schemes** page:

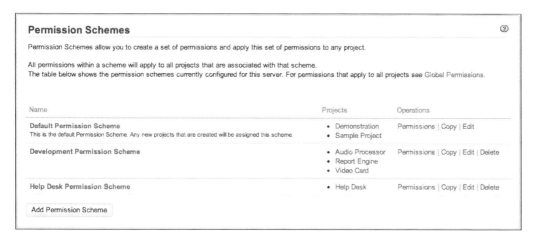

On the **Permission Schemes** page, you will see a list of all the permissions schemes. From here, you will be able to create new schemes, edit and delete existing schemes, as well as configure each scheme's permission settings.

Adding a permission scheme

JIRA comes with a preconfigured permission scheme called **Default Permission Scheme**. This scheme is suitable for most simple software development projects. However, it is often not enough and it is usually a good practice to not modify the Default Permission Scheme directly, so you should create your own permissions schemes:

1. Browse to the **Permission Schemes** pages.
2. Click on the **Add Permission Scheme** button. This will take you to the **Add Permission Scheme** page.
3. Provide a meaningful name and description for the new permission scheme.
4. Click on the **Add** button to create the permission scheme.

For new permission schemes, all of the permissions will have no permission configured. This means that if you start using your new scheme straightaway, you will end up with a project that nobody can access. You will look at how to configure permissions in the later sections.

Editing a permission scheme

You can keep a permission scheme's name and description up to date. You will often need to do this after making a copy of an existing permission scheme. As you will see in the following section, when you copy a permission scheme, JIRA automatically generates a name for your new scheme:

1. Browse to the **Permission Schemes** pages.
2. Click on the **Edit** link for the permissions scheme you wish to update. This will take you to the **Edit Permissions Scheme** page.
3. Update the name and description with new values.
4. Click on the **Update** button to apply the changes.

Deleting a permission scheme

Unlike some other types of schemes, you can delete permissions schemes even if they are being used by projects:

1. Browse to the **Permission Schemes** pages.
2. Click on the **Delete** link for the permissions scheme you wish to remove. This will take you to the **Delete Permissions Scheme** page.
3. Click on the **Delete** button to remove the permission scheme.

If you are deleting a permission scheme that is being used by one or more projects, JIRA will prompt you with the list of projects that are currently using the scheme. If you delete it, all the projects will be automatically updated to use the Default Permission Scheme.

> You cannot delete the Default Permission Scheme.

Copying a permission scheme

It is not always desirable to create permission schemes from scratch, as there are around thirty permissions you will need to set for a new one. JIRA allows you to easily clone existing permissions schemes with the **copy** function:

1. Browse to the **Permission Schemes** pages.

2. Click on the **Copy** link for the permissions scheme you wish to clone. This will immediately create a copy of the permission scheme with the name with **Copy** of appended to the front of the original scheme's name.

One good use of the copy function is to create a backup of an existing permission scheme before you make changes. It is sometimes a good practice to name your permission schemes with a version number, and every time you need to make a change, create a copy and increment the version number in the name. This way, it helps you to keep track of your changes and help you to rollback your changes if things do not work out as planned.

 It is often quicker to clone from an existing permission scheme than starting from scratch.

Configuring a permission scheme

Just like most other schemes in JIRA, you need to further fine-tune your permission scheme to make it useful:

1. Browse to the **Permission Schemes** pages.

2. Click on the **Permissions** link for the permissions scheme you wish to configure. This will take you to the **Edit Permissions** page.

In this page, you will be presented with a list of project-level permissions, along with short descriptions for each, and the users, groups, and roles that are linked to each of the permissions. You will notice that for the Default Permission Scheme, most of the permission options have default users linked to them, through project roles. If you are looking at a new permission scheme, there will be no users linked to any of the permissions. This is your one-page view of permission settings for projects, and you will also be able to add and delete users.

Unlike some other schemes, such as the notification scheme, which allows you to add additional options (through custom events), you cannot define new permissions for a permission scheme:

Permission Helper

Edit Permissions — Help Desk Permission Scheme

Shared by 1 project

On this page you can edit the permissions for the "Help Desk Permission Scheme" permission scheme.
- Grant permission
- **View all permission schemes**

Project Permissions	Users / Groups / Project Roles	Operations
Administer Projects Ability to administer a project in JIRA.	• Project Role (Administrators) (Delete)	Add
Browse Projects Ability to browse projects and the issues within them.	• Project Role (Users) (Delete)	Add
View Issue Source Tab Allows users to view related source code commits on the view issue screen.	• Project Role (Developers) (Delete)	Add
View Read-Only Workflow Users with this permission may view a read-only version of a workflow.	• Project Role (Users) (Delete)	Add

Issue Permissions	Users / Groups / Project Roles	Operations
Create Issues Ability to create issues.	• Project Role (Users) (Delete)	Add
Edit Issues Ability to edit issues.	• Project Role (Developers) (Delete)	Add

Granting a permission

Like the notification scheme, JIRA offers you a range of options to specify which users should have certain permissions. You can specify users through some of the most common options such as groups, but you also have some advanced options, such as using users specified in a custom field.

Again, you have two options to grant permissions to a user. You can add them to specific permissions or multiple permissions at once. Both options will present you with the same interface and there is no difference between the two:

1. Browse to the **Edit Permissions** page for the permission scheme you wish to configure.

2. Click on the **Grant permission** link or the **Add** link for a specific permission. This will take you to the **Add New Permission** page.

3. Select the permissions you wish to grant to the user.

4. Select the user option to specify who to grant the permission to.

5. Click on the **Add** button to grant the selected permission.

Permission options, such as **User Custom Field Value**, is a very flexible way of allowing the end users to control access. For example, you can have a custom field called **Editors**, and set up your **Edit Issues** permission to allow only users specified in the custom field to be able to edit issues.

The custom field does not have to be placed on the usual view/edit screens for the permission to be applied. For example, you can have the custom field appear on a workflow transition called **Submit to Manager**, and once the user has selected the manager, only the manager will have permission to edit the issue.

Revoking a permission

You can easily revoke a permission given to a user, as follows:

1. Browse to the **Edit Permissions** page for the permission scheme you wish to configure.
2. Click on the **Delete** link for the permission you wish to revoke. This will take you to the **Delete Permission** page.
3. Click on the **Delete** button to revoke.

When you are trying to revoke permissions to prevent users from gaining certain access, you need to make sure that there are no other user options granted to the same permission that might be applied to the same user. For example, if you have both the **Single User** and **Group** options set for the **Browse Projects** permission, then you will need to make sure to revoke the **Single User** option and also make sure that the user does not belong to the **Group** option selected, so you do not have a loophole in your security settings.

Applying a permission scheme

We have been saying how permission schemes can be selected by project managers to set permissions for their projects all this time, now we will look at how to apply the scheme to your projects. There really is not anything special, permission schemes are applied to projects in the same way as notification and workflow schemes:

1. Browse to the **Project Administration** page for the project you want to assign project roles for.
2. Select the **Permissions** tab.
3. Select **Use a different scheme** option in the **Actions** menu.
4. Select the permission scheme to use.
5. Click on the **Associate** button.

Permission schemes are applied immediately and you will be able to see the permissions take effect.

Issue security

We have seen how JIRA administrators can restrict general access to JIRA with global permissions, and what project administrators can do to place fine-grained permissions on individual projects through permission schemes. JIRA allows you to go to down yet another level to allow ordinary users to set the security level on the issues they are working with, with **Issue Security**.

Issue security allows users to set view permissions (not edit) on issues by selecting one of the preconfigured issue security levels. This is a very powerful feature, as it allows the delegation of security control to the end users and empowers them (to a limited degree) to decide who can view their issues.

On a high level, issue security works in a similar way to permission schemes. The JIRA Administrator will start by creating and configuring a set of issue security schemes with security levels set. Project administrators can then apply one of these schemes to their projects, which finally at the end allows the users (with Set Issue Security permission) to select the security levels within the scheme and apply them to individual issues.

Issue security scheme

As explained earlier, the starting point of using issue security is the issue security scheme. It is the responsibility of the JIRA administrator to create and design the security levels, so they can be reused as much as possible:

1. Browse to the JIRA administration console

2. Select **Issue Security Schemes** at the bottom to bring up the **Issue Security Schemes** page:

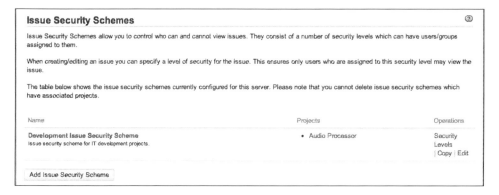

Adding an issue security scheme

JIRA does not come with any predefined issue security schemes, so you will have to create your own from scratch. Perform the following steps to create a new issue security scheme:

1. Browse to the **Issue Security Schemes** page.
2. Click on the **Add Issue Security Scheme** button. This will bring up the **Add Issue Security Scheme** page.
3. Provide a meaningful name and description for the new scheme.
4. Click on the **Add** button to create the new issue security scheme.

Since the issue security scheme does not define a set of security levels like the permission scheme, you will need to create your own set of security levels right after you have created your scheme.

Configuring an issue security scheme

Unlike permission schemes that have a list of predefined permissions, with issue security schemes, you are in full control over how many options you will like to add to the schemes.

The options within an issue security scheme are known as **Security Levels**. They represent the levels of security that users need to meet before JIRA will allow them access to the requested issue. Please note that even though they are called security levels, it does not mean there are any forms of hierarchy amongst the set of levels you create.

Perform the following steps to configure an issue security scheme:

1. Browse to the **Issue Security Schemes** page.

2. Click on the **Security Levels** link for the issue security scheme you wish to configure. This will bring up the **Edit Issue Security Levels** page:

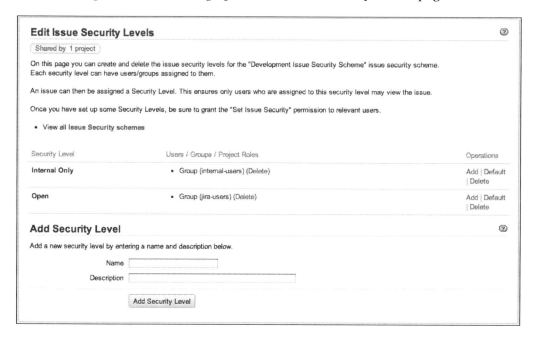

From here, you can create new security levels and assign users to existing security levels.

Adding a security level

Since issue security schemes do not define any security levels, the first step to configure your scheme would be to create a set of new security levels:

1. Browse to the **Edit Issue Security Levels** page for the issue security scheme you wish to configure.

2. Provide a meaningful name and description for the new security level in the **Add Security Level** section.

3. Click on the **Add Security Level** button.

You can add as many security levels as you like in a scheme. One good practice is to design your security levels based on your team or project roles.

Assigning users to a security level

Similar to permission schemes, once you have your security levels in place, you will then need to assign users to each of the levels. Users assigned to the security level will have permissions to view issues with the specified security level:

1. Browse to the **Edit Issue Security Levels** page.

2. Click on the **Add** link for the security level you wish to assign users to. This will bring up the **Add User/Group/Project Role to Issue Security Level** page.

3. Select the option you wish to assign to the security level.

4. Click on the **Add** button to assign the users:

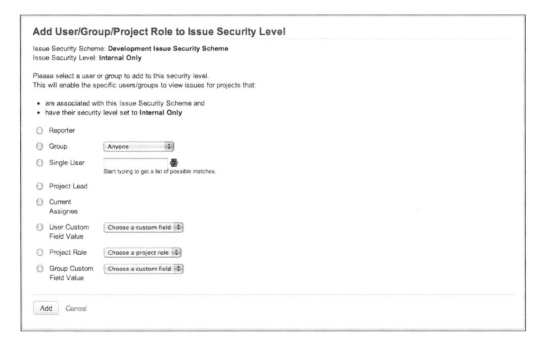

While it may be tempting to use the **Single User** option to add individual users, it is a better practice to use other options such as **Project Role and Group**, as it is more flexible by not tying the permission to individual users, and allows you to control permission with options such as group association.

Setting a default security level

You can set a security level to be the default option for issues if none is selected. This can be a useful feature for projects with high security requirement to prevent users (with **Set Issue Security** permission) from forgetting to assign a security level for their issues:

1. Browse to the **Edit Issue Security Levels** page.
2. Click on the **Default** link for the security level you with to set as default.

Once set as default, the security level will have **Default** next to its name. Now, when the user creates an issue and does not assign a security level, the default security level will be applied.

Deleting a security level

You can revoke users assigned to security levels or remove the security level completely. When you revoke a user, he/she will no longer have access to the issue unless there is another user setting, which the user also belongs to, applied to the same security level.

Perform the following steps to revoke a user from a security level:

1. Browse to the **Edit Issue Security Levels** page.
2. Click on the **Delete** link for the users/groups/project roles you wish to remove. This will take you to the **Delete Issue Security** page.
3. Click on the **Delete** button to revoke the user.

When you delete a security level, you will be affecting all of the issues that are currently set to the security level. JIRA allows you to update those issues to use a different security level (if one is available), or have no security level applied:

1. Browse to the **Edit Issue Security Levels** page.
2. Click on the **Delete** link for the security level you with to remove. This will take you to the **Delete Issue Security Level** page. If there are issues set to the security level, JIRA will list the issues and also ask you to change their security level settings.
3. Select a new security level for the issues affected.
4. Click on the **Delete** button to remove the security level.

Applying an issue security scheme

Just like permission schemes, the project administrators apply issue security schemes to projects. Applying the issue security scheme is similar to applying the workflow scheme, where there is an intermediate migration step involved. This is to ensure that existing issues with issue security levels set can be successfully migrated over to the new security-levels in the scheme:

1. Browse to the **Project Administration** page for the project you want to assign project roles for.
2. Select the **Issue Security** tab.
3. Select **Use a different scheme** option in the **Actions** menu.
4. Select the permission scheme to use.
5. Click on the **Next** button to move to step 2 of the process.
6. Select the new security level to apply to the existing issue that might be affected by this change.
7. Click on the **Associate** button to apply the new issue security scheme:

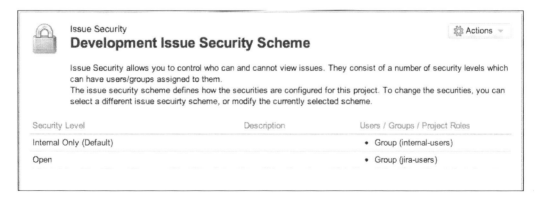

Troubleshooting permissions

Just like notifications, it can be very frustrating to troubleshoot permission settings. To help with this, JIRA also provides a Permission Helper to assist administrators to pinpoint settings that prevent users from accessing certain features.

The Permission Helper works similarly to the Notification Helper:

1. Browse to the JIRA administration console.

2. Select **Permission Helper** from under the **Admin Helper** section.

3. Specify the user that is having access problems in the **User** field.

4. Specify the issue to test with.

5. Select the permission the user does not have (for example, **Edit issue**).

6. Click on **Submit**.

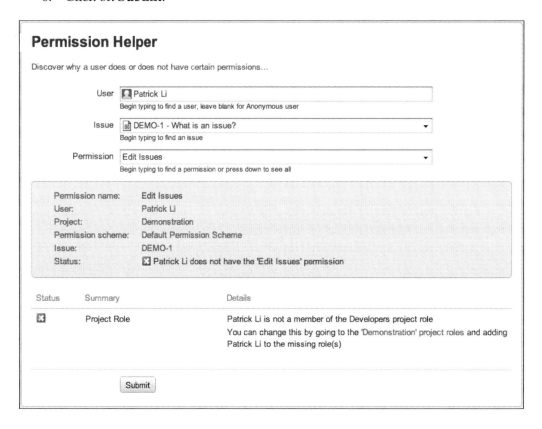

As shown in the preceding screenshot, the user **Patrick Li** cannot edit issues for the **DEMO** project, because he is not a member of the **Developer** project role, which is required as per the **Default Permission Scheme** used.

Workflow security

Security features that we have looked at up until now are not applied to workflows. When securing your JIRA, you will also need to consider who will be allowed to perform certain workflow transitions. For example, only users in the managers' group will be able to execute the **Authorize** transition on issues. For you to enforce security on workflows, you will have to set it on each transition you have, by adding workflow conditions. Please refer to *Chapter 6*, which discusses workflows and conditions in more detail.

The Help Desk project

In the previous chapters, you have configured your JIRA to capture data with customized screens and fields, and processed the captured data through workflows. What you need to do now is secure the data you have gathered to make sure that only the authorized users can access and manipulate issues.

Since your Help Desk Project is used by your internal team, what you really need to do is to put enough permission around your issues to ensure the data they hold do not get modified by other users, usually by mistake. This allows us to mitigate human errors by handling access accordingly.

To achieve this, you need to have the following requirements:

- You need to be able to tell who belongs to the help desk team
- Restrict issue assign operations to only the user that has submitted the ticket and members of the help desk team
- Not to allow tickets to be moved to other projects
- Limit the assignee of tickets to the reporter and members of the help desk team

Of course, there are a lot of other permissions we can apply here; the preceding four requirements will be a good starting point for us to build on further.

Setting up groups

The first thing you need to do is to set up a new group for your help desk team members. This will help you distinguish normal JIRA users from your help desk staff:

1. Browse to the **Group Browser** page.
2. Name the new group `help-desk-team` in the **Add Group** section.
3. Click on the **Add Group** button.

You can create more groups for other teams and departments, for your scenario here. Since anyone can log a ticket in your project, there is no need to make that distinction.

Setting up user group association

With your group set up, you can start assigning members of your team to the new group:

1. Browse to the **Group Browser** page.
2. Click on the **Edit Members** link for the `help-desk-team` group.
3. Select users with the user picker or simply type in the usernames separated with a comma. This time, let's add our admin user to the group.
4. Click on the **Join** button.

Setting up permission schemes

The next step is to set up permissions for our Help Desk project, so you need to have your own permission scheme. As always, it is more efficient to copy the Default Permission Scheme as a baseline and make your modifications on top, since we are only making a few changes here:

1. Browse to the **Permission Schemes** pages.
2. Click on the **Copy** link for **Default Permission Scheme**.
3. Click on the **Edit** link for the new copy of **Default Permission Scheme** created.
4. Name the new permission scheme `Help Desk Permission Scheme`.
5. Change the description to `Permission scheme designed for Help Desk team projects`.

Now we have our base permission scheme setup, we can start on the fun part, interpreting requirements and implementing them in JIRA.

Setting up permissions

The first thing you need to do when you start to set up permissions is try to match up existing JIRA permissions to your requirements. In our case, we want to restrict the following:

- Who can assign issues?
- Who can be assigned to an issue?
- Disable issues from being moved

Looking at the existing list of JIRA permissions, you can see that we can match up the requirements with the **Assign Issues**, **Assignable Users**, and **Move Issues** permissions respectively.

Once you have worked out what permissions you need to modify, the next step is to work out a strategy to specify the users that should be given the permissions. Restricting move issue options is simple. All you have to do is remove the permission from everyone, thus effectively preventing anyone from moving issues in your project.

The next two requirements are similar, as they are both granted to the reporter (user that submitted the ticket), and our new `help-desk-team` group:

1. Browse to the **Permission Schemes** pages.
2. Click on the **Permissions** link for **Help Desk Permission Scheme**.
3. Click on the **Grant permission** link.
4. Select both Assign Users and **Assignable Users** permissions.
5. Select the **Reporter** option.
6. Click on the **Add** button.
7. Repeat the steps and grant the `help-desk-team` group both permissions.

By selecting both the permissions in one go, you have quickly granted multiple permissions to users. Now, you need to remove all the users granted with the **Move Issues** permission. There should be only one granted at the moment, **Project Role (Developer)**, but if you have more than one granted, you will need to remove all of them:

1. Browse to the **Permission Schemes** page.
2. Click on the **Permissions** link for **Help Desk Permission Scheme**.
3. Click on the **Delete** link for all the users that have been granted **Move Issues** permission.

That's it! You have addressed all of our permission requirements with just a few clicks.

Putting it together

Last but not least, you can now put on our project administrator's hat and apply your new permission scheme to your Help Desk project:

1. Browse to the **Project Administration** page for your Help Desk project.
2. Click on the **Select** link for **Permission Scheme**.
3. Select **Help Desk Permission Scheme**.
4. Click on the **Associate** button.

By associating the permission scheme with our project, you have applied all of your permission changes. Now if you create a new issue or edit an existing issue, you will notice that the list of assignees will no longer include all the users in JIRA.

Summary

In this chapter, we first looked at how we can integrate JIRA with user repositories, such as LDAP, through user directories. We then looked at JIRA's user management options with groups and project roles. While both are very similar, groups are global, while project roles are specific to each project.

We have also learned how JIRA hierarchically manages permissions. We discussed each permission level in detail and how to manage them.

In the next chapter, we will take a different angle and start looking at another powerful use of JIRA, getting your data out through reporting.

9

Searching, Reporting, and Analysis

From *Chapter 2*, *Project Management*, to *Chapter 5*, *Screen Management*, we looked at how JIRA can be used as an information system to gather data from users. In *Chapter 6*, *Workflows and Business Processes*, and *Chapter 7*, *E-mails and Notifications*, we discussed some of the features that JIRA provides to add values to the gathered data through workflows and notifications. In this chapter, we will look at the other half of the equation, getting the data out and presenting it as useful information to the users.

By the end of this chapter, you will have learned the following:

- Utilizing the search interface in JIRA
- The different search options available in JIRA.
- About filters and how you can share search results with other users
- Generating reports in JIRA
- Sharing information with dashboards and gadgets

Search interface and options in JIRA

As an information system, JIRA comes fully loaded with features and options to search for data. It allows you to search for issues quickly through simple text-based, more refined searches by specifying issue field criteria that must be fulfilled, and more advanced searches through JIRA's own search language.

However, before we start looking into the in-depth details of all the search options JIRA provides, let's first take a look at the main search interface that you will be using in JIRA while performing your searches.

Issue navigator

The **Issue Navigator** is the primary location, where you will be performing all of your searches in JIRA. You can access the issue navigator by clicking on the **Issues** link in the top menu bar.

The issue navigator is roughly divided into three to four sections. The first section is where you will specify all of your search criteria, such as the project you want to search in and the issue type you are interested in. The second section is a table that lists the search results brought back. The third section includes the operations that you can perform on the search results, such as exporting them in a different format. The fourth and last section lists a number of useful, preconfigured filters and user-created filters.

When you access the issue navigator for the first time, you will be in **Basic Search** (we will discuss the different search options in more detail later in this chapter). If you have previously visited the issue navigator and chosen to use a different search option, such as Advanced Search, then JIRA will remember this and open up Advanced Search instead.

The following screenshot shows the issue navigator in the Basic Search mode. In Basic Search, you specify your search criteria with field controls at the top, selecting the values for each field:

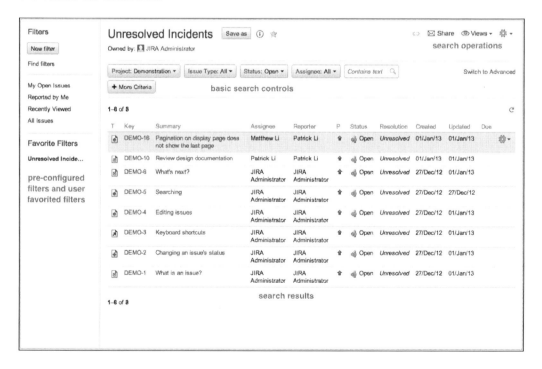

Basic search

Also known as **Simple Search**, basic search allows you to construct your search criteria with a simple-to-use interface. The basic search interface lets you select the fields you want to search with, such as projects and issue types, and specify the values for these fields. As shown in the following screenshot, we are searching for issues of the type **Bug** in the project **Audio Processor**, and with the status as **Open**.

With basic search, JIRA will prompt you for the possible search values for the selected field. This is very handy for fields such as status- and select list-based custom fields, so you do not have to remember all the possible options. For example, for the status field, JIRA will list all the available statuses:

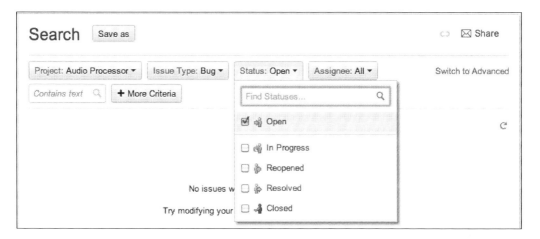

While working with the basic search interface, JIRA will have the default fields of project, issue type, status, and assignee visible. You can add additional fields to the search by clicking on the **More Criteria** button and then selecting the field you want to use in the search. Perform the following steps to construct and run a basic search:

1. Browse to **Issue Navigator**. If you do not see the basic search interface and the Switch to Basic link is showing, Click on it to switch to basic search.

2. Click on the **New filter** button at the left to start a new search.

3. Select and fill in the fields in the basic search interface.

JIRA will automatically update the search results every time you make a change to the search criteria.

When working with basic search, one thing to keep in mind is that the project and issue type context of the custom fields are taken into consideration (please see *Chapter 4, Field Management*, for field configuration). If a custom field is set to be applicable to only specific projects and/or issue types, then you have to select the project and issue type as part of your search for the custom field to show up.

Advanced search (JQL)

Basic search is useful and will fulfill most of the users' search needs. However, there are still some limitations. One such limitations is that basic search allows you to perform searches based on inclusive logic, but not exclusive logic. For example, if you need to search for issues in all but one project, with basic search, you will have to select every project except for the one to be excluded, since the basic search interface does not let you specify exclusions, and this is where advanced search comes in.

With advanced search, instead of using a field selection-based interface as in basic search, you will be using what is known as the **JIRA Query Language (JQL)**. JQL is a custom query language developed by Atlassian. If you are familiar with the **Structured Query Language (SQL)**, then you will notice that it has a similar syntax, however, JQL is not the same as SQL.

One of the most notable differences between JQL and SQL is that JQL does not start with a select statement. A JQL query consists of a field, followed by an operator, and then by a value or a function (which will return a value). You cannot specify what fields to return from a query with JQL, which is different to SQL. You can think of a JQL query as the part that comes after the `where` keyword in a normal SQL `select` statement. The following table summarizes the components in JQL:

JQL component	Description
Keyword	Keywords in JQL are special reserved words that do the following: <ul><li>Join queries together, such as AND</li><li>Determine the logic of the query, such as NOT</li><li>Have special meaning, such as NULL</li><li>Provide specific functions, such as ORDER BY</li></ul>

JQL component	Description
Operator	Operators are symbols or words that can be used to evaluate the value of a field on the left and the values to be checked on the right. Examples include the following: • **Equals**: = • **Greater than**: > • **IN:** When checking if the field value is in one of the many specified values specified in parentheses
Field	Fields are JIRA system and custom fields. When used in JQL, the value of the field for issues is used to evaluate the query.
Functions	Functions in JQL perform specific calculations or logic and return the result as values that can be used to for evaluation with an operator.

Each JQL query is essentially made up of one or more components. A basic JQL query consists of the following three elements:

- **Field**: This can be an issue field (for example, status) or a custom field.
- **Operator**: This defines the comparison logic (for example, = or >) that must be fulfilled for an issue to be returned in the result.
- **Value**: This is what the field should be compared to. It can be a literal value expressed as text (for example, Bug) or a function that will return a value.

Queries can then be linked together to form a more complex query with keywords such as logical AND or OR. For example, a basic query to get all the issues with a status of Resolved will look similar to the following:

```
status = Resolved
```

A more complex query to get all the issues with a status of Rcsolved, issue type of Bug, and assigned to the currently logged-in user will look similar to the following (where currentUser() is a JQL function):

```
issuetype = Bug and status = Resolved and assignee = currentUser()
```

Discussing each and every JQL function and operator is out of the scope of the book, but you can get a full reference by clicking on the **Syntax Help** link in the advanced search interface. The full JQL syntax reference can be found at http://confluence.atlassian.com/display/JIRA/Advanced+Searching.

You can access the advanced search interface from the Issue Navigator, as follows:

1. Browse to the Issue Navigator.
2. Click on the **Switch to Advanced** link in the top-left corner.
3. Click on the **New filter** button on the left to start a new search.
4. Construct your JQL query.
5. Click on the **Search** button or press the *Enter* key on your keyboard.

As JQL can has a complex structure and it takes some time to get familiar with, the advanced search interface has some very useful features to help you construct your query. The interface has an **auto-complete feature** (which can be turned off) that can help you pick out keywords, values, and operators to use. It also validates your query in real time and informs you if your query is valid:

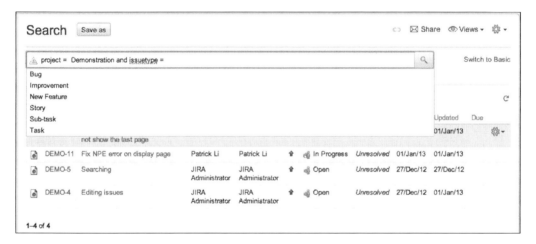

If there are no syntax errors with your JQL query, JIRA will display the results in a table below the JQL input box.

You can switch between the basic and advanced search by clicking on the **Switch to Basic/Advanced** link while running your queries, and JIRA will automatically convert your search criteria into and from JQL. In fact, this is a rather useful feature and can help you learn the basic syntax of JQL when you are first starting up, by first constructing your search in basic and then seeing what the equivalent JQL is. You need to a take note that, however, not all JQLs can be converted into basic search since you can do a lot more with JQL than with the basic search interface.

Switching between the simple and advanced search can help you get familiar with the basics of JQL.

Quick search

JIRA provides a quick search functionality, which allows you to perform quick simple searches based on text contained in the issue's summary, description, or comments. This allows you to perform quick text-based searches on all issues in JIRA.

The quick search function has several additional features to let you perform more specialized searches with minimal typing, through smart querying. JIRA has a list of built-in queries, which you can use as your quick search terms to pull up issues with a specific issue type and/or statuses. Some useful queries include the following:

Smart query	Result
Issue key (for example, HD-12)	Takes you directly to the issue with the specified issue key.
Project key (for example, HD)	Displays all the issues in the project specified by the key in the Issue Navigator.
my or my open bugs	Displays all the issues that are assigned to the currently logged-in user.
overdue	Displays all issues that are due before today.
Issues with a particular status (for example, open)	Displays all issues with the specified status.
Issues with a particular resolution (for example, resolved)	Displays all issues with the specified resolution.

You can combine these queries together to create quick and yet powerful searches in JIRA. For example, the following query brings back all the resolved issues in the HD project:

```
HD resolved
```

Running a quick search is much simpler than either basic or advanced searches. All you have to do is to type in either the text you want to search with or the smart query in the **Quick Search** box in the top-right corner, and hit *Enter* on your keyboard.

As you can see, the goal of quick search is to allow you to find what you are looking for in the quickest possible way, and with smart query, you are able to perform more than just simple text-based searches.

 It is important to note that **Quick Search** is case-sensitive. For example, searching with the term My instead of my will become a simple text search, rather than issues that are assigned to the currently logged-in user.

Working with search results

You have seen how you can execute searches in JIRA. With the exception of using the issue key smart query, which will take you directly to the target issue, all other search results will be shown in the issue navigator.

The issue navigator is capable of more than letting you run searches and presenting you with the results; it also has other features including the following:

- Export search results into different views
- Select the columns you want to see for the issues in the results
- Share your search results with other people
- Create and manage filters

Exporting search results

From the Issue Navigator, JIRA allows you to export your search results in a variety of formats, such as MS Word and Excel. In JIRA, these are called **views**. JIRA is able to present your search results in different views such as XML or print-friendly pages. When you select views, such as MS Word, JIRA will generate the appropriate file and let you download it directly. Perform the following steps to export your results to a different format:

1. Browse to the **Issue Navigator** page.
2. Execute a search.
3. Bring down the **Views** drop-down menu in the top-right corner.
4. Select the view you wish to see your search results in.

Depending upon the view you select, some views will be on screen (printable), while others will prompt you with a download dialog box (MS Word).

Customizing the column layout

JIRA lets you configure the columns in your issue navigator to specify which fields are displayed when showing your search results. In JIRA, you can customize your issue navigator at a global level, which will affect all your searches, and also on a per search level with filters (see later in the chapter). Perform the following steps to customize your global issue navigator's column layout:

1. Browse to the **Issue Navigator** page.
2. Bring down the **Tools** drop-down menu in the top-right corner.
3. Select the **Configure Columns** option. This will bring you to the **Issue Navigator Columns** page.

In the **Issue Navigator Columns** page, you can add new columns to the navigator layout, remove existing columns, and reorder columns. There is also an option to hide the **Actions** column, which is always the last column and shows some short-cut links for the actions you can perform on issues directly from the navigator.

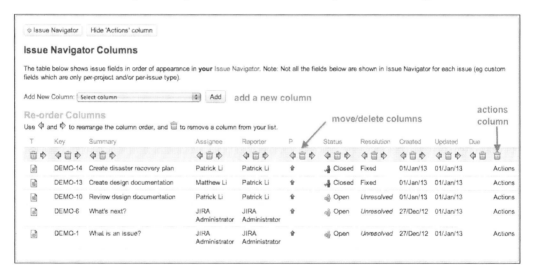

Once you have updated the column layout of the issue navigator, the layout will be used for all future searches you perform. If you want to have dedicated layouts for searches, you need to create named searches called **filters** and configure the column layout on the filters. We will look at filters in the later sections of this chapter.

Sharing search results

After completing a search, you might want to share the results with your colleagues. Now, you can tell your colleagues to run the same search or as we will see later in the chapter, save your search as a filter and then share it with people, but a more convenient way is to use the built-in **share feature**, especially if this is a one-off sharing.

To share your current search results, all you have to do is click on the **Share** link in the top-right corner and type in the user's name or an e-mail address (using an e-mail address lets you share your search results with people who are not JIRA users), and you can add multiple users or e-mail addresses, so you can share this with more than one person. You can also add a quick note, letting people know the purpose, and JIRA will send out e-mails to all the selected users and e-mail addresses.

Filters

After you have performed a query, sometimes it will be useful to save the query for later use. For example, you might have created a query to list all the open bugs and new features in a project that are to be completed by a certain date in several projects, so you can keep an eye on their progress. Instead of recreating this search query every time you want to check up on the statuses, you can save the query as a filter, which can be reused at a later stage. You can think of filters as named search queries that can be reused.

Other than being able to quickly pull up a report without having to recreate the queries, saving search queries as filters provides you with other benefits, including the following:

- Share saved filters with other users
- Use the filters as a source of data to generate reports
- Display results on a dashboard as a gadget
- Subscribe to the search queries to have results e-mailed to you automatically

We will explore all of the advanced operations you can perform with filters and explain some of the new terms and concepts, such as dashboard and gadgets in later sections, but first, let's look at how we can create and manage filters.

Creating a filter

To create a new filter, you will first have to construct and execute your search query. You can do this with any of the three available search options provided in JIRA, but please note that the search result must bring you to the Issue Navigator. So if you are using the quick search option and search by issue key, you will not be able to create a filter. Once you have executed your query, regardless of if it brings back any result, you will be able to create a new filter based on the executed search:

1. Browse to **Issue Navigator**.
2. Click on the **New filter** button in the left-hand side.
3. Construct and execute a search query in JIRA.
4. Click on the **Save as** button at the top.
5. Provide a meaningful name for the filter.
6. Click on the **Submit** button to create the filter.

Once you have created the filter, all your search parameters will be saved. In future, when you re-run the saved filter, JIRA will retrieve the updated results based on the same parameters.

Take note that you need to click on the **New filter** button to start a new search. Since issue navigator remembers your last search, if you were working with an existing filter, without starting a new search, you will be in fact modifying the current filter instead.

 Always click on **New filter** to start a new search session to avoid accidentally modifying an existing filter.

Managing filters

As the number of created filters grows, you will need a centralized location to manage and maintain them. There are two ways to access the **Manage Filters** page. You can access the page through the issue navigator, as follows:

1. Browse to **Issue Navigator**.
2. Click on the **Find Filters** link at the left-hand side. This will bring you to the **Manage Filters** page.

You can also access the **Manage Filters** page by going through the top navigator bar:

1. Bring the drop-down menu from **Issues**.
2. Click on the **Manage Filters** option at the bottom of the list.

The **Manage Filters** page displays the filters that are visible to you in three main categories, as set out in the tabs to the left, along with the option to search for existing filters:

- **Favorite**: This option filters with a golden star next to their names. These filters will be listed in the **Issues** drop-down menu. You can mark a filter as favorite by clicking on the star directly.

- **Popular**: This option lists the top 20 filters that have the most people marking them as favorite.

- **My**: This option lists the filters that are created by you.

- **Search**: This option searches for existing filters that are shared by other users.

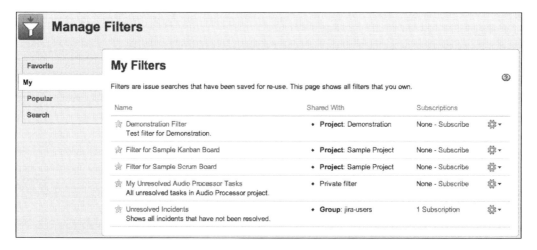

As shown in the preceding screenshot, both the **Demonstration Filter** and **Unresolved Incidents** filters are marked as favorite, and the **My Unresolved Audio Processor Tasks** filter is set to private.

Editing and sharing a filter

After creating a filter, you can update its details such as name and description, sharing permission, and search parameters:

1. Browse to the **Manage Filters** page.

2. Click on the **Edit** link for the filter you wish to edit. This will bring you to the **Edit Current Filter** page.

3. Update the details of the filter.

4. Select the group/project role to share the filter with.

5. Click on the **Save** button to apply the changes:

For you to be able to share a filter, you will also need to have the **Create Shared Object** global permissions (please refer to *Chapter 8, Securing JIRA,* for more information on global permissions).

After you have shared your filter, other users will be able to search for it and subscribe to it. They, however, will not be able to make changes to your filter. Only the owner of the filter is able to make changes to its search parameters. As we will see later, ownership of a filter can only be changed by a JIRA administrator.

Subscribing to a filter

You have seen in *Chapter 7, E-mails and Notifications*, that JIRA is able to send out e-mails when certain events occur to keep the users updated. With filters, JIRA takes this feature one step further, by allowing you to subscribe to a filter.

When you subscribe to a filter, JIRA will run a search based on the filter and send you the results in an e-mail. You can specify the schedule of when and how often JIRA should perform this. For example, you can set up a subscription to have JIRA send you the results every morning before you come to work, so when you open up your mail inbox, you will have a full list of issues that require your attention.

To subscribe to a filter, you will need to be able to see the filter (either created by you or shared with you by other users):

1. Browse to the **Manage Filters** page.

2. Locate the filter you wish to subscribe to.

3. Click on the **Subscribe** link for the filter. This will take you to the **Filter Subscription** page.

4. Select the recipient of the subscription. Normally, this will be you (**Personal Subscription**). But you can create subscriptions for other people by selecting a group.

5. Select **Email this filter, even if there are no issues found option if you wish to have an e-mail sent to you if there are no results returned from the filter**. This can be useful to make sure that the reason you are not getting e-mails is not due to other errors.

6. Specify the frequency and time when JIRA should send you the e-mails.

7. Click on the **Subscribe** button. This will create the subscription and take you to the **Subscription Summary** page.

8.   Click on the **Run Now** link to test your new subscription:

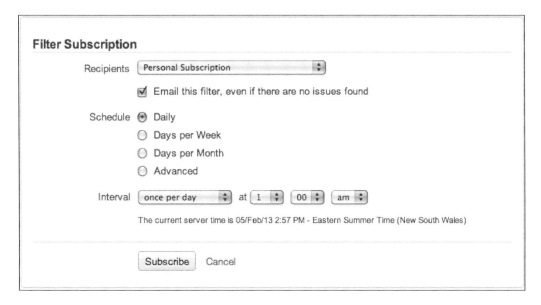

Deleting a filter

You can delete a filter when it is no longer needed. However, since you can share your filters out with other users and they can create subscriptions, you need to keep in mind that if you are deleting a shared filter, you might impact other users. Luckily, when you delete a filter, JIRA will inform you if other people are using the filter:

1.   Browse to the **Manage Filters** page.

2.   Click on the **Delete** link for the filter you wish to remove. This will bring up the **Delete Filter** confirmation dialog box.

3.   Make sure that the removal will not impact other users.

4. Click on the **Delete** button to remove the filter:

In your example, the **Unresolved Incidents** filter is shared and there is one user subscribing to it. JIRA informs you of that and by clicking on the **1** link, you will be taken to the **View Subscription** page, where you can see a list of users that are subscribed to the filter. You can then decide either to proceed with deleting the filter and letting the other users know, or leave the filter in JIRA.

Changing the ownership of a filter

JIRA only allows the filter's owner to make changes, such as the search criteria. This is usually not a problem for most cases, but when a filter is shared with other users, this can be problematic when the owner leaves the organization.

In JIRA 5, `jira-administrators` changes a filter's ownership to address situations like this. Perform the following steps to change a filter's ownership:

1. Browse to the **JIRA Administration** console.
2. Click on the **Shared Filters** link under the **Users** section.
3. Search for the filter you wish to change ownership of.
4. Bring down the **Actions** menu for the filter and select the **Change Owner** option.
5. Search and select the user that will be the new owner.

6. Click on the **Change Owner** button:

Reports

Apart from JQL and filters, JIRA also provides specialized reports to help you get a better understanding of the statistics for your projects, issues, users, and more.

Most reports in JIRA are designed to report on issues from a specific project, however, there are some reports that can be used globally across multiple projects, with filters. The following table shows all the reports that come with JIRA out of the box:

Report type	Description
Workload Pie Chart Report	Shows the relative workload for assignees of all issues in a particular project or issue filter.
User Workload Report	Shows how much work a user has been allocated and how long it is estimated to take, based on values in the estimate fields.
Version Workload Report	Shows how much outstanding work there is (per user and per issue) before a given version is complete.
Version Time Tracking Report	Shows progress towards completing a given version, based on issues' work logs and time estimates.
Single Level Group By Report	Shows the search results from an issue filter, grouped by a field of your choice.
Created versus Resolved Issues Report	Shows the number of issues created versus the number of issues resolved over a given period of time.
Resolution Time Report	Shows the average time taken to resolve issues.

Report type	Description
Pie Chart Report	Shows the search results from a specified issue filter (or project) in a pie chart, based on a statistic of your choice.
Average Age Report	Shows the average age (in days) of unresolved issues.
Recently Created Issues Report	Shows the rate at which issues are being created in the current project.
Time Since Issue Report	Shows the number of issues for which your chosen date field (for example **Created**) was set on a given date.

Generating a report

All JIRA reports are accessed from the **Browse Project** page of a specific project, regardless of if the report is project-specific or global. The difference between the two types of report is that a global report will let you choose a filter as a source of data, while a project-specific report will have its source of data predetermined based on the project you are in.

When generating a report, you will often need to supply several configuration options. For example, you might have to select a filter, which will provide the data for the report, or select a field to report on. The configuration options vary from report to report, but there will always be hints and suggestions to help you work out what each option is.

Perform the following steps to create a report; you will first need to get to a project's browse page:

1. Bring up the drop-down menu from **Projects**.
2. Select the project you wish to report on, or **View All Projects** if the project does not show up in the list.
3. Click on the **Summary** tab if it is not already selected.
4. Select the report you wish to create under the **Reports** heading. This will often bring you to the **Report Configuration** page.
5. Specify the configuration options for the report.
6. Click on the **Next** button to create the report.

In the following example, we will be creating a pie chart report. We will first select the type of report to be generated by selecting it from a list of available report types that come with JIRA:

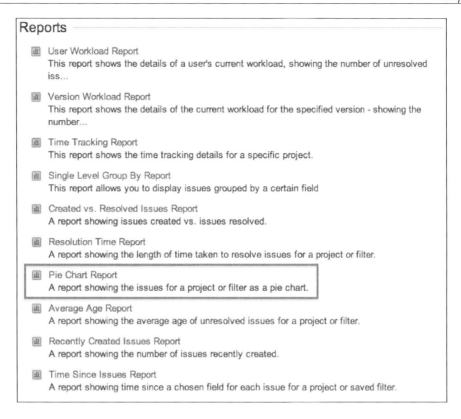

We will then configure the necessary report parameters. In this case, you need to specify if you are generating a report based on a project or an existing filter; by default, the current project will be preselected. You also need to specify which issue field you will be reporting on:

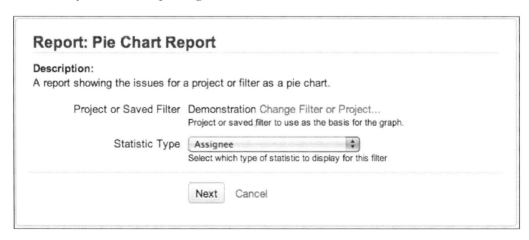

Once you have configured the report and hit on the **Next** button, JIRA will generate the report and present it on the screen:

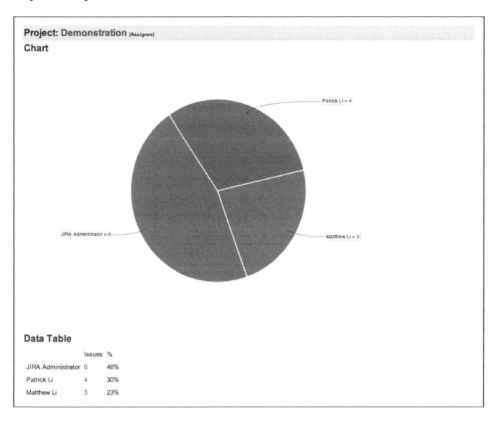

The report type determines the report's layout. Some reports have a chart associated with it (for example, **Pie Chart Report**), while other reports will have a tabular layout (for example, **Single Level Group By Report**). Some reports will even have an option for you to export its content into formats such as Microsoft Excel (for example, **Time Tracking Report**).

Dashboard

The dashboard is the first page you see when you access JIRA. Dashboards host "mini-applications" known as **Gadgets**, which provide various data and information from your JIRA instance. The dashboard acts as a portal, which provides users with a quick one-page view of information that is relevant or of interest to them.

Managing dashboards

When you first install JIRA, the default dashboard you see is called the **System Dashboard**, and it is preconfigured to show some useful information, such as all issues that are assigned to you.

Since everyone shares the system dashboard, you as a user cannot make changes to it, but can create your own dashboards, and each dashboard's functions are configured independently:

1. Bring down the drop-down menu from **Dashboards**.

2. Select the **Manage Dashboards** option. This will bring you to the **Manage Dashboards** page:

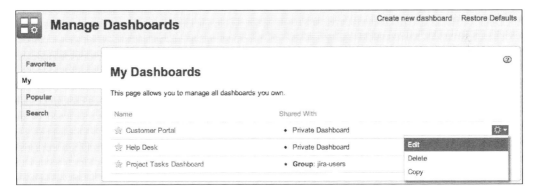

From this page, you can edit and maintain dashboards created by you, search dashboards created and shared by others, and mark them as favorite, so that they will be listed as tabs for easy access.

When a dashboard is marked as favorite by clicking on the star icon in front of its name, the dashboard will be accessible when you click on the **Dashboards** link at the top menu bar. If you have more than one favorite dashboard, each will be listed in the tabs and you can select which one to display.

Creating a dashboard

The default **System Dashboard** cannot be changed by users, so if you want to have a personalized dashboard displaying information that is specific to you, you will need to create a new dashboard. Perform the following steps to create a new dashboard:

1. Bring up the drop-down menu from **Tools**.

2. Select the **Create Dashboard** option. This will bring you to the **Create New Dashboard** page.

3. Provide a meaningful name and description for the new dashboard.

4. Select if you wish to copy from an existing dashboard or start with a blank one. This is similar to creating a new screen from scratch or copying an existing screen.

5. Select whether or not the new dashboard should be a favorite dashboard (for easy access) by clicking on the star icon.

6. Select if you wish to share the dashboard with other users. If you share your dashboard with the **Everyone** option, then users that are not logged in will also be able to see your dashboard.

7. Click on the **Add** button to create the dashboard.

The following screenshot shows how you can create a new dashboard from scratch (blank dashboard) and share it with the members of the jira-users group, which by default, are all logged-in users:

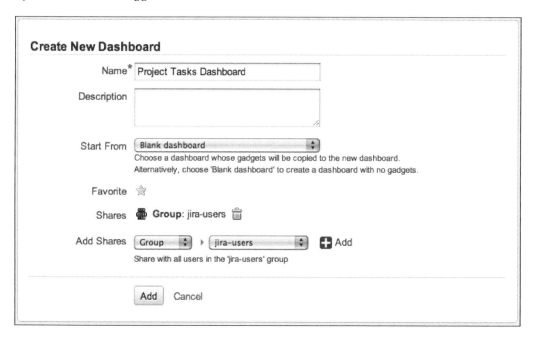

Once you have created the new dashboard, you will be taken immediately to it. As the owner of the new dashboard, you will be able to edit its layout and add gadgets to it. We will be looking at these configuration options in the next section.

Editing and sharing a dashboard

For dashboards created by you, you can edit its name and description, and choose to share it with other users so that they can access the dashboard by choosing it as a favorite:

1. Browse to the **Manage Dashboards** page.

2. Click on the **Edit** option for the dashboard you with to edit. This will bring you to the **Edit and Share Dashboard** page.

3. Update the details of the dashboard.

4. Select the group/project role to share the dashboard with.

5. Click on the **Update** button to apply the changes.

For you to be able to share a dashboard, you will also need to have the **Create Shared Object** global permissions (please refer to *Chapter 8, Securing JIRA,* for more information on global permissions).

Deleting a dashboard

Dashboard creators can also delete dashboards they have created. However, it is important to note that if you have shared the dashboard, by removing it from JIRA, all other users that are using it will be affected:

1. Browse to the **Manage Dashboards** page.

2. Click on the **Delete** option for the dashboard you wish to remove. This will bring up the **Delete Dashboard** confirmation dialog box.

3. Click on the **Delete** button to remove the dashboard.

The **Delete Dashboard** dialog box will alert you if there are users who have added the dashboard as favorite.

Configuring a dashboard

All custom created dashboards can be configured once they have been created. As the owner, there are two aspects of a dashboard you can configure:

• **Layout**: This describes how the dashboard page should be divided.

• **Contents**: This describes the gadgets that are to be added to the dashboard.

Setting a layout for the dashboard

You have to be the owner of the dashboard (created by you) to set the layout. Setting a dashboard's layout is quite simple and straightforward. If you are the owner, you will have the **Edit Layout** option at the top-right corner while you view the dashboard.

JIRA comes with five layouts that you can choose from. These layouts differ in how the dashboard page's onscreen real estate is divided. By default, new dashboards have the second layout, which divides it into two columns of equal size:

1. Bring up the drop-down menu from **Dashboards**.

2. Select the dashboard you wish to edit the layout for.

3. Click on the **Edit Layout** option at the top-right corner. This will bring up the **Edit Layout** dialog box.

4. Select the layout you wish to change to:

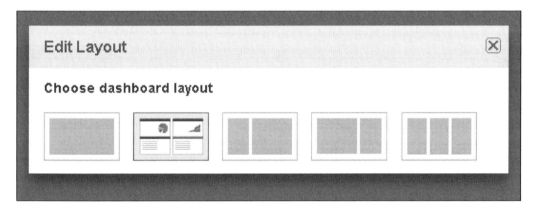

After selecting a layout from the dialog box, it will be immediately applied to the dashboard. Any existing contents will automatically have their size and positions adjusted to fit within the new layout.

After you have decided on your dashboard's layout, you can start adding contents, known as **gadgets**, onto your dashboard. But before you get to that, let's first take a brief look at what gadgets are.

Gadget

If you are familiar with the personalized Google homepage (**iGoogle**), you should be fairly familiar with gadgets by now. As a matter of fact, JIRA and iGoogle gadgets are built on the same technology.

Gadgets are like mini applications that live on a dashboard in JIRA. Each gadget has its own unique interface and behavior, for example, the **Pie Chart** gadget displays data in a pie chart while the **Assigned to Me** gadget lists all the unresolved issues that are assigned to the current user in a table.

To discuss the in-depth details of gadgets and OpenSocial is beyond the scope of this book, but there is much information on this topic available on the Internet, if you are interested in creating your own gadgets to use with JIRA. A good place to start will be the Atlassian documentation at `http://confluence.atlassian.com/display/GADGETDEV/Getting+Started+with+Gadget+Development`.

Placing a gadget on the dashboard

All gadgets are listed in the **Gadget Directory**. JIRA comes with a number of useful gadgets, such as the Assigned to Me gadget that you see on the System Dashboard. The next screenshot shows the gadget directory, listing all the bundled gadgets in JIRA.

Perform the following steps to place a gadget onto your dashboard:

1. Bring up the drop-down menu from **Dashboards**.
2. Select the dashboard you wish to add a gadget to.
3. Click on the **Add Gadget** option at the top-right corner. This will bring up the **Gadget Directory** window:

4. Click on the **Add it Now** button for the gadget you wish to add.

5. Click on the **Finish** button to return to the dashboard:

Depending on the gadget you have selected, some gadgets will require additional options to be configured. For these gadgets, you will be presented with their configuration screen on the dashboard. Fill in the options and click on the **Save** button.

The next screenshot shows the configuration screen for the **Assigned to Me** gadget, where you can control the number of results to show and the fields to include. One common parameter is the **Refresh Interval** option, where you can decide how often the gadget should refresh its content, if you stay on the dashboard or stay static if you choose never. Whenever you refresh the entire dashboard, all gadgets will load the latest data, but if you stay on the dashboard for an extended period of time, each gadget can automatically refresh its data, so the content will not become stale overtime:

Assigned to Me

Number of Results: | 10
Number of results to display (maximum of 50).

Fields to display

⠿ Issue Type 🗑
⠿ Key 🗑
⠿ Priority 🗑
⠿ Summary 🗑

Drag-drop to reorder the fields.

Select a field... ⬍ (Add)
Add fields to the list above by selecting them and clicking 'Add'.

Refresh Interval: | Never ⬍
How often you would like this gadget to update

(Save) (Cancel)

Moving a gadget

When you add a gadget, it's usually added to the first available spot on the dashboard. This sometimes may not be where you want the gadget to display, and in other cases, you might want to move the existing gadgets around from time to time. As the owner of the dashboard, you can easily move gadgets on a dashboard, through a simple drag-and-drop interface:

1. Browse to the dashboard that has gadgets you wish to move.
2. Click on the gadget's title and drag it to the new position on the dashboard.

As soon as you drop the gadget to its new location (release your mouse button), the gadget will be moved permanently until you decide to move it again.

Editing a gadget

After configuring your gadget when you first place it onto your dashboard, the gadget will remember this and use it to render its content. You can update the configuration details or even its look and feel.

1. Browse to the dashboard that has gadgets you wish to update.
2. Hover over the gadget and click on the down arrow button at the top-right corner of it. This will bring up the gadget configuration menu.

3.   Click on the **Edit** option.

4.   This will change the gadget into its configuration mode.

5.   Update the configuration options.

6.   Click on the **Save** button to apply the changes:

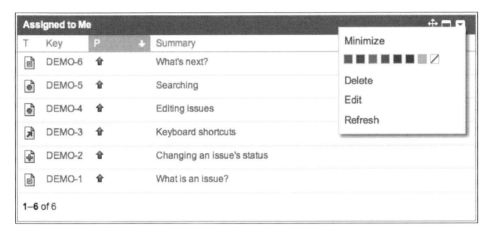

The preceding screenshot shows the edit menu for the **Assigned to Me** gadget. You can force a refresh with the **Refresh** option. Since gadgets retrieve their data asynchronously via AJAX, you can use this option to refresh the gadget itself, without refreshing the entire page. The edit, delete, and color options are only available to the owner of the dashboard.

Deleting a gadget

As the owner of the dashboard, you can remove the existing gadgets from the dashboard when they are no longer needed. When you remove a gadget from a dashboard, please note that that all the other users who have access to your dashboard will no longer see it:

1.   Browse to the dashboard that has gadgets you wish to delete.

2.   Hover over the gadget and click on the down arrow button at the top-right hand corner of it. This will bring up the gadget configuration menu.

3.   Click on the **Delete** option.

4.   Confirm the removal when prompted.

Once removed, the gadget will disappear from the dashboard. If you choose to re-add the same gadget again at a later stage, you will have to reconfigure it again.

The Help Desk project

In our previous chapters and exercises, we have built and customized a JIRA project to collect data from users. What we need to do now is to process and present this data back to the users. The goal we are trying to achieve in this exercise is to set up a portal page for our `Help Desk` team, which will have useful information such as statistics and issue listings that can help our team members to better organize themselves, to provide better services to other departments.

Setting up filters

The first step is to create a useful filter that can be shared with the other members of the team and also act as a source of data to feed our gadgets. We will use the advanced search to construct our search:

1. Browse to **Issue Navigator**.

2. Click on the **Switch to advanced searching** link to bring up the JQL interface.

3. Type in the following JQL search query:

   ```
   project = HD and issuetype = Incident and status != Resolved and
   status != Closed order by priority
   ```

4. Click on the **Search** button to execute the search.

5. Click on the **Save it as a filter** link to bring up the **Save Current** Filter page.

6. Name the filter as `Unresolved Incidents`.

7. Mark the filter as favorite.

8. Share the filter with `help-desk-team` group setup from *Chapter 8, Securing JIRA*.

9. Click on the **Save** button to create the filter.

This filter searches and returns a list of unresolved issues of type **Incident** from our Help Desk project. The search results are then ordered by their priority, so users can determine the urgency. As you will see in the later steps, this filter will be used as the source of data for your gadgets to present information on your dashboard.

Setting up dashboards

The next step is to create a new dashboard for your help desk team. What you need is a dashboard specifically for your team, so that you can share information easily. For example, you can have the dashboard displayed in a large overhead projector showing all the high priority incidents that need to be addressed:

1. Bring up the drop-down menu from **Tools**.
2. Select the **Create Dashboard** option. This will bring you to the **Create New Dashboard** page.
3. Name the new dashboard Help Desk.
4. Select **Blank dashboard** as your base.
5. Tick the new dashboard as favorite.
6. Share the filter with the **help-desk-team** group.
7. Click on the **Save** button to create the dashboard.

In your example, we will use the default two columns layout for your new dashboard. But you are free to experiment with other layouts and find the ones that best suit your needs.

Setting up gadgets

Now that you have set up your portal dashboard page and shared it with the other members of the team, you need to start adding some useful information to it. One example would be to have the dashboard display all the unresolved incidents that are waiting to be processed. JIRA has an **Assigned to Me** gadget, which shows all the issues that are assigned to the currently logged-in user, but what you need is a global list irrespective of the assignee of the incident.

Luckily, JIRA also has a **Filter Results** gadget, which displays search results based on a search filter. Since you have already created a filter that returns all the unresolved incidents in your Help Desk project, the combination of both will nicely solve your problem:

1. Browse to the **Help Desk** dashboard you have just created.
2. Click on the **Add Gadget** option at the top-right corner. This will bring up the **Gadget Directory** window.
3. Click on the **Add it Now** button for the **Filter Results** gadget.
4. Click on the **Finish** button to return to the dashboard.
5. Select the **Unresolved Incidents** filter you have created.

6. Select **Default Columns** and any additional fields you wish to add.

7. Set **Refresh Interval** to **15** minutes.

8. Click on the **Save** button.

This will add a new **Filter Results** gadget to your new dashboard, using your filter as the source of data. The gadget will auto-refresh its contents every 15 minutes, so you will not need to refresh the page all the time. You can add some other gadgets to the dashboard to make it more informative and useful. Some other useful gadgets include the **Activity Stream** and **Assigned to Me** gadgets.

Putting it together

This is pretty much all you have to do to set up and share a dashboard in JIRA. After you have added the gadget to it, you will be able to see it in action. The great thing about this is, since you have shared the dashboard with others in the team, they will be able to see the dashboard too. Members of the team will be able to search for your new dashboard or mark it as favorite to add it to their list of dashboards.

You do have to keep in mind that, if you are using a filter as a source of data for your gadget, then you have to share the filter with other users too, or they will not be able to see anything from the gadget.

Summary

We have covered how users can search and report on the data they have put into JIRA, which is an essential component for any information system. JIRA provides a robust search facility by offering many different search options to users, including quick, simple, and advanced searches. You can save and name your searches by creating filters which can be re-run at later stages to save you from re-creating the same search again.

JIRA also allows you to create configurable reports on projects or results brought back from search filters. Information can be shared with others through a dashboard, which acts as a portal for users to quickly get a glance of the data kept in JIRA.

In the next chapter, we will look at various other value added features and administration options in JIRA, including the built-in backup/restore utility, and extend JIRA's core features and functionalities through plugins/add-ons.

10
General Administration

JIRA is a very powerful and flexible application. You have seen how you can customize its functionalities by building new fields, screens, workflows, notifications, and permission rules. Apart from the major areas we have covered up until now, there are some other useful features that you can customize.

You can change the appearance of JIRA, so that its look and feel will be more consistent with other web applications that you have in your organization. You can also select the language JIRA will use to display its content, perform quick backups, and restore with the built-in tools. Finally, we will take a look at how you can extend the power of JIRA through custom add-ons.

In this chapter, we will cover the following topics:

- How to customize JIRA's look and feel
- General administration options in JIRA
- Backing up and restoring data in JIRA
- How to keep search index in sync with data
- Extending JIRA's functionalities through custom add-ons

Customizing the look and feel

While the default appearance that is configured with JIRA upon installation is sufficient for most intents and purposes, organizations often require their applications and websites to be branded to have a standardized look and feel. JIRA allows for this level of flexibility by allowing you to configure its colors, date representations, and even lets you add a logo to it:

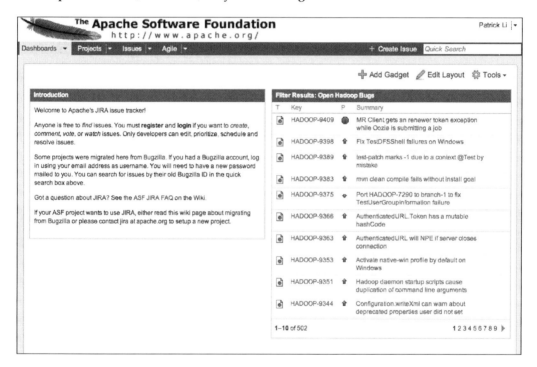

As an example, the preceding screenshot shows a branded version of JIRA to demonstrate what you can do with its look and feel configurations:

Since the look and feel is something that is global across JIRA, you will need to be a JIRA or system administrator to configure these settings.

1. Browse to the JIRA administration console.
2. Click on **Look and Feel** under the **User Interface** section. This will bring up the **Look and Feel Configuration** page.

From this page, you will be able to customize the color, logo, and date format settings of your JIRA instance.

Changing the JIRA logo

People often say that a picture is worth a thousand words, and a logo is usually the first thing when it comes to branding a website. JIRA lets you assign a logo, which will be displayed at top of every page in JIRA:

1. Browse to the **Look and Feel Configuration** page.
2. Specify the URL or the file path (on the JIRA server) of your logo image under the **Logo** section.
3. Specify the width and height of the image.
4. Click on the **Update** button to set your logo.

Once you have set your logo, JIRA will display the logo in the preview section with your specified dimension. The logo will be applied immediately at the top left-hand corner.

Customizing colors

JIRA divides its user interface into a number of elements, and each element can be assigned its own color. For example, you can set a different color for the top navigation bar and the hyperlink colors. This allows you to have a degree of flexibility to configure the color of JIRA to be more consistent with your organization's branding standards:

1. Browse to the **Look and Feel Configuration** page.
2. Click on the **Edit Configuration** link at the bottom of the page. This will allow you to edit the look and feel settings.

3. Specify the colors for each component/section under the **Colours** section. You can either specify the hexadecimal color code directly or use the color picker to select the color you want:

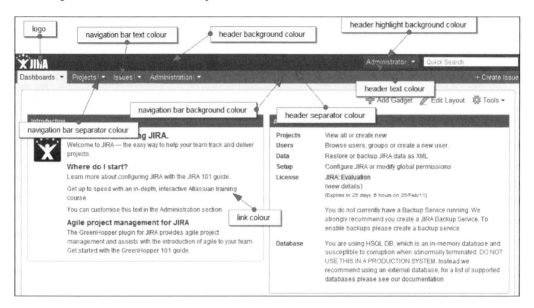

The preceding screenshot shows a breakdown of the different sections in JIRA and what color options will be applied:

Color option	Description
Header Background Colour	The background color of the top bar (where the logo image is displayed).
Header Highlight Background Colour	The background color of the text that sits inside the top bar when highlighted (hovered over).
Header Text Colour	The color of the text that sits inside the top bar.
Header Text Highlight Colour	The color of the text that sits inside the top bar when highlighted.
Header Separator Colour	The color of the horizontal line between the top bar and the navigation bar.
Navigation Bar Background Colour	The background color of the bar that contains the navigation links, such as **Dashboard** and **Administration**.
Navigation Bar Text Colour	The color of the link texts in the navigation bar.
Navigation Bar Separator Colour	The color of the vertical dotted line between each menu item in the navigation bar.

Color option	Description
Link Colour	The color of the text links in JIRA.
Link Active Colour	The color of the text links in JIRA when selected.
Heading Colour	The color of the text headings in JIRA.

Changing gadget colors

In *Chapter 9, Searching, Reporting, and Analysis,* we introduced dashboards and gadgets in JIRA. A gadget's color is independent to the rest of JIRA. As a matter of fact, JIRA allows the administrator to create a set of colors for users to pick from. Perform the following steps to create your custom color set:

1. Browse to the **Look and Feel Configuration** page.

2. Hover over the color you want to change under the **Gadget Colors** section, and click on the color icon.

3. Specify the colors for your gadgets. The first color (**Color 1**) will be the default color for all the gadgets, without a color selected:

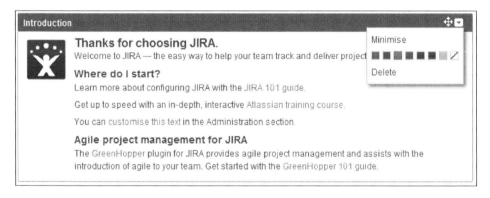

After saving your set of gadget colors, they will be made available for users to select from. For gadgets that do not have a color selected, the default color will be applied automatically.

Setting the date/time format

Another aspect of JIRA's look and feel that can be customized is how dates are displayed and entered. Different countries display dates differently. For example, some countries display dates in the month/day/year format, while others use the day/month/year format. JIRA allows you to set how you will like dates to be handled to better suit your environment.

JIRA follows the date format set by Java, the technology JIRA is built on. You can find the full explanation on the format at `http://download.oracle.com/javase/6/docs/api/java/text/SimpleDateFormat.html`:

1. Browse to the **Look and Feel Configuration** page.

2. Hover over the date-time setting you want to change, and click on the edit icon.

3. Update the configuration value.

4. Click on the **Update** button:

Date/Time Formats

Documentation on date/time formats can be found online.

Time Format	h:mm a ✎ E.g. 8:55 PM → click to edit
Day Format	EEEE h:mm a E.g. Tuesday 8:55 PM
Complete Date/Time Format	dd/MMM/yy h:mm a E.g. 22/May/07 8:55 PM
Day/Month/Year Format	dd/MMM/yy E.g. 22/May/07
Use ISO8601 standard in Date Picker Turning it on will cause Monday to be the first day of week in the Date Picker, as specified by the ISO8601 standard	No

After you have updated the date/time format settings, all date and date-time fields in JIRA, such as due date, will adopt the new format to display dates, and users will be required to enter them in the new format.

General configurations

In the past few chapters, we have been focusing on how to customize JIRA's issue management features and options. As an application, there are also several system configuration options that can be configured. These include the maximum failed login attempts allowed before locking the user out, setting the default language used by JIRA, and other miscellaneous options.

JIRA groups these options under **General Configurations**, and you can fine-tune these settings:

1. Browse to the JIRA administration console.
2. Click on **General Configuration** under the **System** section. This will bring up the JIRA **General Configuration** page.

From here, you will be able to set the configuration settings for options that are not related to JIRA projects and issues.

Settings

The **Settings** section contains several system-wide configuration settings that control some generic behaviors of JIRA:

Setting	Description
Title	This is the name of your JIRA instance. This name will appear in the **Introduction Gadget** section on the dashboard.
Mode	This option lets you decide if JIRA will allow users to sign up/create an account on JIRA" • **Public**: Anyone can create an account by signing up • **Private**: Only the JIRA administrator can create new accounts
Maximum Authentication Attempts Allowed	This is the number of failed login attempts allowed before the CAPTCHA challenge is required. This is helpful to prevent brute force login attacks, where malicious users continuously attempt to log in to an account by trying and guessing password combinations.
CAPTCHA on signup	This option enables/disables the CAPTCHA challenge when users sign up for new accounts. It's useful to prevent bots from signing up.

Setting	Description
Base URL	This is the base URL of your JIRA. It is usually the URL used by users to access your JIRA. For example, the base URL in your example will be `http://localhost:8080/jira`. This is used by JIRA internally for things such as links in notification e-mails sent out by JIRA, and **Gadgets**. It is important that this is set correctly.
Email from	This is the **From:** header used by JIRA when sending out notifications.
Introduction	This is a short introduction to be displayed on the dashboard in the **Introduction** gadget.

Internationalization

The **Internationalization** section lets you set the language that JIRA will use while displaying its content. JIRA comes with a wide range of languages to choose from. If the language you are looking for is not available, then you can check the Atlassian Marketplace (see later section) to see if someone has created a translation that you can use.

Setting default language

Perform the following steps to set the default language for JIRA:

1. Browse to the **General Configuration** page.
2. Click on the **Edit Configuration** button at the bottom of the page.
3. Select **Default language** under **Internationalization**.
4. Click on the **Update** button to set the default language:

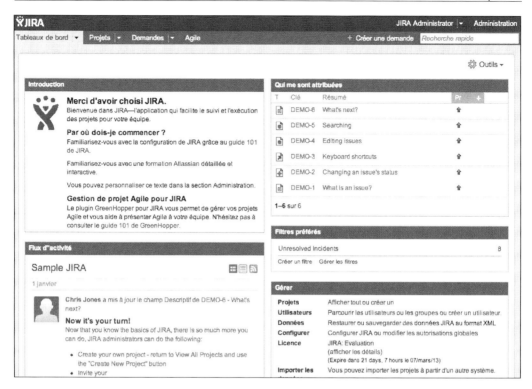

After choosing the default language, the change will be applied immediately. The selected default language will be used by JIRA for users who have not set up a personal language preference. The preceding screenshot shows JIRA in French, one of the languages shipped with JIRA.

Setting user language

For multinational organizations, sometimes multiple teams use a single JIRA instance across the globe. In these cases, it becomes desirable to be able to have different languages available to users depending on where the user comes from. This is where user-based language setting comes in. JIRA lets each user select the language of their choice, which will take precedence over the default language setting applied by the administrator. This selection needs to be done by each user individually. Perform the following steps to select a language:

1. Log in to JIRA with your own account.

2. Click on your username at the top-right corner of the page. This will bring up your **User Profile** page.

3. Click on the edit icon in the **Preferences** section. This will bring up the **Update User Preference** page.

4. Select the language you wish to use.

5. Click on the **Update** button to apply the change.

```
Preferences                                                              ✎

   Page Size:                     50
   Email Type:                    HTML
   Language:                      English (United States) [Default]
   Time Zone:                     JIRA default (GMT-08:00) Los Angeles
   My Changes:                    Do not notify me
   Filter and Dashboard Sharing:  Unshared
   Keyboard shortcuts:            Enabled
   Navigator Columns:             View Navigator Columns
   Autowatch:                     Inherit from global settings
```

Once selected, the change will be applied immediately, and you should see **JIRA** displayed in the language of your choice.

Options

The **Options** section contains a list of on/off options, which you can use to control if certain features of JIRA should be enabled. JIRA comes with sensible default settings for these options. However, very often you will need to change these settings to better suit your environment:

Options	Description
Allow users to vote on issues	This option enables/disables voting in JIRA.
Allow users to watch issues	This option enables/disables issue watching in JIRA.
Allow unassigned issues	When enabled, issues can be set to unassigned. If disabled, issues MUST have assignees.
External user management	When enabled, this option tells JIRA that you are using an external application to manage users (for example, LDAP and Atlassian Crowd). JIRA will disable user management features so you will not be able to create, edit, and delete user/groups.
External password management	When enabled, this option tells JIRA that you are suing an external application to manage user passwords. JIRA will not allow users to change their password and remove the **Forgot Password** link on the login screen.

Options	Description
Logout confirmation	This option controls whether or not a confirmation prompt will be displayed when users logs out.
Use gzip compression	This option controls whether or not compression should be applied when JIRA serves out pages to the browser.
Accept remote API calls	This option controls whether or not JIRA will accept web service calls (XML-RCP or SOAP). This option needs to be enabled if other applications attempt to access/integrate JIRA with these services.
User email visibility	This option controls whether or not a user's e-mail address will be viewable.
Comment visibility	This option determines the options available when users restrict their comment visibility.
Exclude email header "Precedence: bulk"	This option controls whether or not to prevent the **Precedence: Bulk** header on JIRA notification e-mails.
Issue Picker Auto-complete	This option enables/disables the auto-completion of issue keys in the **Issue Picker** pop-up screen.
User Searching By Full Name	This option enables/disables the auto-completion feature while searching for users by their full name instead of the username.
JQL Auto-complete	This option enables/disables the auto-completion feature while constructing JQL queries.
Internet Explorer MIME Sniffing Security Hole Workaround Policy	This option enables cross-site scripting vulnerabilities present in Internet Explorer 7 and earlier. <ul><li>**Insecure: inline display of attachments**: This allows all attachments to be displayed inline. It is the least secure option.</li><li>**Secure: force download of all attachments for all browsers**: This will force downloads of all attachments. It is the most secure option, but less convenient.</li><li>**Work around Internet Explorer security hold**: This will force download attachments that IE would mistakenly detect as an HTML file. It is the preferred and default option.</li></ul>
Contact Administrators Form	This option provides a form for users to contact the JIRA administrators (users with JIRA Administrator global permission). You can also provide a custom message to the users with the **Contact Administrator Message** option below.

Options	Description
Contact Administrators Message	This option lets you set a custom message that will be displayed on the **Contact Administrators Form**.
Use Gravatar for user avatars	This option uses the Gravatar (`http://en.gravatar.com`) service for managing user avatars.
Inline edit	This option enables/disables the new inline editing feature, where users can edit the value of a field by simply clicking on it.
Auto-update search results	When enabled, JIRA will automatically update the search results in the issue navigator when the search criteria is changed in the basic search mode.

Setting the announcement banner

There will often be times when you will need to make a change to the system, where you need to take JIRA down for a period of time. In a production environment, where there is a high reliance on the uptime, this can lead to unnecessary disruption to the users if not planned and communicated accordingly. JIRA recognizes this and provides a facility to help by letting administrators place an announcement banner on every page in JIRA. Together with traditional methods, such as e-mail alerts, day-to-day business disruptions caused by system downtime can be minimized.

Perform the following steps to put up an announcement banner in JIRA:

1. Browse to the JIRA administration console.
2. Click on **Announcement Banner** in the left panel. This will bring up the **Edit Announcement Banner** page.
3. Specify the announcement. This can be any simple text, valid HTML markup, CSS, or JavaScript.
4. Select if you want this announcement to be public, where everyone will be able to see, or private where only logged-in users can see.
5. Click on the **Set Banner** button to put up the announcement.

In the following screenshot, we create an announce banner that will warn users about a planned outage. We also use some JIRA CSS classes, so the output will be consistent with the general look and feel of JIRA:

Edit Announcement Banner

You can set HTML text which will display as a banner at the top of all pages in JIRA. This is useful for alerting users of upcoming system-wide changes.

Announcement

```
<div class="aui-message info">
<span class="aui-icon icon-info"></span>
<b>JIRA will be down on 22/Feb/2012 at 6:00PM for maintenance for 2 hours.
Please make sure you save your work.</b>
</div>
```

Visibility Level
○ Public - Show to anyone
◉ Private - Show to logged in users only

Set Banner

The following screenshot shows the result of the announcement banner we have set up. The banner will be at the top of page and will be visible on every page in JIRA until you remove it:

Backing up and restoring JIRA

For any applications running in a production environment, it is critical that their data is backed up regularly, so that they can be restored in case of a disaster.

The first thing you will need is to have a disaster recovery plan in place. This plan should outline the details of the strategy in place to back up JIRA's data and where the backups should be stored, and the recovery process of restoring the data. In context of JIRA, there are typically two items you will need to backup:

- **Database**: This is where JIRA stores most of its critical data, such as issues and configuration settings. It is recommended to use the native database backup tools available for your database (for example, `mysqldump` for MySQL).

- **JIRA_HOME**: This is where JIRA stores other important files, such as attachments and third-party add-ons. Since this is a directory sitting on the filesystem, you will need a native tool to back up the files (for example, **Scheduled Tasks in Windows**).

JIRA also comes with an XML backup/restore feature, which will back up the data from the database into an XML file. This utility, however, is not designed to be used for large JIRA instances (for example, with 200,000 issues or more). It is important to note that data kept in JIRA_HOME is not backed up.

> You should always use proper backup tools instead of relying on the built-in XML backup system.

Creating an XML backup

JIRA comes with a simple backup utility that lets you backup your data into an XML file, which can be later imported back in to restore JIRA. However, you must keep in mind that you should not rely on this utility as your sole backup strategy, as this option has several limitations:

- It cannot be used to back up large JIRA installations. JIRA is unable to restore backup files that are 2 GB or greater in size.
- It does not back up data on the filesystem, such as attachments.

Nonetheless, this can still be very handy when you need a quick way to perform a one-off backup before you make some system-wide changes such as an upgrade, or you need to copy data from one JIRA to another. Perform the following steps to create an XML backup:

1. Browse to the JIRA administration console.
2. Click on **Backup System** under **Import & Export**.
3. Specify the name of your exported XML file. The created backup file will always be a ZIP file.

4. Click on the **Backup** button:

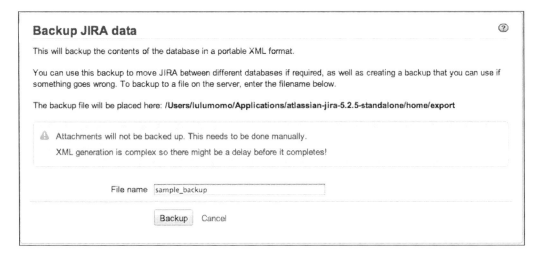

Depending upon the size of your JIRA, the backup process will take some time to complete. Once the backup process completes, JIRA will display the confirmation page with the full path to the exported XML file. If your JIRA has too much data, the backup will fail with an error. If this occurs, you will have to back up your data using your database backup tools.

Restoring from an XML backup

Once you have generated an XML backup, you can use that to restore your JIRA by importing it back in. Please note that when you perform a restore, the existing data will be completely wiped, including your JIRA license information, which will also be restored from the XML backup:

1. Browse to the JIRA administration console.

2. Click on **Restore System** under **Import & Export**.

3. Specify the XML backup file to restore from. Note that JIRA will look for the file inside the JIRA_HOME/import directory.

4. Optionally, supply a new JIRA license. You will need to do this if you want to override the license information from the backup file.

5. Click on the **Restore** button to start the restore process:

Since attachments are not a part of the XML backup, the restore process will not restore the attachments, however, if you are restoring a backup from the same instance, attachments will be automatically located. While JIRA is in the process of restoring from a backup, users will not be able to access JIRA.

You can only restore an export from the same or an older version of JIRA. For example, you cannot restore an export from JIRA 5.2 into JIRA 5.1.

Searching and indexing

In *Chapter 9, Searching, Reporting, and Analysis*, you looked at how you can search for data in JIRA. In order to support large instances with thousands of issues, JIRA creates and maintains search indexes on the filesystem. This index is added and modified whenever issues are created or updates are made, automatically in the background. Sometimes, however, JIRA will require you to perform a manual reindexing. This may occur when the index files are corrupt or missing, or changes are made directly in the database causing the index to be out of sync. You will notice this when your searches are constantly returning with the wrong set of issues.

When you reindex, you effectively recreate the search index on the filesystem based on the most current data in the database. This ensures that the values in both are in sync. It is important to note that as the amount of data grows in your database, so will the search index, so you will need to allocate enough disk space to the server where you install JIRA. Perform the following steps to reindex your JIRA:

1. Browse to the JIRA administration console.
2. Click on **Indexing** in the left panel. This will bring up the **Re-Indexing** page.
3. Select the re-index option, either in the background or a locked rebuild (in JIRA 5.2).
4. Click on the **Re-Index** button to start the reindexing process:

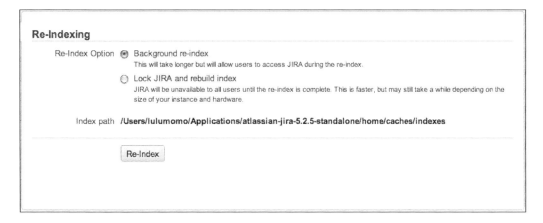

Starting with JIRA 5.2, you can choose to reindex JIRA either in the background, or fully lock down JIRA to rebuild the index from scratch. When you choose the **Lock JIRA and rebuild index** option, you will not be able to use JIRA until the reindex process completes.

When you run reindexing in the background, you can continue using JIRA while the reindex process is running. This is very useful when you make changes, such as the search template for a custom field, and need to reindex JIRA to reflect the change during working hours.

Depending upon the size of your JIRA instance, the reindex process can take some time to complete (several hours for some large installations; for example, 200 thousand issues).

Add-ons

In the previous chapters, we have illustrated JIRA's flexibility by allowing you to add new custom fields to capture data, and created new workflows to model business processes, but it does not stop here. Another powerful feature of JIRA is its built-in plugin system.

Generally, an add-on (also known as a plugin) is a self-contained extension with a `.jar` or `.obr` file extension that can be installed into JIRA to add new functionalities or enhance existing features.

Atlassian Marketplace

Atlassian hosts add-ons on its Atlassian Marketplace website. The Marketplace hosts a rich set of add-ons from both Atlassian and third-party vendors, for all Atlassian products such as JIRA, Confluence, and Stash. From here, you will be able to search useful add-ons, read reviews on add-ons you are interested in, and download/buy add-ons directly.

Add-ons hosted on the Marketplace come in several flavors:

- **Free/open source**: These are usually created and maintained by the community, are free to use, and are usually unsupported and "use at your own risk".
- **Paid via vendor**: These are commercial add-ons with payments and licenses processed by the vendor.
- **Paid via Atlassian**: These are commercial add-ons with payments and licenses processed by Atlassian (via Marketplace). You can purchase and obtain the license directly from the Marketplace within JIRA.

You can access the Atlassian Marketplace site at `https://marketplace.atlassian.com`.

Universal Plugin Manager

The **Universal Plugin Manager** (**UPM**) for short, is where you can find and install new add-ons and manage installed add-ons directly from inside JIRA. The UPM has two main interfaces:

- **Find new add-ons**: This is used for searching the Marketplace for add-ons and installing them directly.
- **Manage add-ons**: This manages the existing add-ons in your JIRA, and also lets you manually install add-ons that you have downloaded.

Finding new add-ons

The find new add-ons interface allows you to search add-ons that are available on the Marketplace directly inside JIRA. You can filter your searches with criteria such as category and licensing requirement.

Once you have found the add-on you want, you can install it directly by clicking on the **Install** button (if it is free), or **Buy/Evaluate the add-on** (if it is commercial):

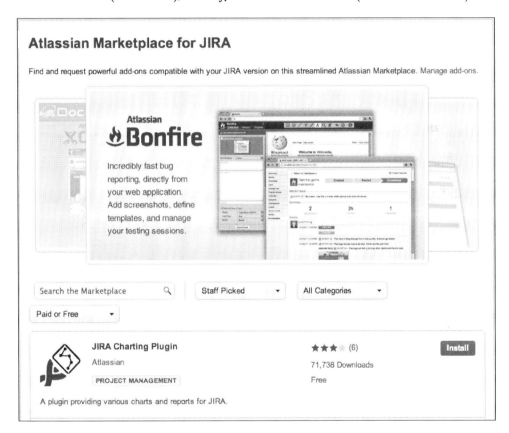

Managing add-ons

The manage add-ons interface allows you to manage all installed add-ons in JIRA. The page is divided into three major sections:

- **Available Updates**: The UPM will automatically detect the add-ons that are currently installed and search for available updates that are compatible with your JIRA version. The results will be listed under this section.

- **User-installed Add-ons**: These add-ons are installed by you and other administrators. You will usually find and install them from the Marketplace.

- **System Add-ons**: These are the important add-ons that are bundled with JIRA and cannot be uninstalled. You can, however, disable them, but doing so is not recommended.

The following screenshot shows that we have one add-on, **JIRA iCalendar Plugin**, which can be updated, and we currently have six user-installed add-ons:

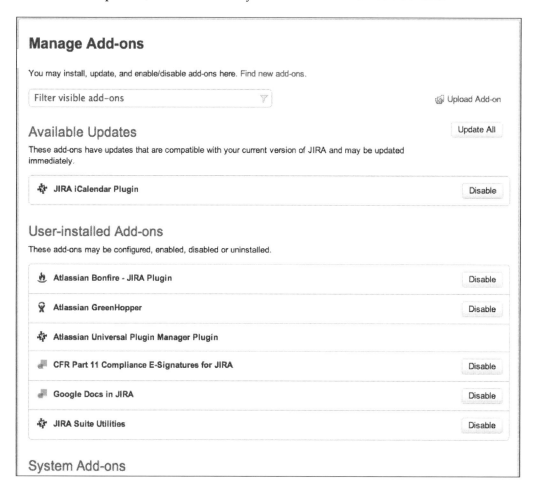

Installing an add-on

Installing a new add-on from the UPM is usually just a matter of clicks. There are two options when installing add-ons. The first option is to install it via the Marketplace; this will require you to have a working connection between your JIRA and the outside Internet:

1. Browse to the UPM.
2. Select the **Find New Add-ons** tab.
3. Search for the add-on you want.
4. Click on on **Install**, **Buy Now**, or **Free Trial**, depending upon the add-on's license requirement.

The second option to install an add-on is to manually obtain the add-on file yourself, and then upload/install it via the UPM. This method is suitable when your JIRA does not have a working connection with the Internet. Some add-ons may also require this manual installation:

1. Browse to the UPM.
2. Select the **Manage Add-ons** tab.
3. Click on the **Upload Add-on** link.
4. Select the add-on file by clicking on **Choose File**.
5. Click on the **Upload** button.

Once the add-on is installed, the UPM will display additional information on the add-on. In the following screenshot, we have just installed the **Atlassian GreenHopper** add-on:

Configuring an add-on

Simple add-ons that add additional custom field types and workflow post functions can be used straight out of the box after installation. Some other more complex add-ons would require additional configuration, such as licensing information and custom field mappings. Each add-on will have different ways to set the configuration options, so you will need to consult the add-on's usage instructions. Generally, if an add-on requires configuration, there will be a **Configure** button available.

Enabling/disabling an add-on

Almost all add-ons can be enabled and disabled. This is useful when you troubleshoot problems, and you can just disable the add-on or specific modules within it, which you suspect to be the cause of the problem rather than uninstall it completely.

Perform the following steps to enable or disable an add-on in a simple and straightforward manner:

1. Locate the add-on you with to enable/disable.
2. Click on the **Enable/Disable** button.

Updating an add-on

As you have seen, the UPM automatically detects the available updates for your installed add-ons. All you have to do is to click on on the add-on you wish to update, and then click on on the **Update** button:

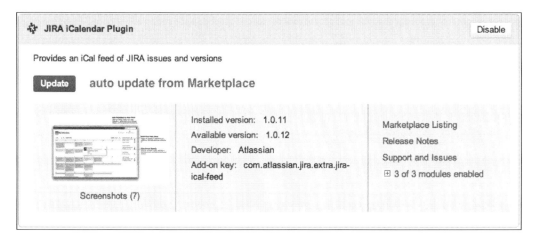

You can also update your add-ons by manually uploading and installing them. You will also need to read the vendor's documentation on any special requirements for the update.

Uninstalling an add-on

Uninstalling an existing plugin is a simple process:

1. Browse to the **Manage Add-ons** page.
2. Click on the add-on to remove.
3. Click on the **Uninstall** button for the add-on.
4. Click on **Continue** on the confirmation dialog box.

Before you uninstall an add-on, you need to first make sure that the add-on does not contain critical functionalities that are currently being used by JIRA. For example, if the add-on has a custom field type that is being used by a workflow condition, uninstalling the add-on may cause the condition to fail. It is best to test this out in a test environment before uninstalling from production, or disable the add-on first so you can recover from problems quickly by re-enabling the add-on again.

Viewing the audit log

The **Universal Plugin Manager** keeps track of all the changes that have been made to add-ons in an audit log. This will include activities such as installing new add-ons, upgrading the existing add-ons, enabling/disabling of add-ons, and more. The audit log will also keep a record of when each of the activities was performed, and which user performed them. Perform the following steps to view the audit log:

1. Browse to **Universal Plugin Manager**.
2. Select the **Manage Add-ons** tab.

3.   Click on the **Audit Log** link at the bottom of the page:

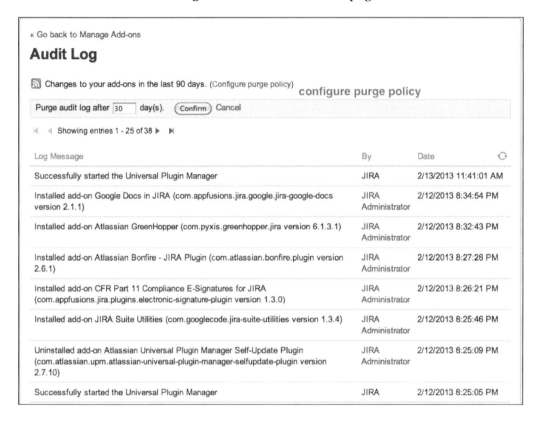

JIRA will automatically purge audit log entries after a period of time. By default, entries that are older than 90 days will be removed from the system. You can modify the period by clicking the **Configure purge policy** link at the top and setting a new period.

Enabling the safe mode

The Universal Plugin Manager allows you to disable all user-installed add-ons with the **Safe Mode** option. This is helpful when troubleshooting problems with JIRA, and you can very quickly determine if the problem is caused by a misconfiguration or by an add-on that has been installed recently. Perform the following steps to run your JIRA in safe mode:

1. Browse to **Universal Plugin Manager**.
2. Select the **Manage Add-ons** tab.
3. Click on the **Enable Safe Mode** link at the bottom of the page.
4. Click on **Continue** on the confirmation prompt.

Summary

In this chapter, we have rounded up our discussion of JIRA by covering some value-added features, such as customizing JIRA's look and feel, and how to extend JIRA's functionalities through the use of add-ons. JIRA is a great product, both powerful and flexible, and best of all, it allows you to further enhance it with new features through its robust plugin system. Atlassian has a great community and ecosystem with people offering advices and solutions to your problems on the forum, and with over 500 add-ons (and growing) for JIRA in the Atlassian Marketplace, you are sure to find the add-on that will meet your needs.

In the next chapter, we will introduce some advanced features and uses of JIRA, such as using JIRA as a public feedback collection system, and using JIRA to run agile projects.

11
Advanced Features

In previous chapters, we covered all the basic features of JIRA and showed how you can customize many of its out-of-box features to make JIRA work for you. In *Chapter 10*, *General Administration*, we also introduced add-ons, small self-contained extensions that can expand JIRA's existing features. In this chapter, we will take a look at two add-ons that can transform your JIRA to be more than just a simple issue-tracking system.

By the end of the chapter, you will have learned how to:

- Run agile projects in JIRA with GreenHopper
- Collect feedback from visitors directly on your website with Issue Collector

GreenHopper

So far, you have seen and used JIRA as a traditional issue-tracking system, where users can log issues and transition them through workflows. With the recent increased adoption of agile development methodologies, it is clear that JIRA by itself is not enough, and this is where GreenHopper comes in.

GreenHopper adds the power of agile methodologies to JIRA, by providing a new user interface to help you and your team plan and visualize the tasks you have at hand. GreenHopper is a separate product and does not come with JIRA. So the first step for us is to install it via the Marketplace.

Getting GreenHopper

GreenHopper is a commercial add-on provided by Atlassian. As we have seen in *Chapter 10, General Administration*, we can discover and install add-ons directly from JIRA through the Universal Plugin Manager. Perform the following steps to install GreenHopper via the UPM:

1. Browse to **Universal Plugin Manager**.

2. Select the **Find New Add-ons** tab.

3. Search for GreenHopper in the search box. This will locate the add-on **GreenHopper - Agile project management for JIRA**.

4. Click on on the **Free Trial** button if you want to evaluate GreenHopper before purchasing, or click on the **Buy Now** button to purchase directly. This will prompt the UPM to start downloading and installing the add-on.

5. Click on the **Get License** button when prompted, and follow the steps to either generate a trial license or purchase a full license:

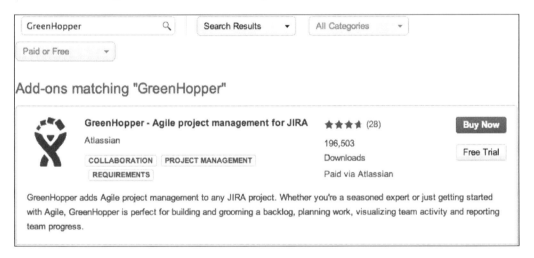

After you have successfully installed GreenHopper, there will be a new item added to JIRA's top menu bar called **Agile**, as shown in the following screenshot:

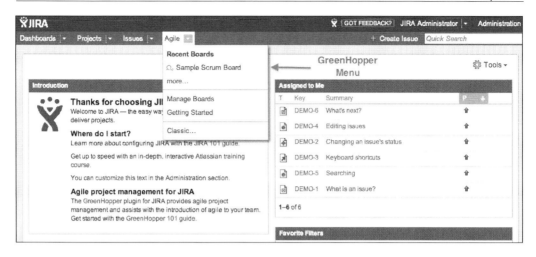

Starting with GreenHopper

Before we start using GreenHopper, the first thing you need to understand is that GreenHopper adds a new user interface to JIRA, allowing you to better visualize the data you already have in JIRA. For example, an issue in GreenHopper is the same as an issue in JIRA, and you can go back and forth between the two user interfaces.

Now that the relationship between GreenHopper and JIRA is clear, we need to familiarize ourselves with a number of new terminologies that we will be using.

Scrum

Scrum is an agile software development methodology, where the development team plans and works on the project iteratively and incrementally to complete the project.

You can read more on Scrum at
`http://en.wikipedia.org/wiki/Scrum_(development)`.

Kanban

Kanban is a methodology where the focus is to visualize and limit the amount of work that is in progress. Kanban allows the project team to focus on delivering custom value.

You can read more on Kanban at
`http://en.wikipedia.org/wiki/Kanban_(development)`.

Board

A **board** is what GreenHopper uses to display and visualize issues in JIRA. You can think of it as a traditional white board, where you will have sticky notes representing the tasks to be completed.

Card

Following the preceding white board analogy, a **card** is the sticky note that represents the task to be done. With GreenHopper, a card is an issue, visualized differently:

Story

Stories or **user stories** represent requirements or features that are to be implemented. They are usually written in a non-technical language and describe what needs to be done and whom the requirement is designed for (e.g. the end user, the administrator), in a few short sentences.

In GreenHopper, a story is represented as an issue of type User Story.

Sprint

Sprints also known as **iterations**, are used in iterative agile development methodologies, such as Scrum. A sprint has a specific duration (that is, a start and end date) and is usually between one to four weeks, in which the team works to deliver a portion or an improvement of the whole product or project.

Epic

An **epic** is a large user story that has not yet been broken down into smaller, more manageable stories, usually a group of related stories. Epics should be broken down into their component stories during the planning session, before becoming part of a sprint.

In GreenHopper, an epic is represented as an issue of type Epic.

Backlog

The **backlog** contains all the issues that have not yet been included in a sprint.

Working with boards

To start working with GreenHopper, you need to get familiar with boards. You can view and access boards from the **Manage Boards** page, by pulling down the **Agile** menu and selecting **Manage Boards**. From the **Manage Boards** page, you will see all the boards that are shared with you. The following screenshot shows three boards, two are shared with **Sample Project**, and one is not shared at all, making it a private board:

GreenHopper has two types of boards, Scrum and Kanban. The **Scrum** board is designed to support the Scrum methodology, where teams plan and work in sprints. Scrum boards have access to all three modes mentioned above.

The **Kanban** board is designed to support the Kanban methodology, where teams focus on managing and constraining their work in progress. Since Kanban does not have a planning session like Scrum, its boards do not have the Plan mode.

There are three modes for GreenHopper boards, namely Plan, Work, and Report:

- **Plan**: This is where you plan your sprints. This mode is only available to Scrum boards.
- **Work**: This is where cards (issues) are progressed (workflow transition) from one column (issue status) to another.
- **Report**: This contains a number of built-in reports and charts such as the Burndown chart (Scrum) and Control chart.

The following screenshot shows an example of a Scrum board in the Plan mode:

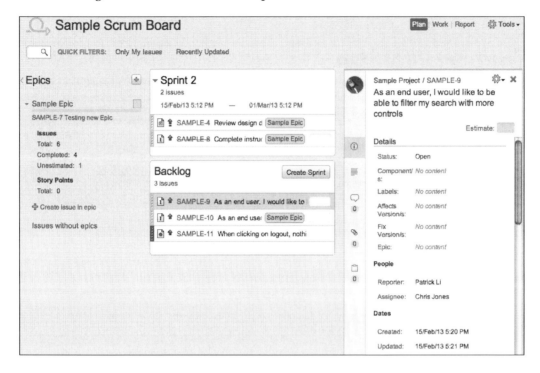

Creating a new board

There are two ways to create a new board. You can create either a new Scrum or Kanban board. Perform the following steps to create a new board from presets:

1. Bring down the **Agile** menu and select **Manage Boards**.

2. Click on the **Tools** option at the top-right and select **Create Board**.

3. Choose to create either a Scrum or Kanban board.

4. Provide a name for the new board.

5. Select the project the new board is for.

6. Click on the **Create** button.

When creating a new board based on the presets, GreenHopper will automatically generate the necessary JQL queries based on the selected project. For a Scrum board, it will include all the issues in the project, while for a Kanban board, it will include all the issues that do not belong to a released version.

Creating a new board based on the presets is simple and fast but each board is linked to a project only. You can also create a new board with a filter, and this way, you can control what issues will be added to the board. One thing to keep in mind is that you can only create Kanban boards this way. You cannot create a Scrum board with a filter.

Perform the following steps to create a new Kanban board with a filter:

1. Bring down the **Agile** menu and select **Manage Boards**.
2. Click on the **Tools** option at the top-right and select **Create Board**.
3. Select the **Advanced** option.
4. Provide a name for the new board.
5. Select a filter you want to use.
6. Click on the **Create** button.

Working with Scrum boards

Teams that work with the Scrum agile methodology should use Scrum boards, which as we have seen, can be created with the Scrum preset. Scrum boards have a Plan mode, which lets you create epics, add stories to epics, and set up sprints.

Working with Epics

As you have already seen, an epic is a large user story, which needs to be broken down during the planning session before the start of a sprint.

You can create epics directly on your Scrum board in GreenHopper. Perform the following steps to create a new epic:

1. Browse to your Scrum board and make sure you are in the Plan mode by clicking on **Plan** at the top-right.
2. Click on the plus (+) button in the **Epic Panel** to the left.
3. Provide a name for your new epic in the **Epic Name** field. The epic name is what will be used to identify other issues, such as stories that are linked to it.
4. Provide a summary for the new epic. It should be a short.

As shown in the following screenshot, the **Create Epic** dialog box looks very similar to the normal **Create Issue** dialog box. In GreenHopper, when creating a new epic, you just create a new issue of type epic in JIRA. This means that you can create epics via the traditional method as well:

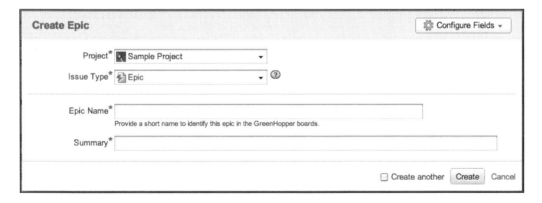

After you have created your epic, you can start adding issues to it. Adding issues to an epic allows you to group similar stories together. You can add new as well as existing issues to an epic.

Perform the following steps to add a new issue to an epic:

1. Browse to your Scrum board and make sure you are in the Plan mode by clicking on **Plan** at the top-right.

2. Click on the triangle icon next to the epic's name to expand the epic's details.

3. Click on the **Create issue in epic** link.

4. Create the issue as per normal.

By default, GreenHopper will assume that you are creating a new story under the epic, but you can change the issue type for other types of issues.

Perform the following steps to add an existing issue to an epic:

1. Browse to your Scrum board and make sure you are in the Plan mode by clicking on **Plan** at the top-right.

2. Drag-and-drop the issue onto the epic you want to add it to. The epic will turn green when the issue is dragged onto it.

Working with sprints

During your planning sessions, you and your team will need to decide what issues in the backlog will be in your next sprint. To create a new sprint in GreenHopper, all you have to do is to click on the **Create Sprint** button in your backlog.

After creating your new sprint, you can drag-and-drop issues from your backlog into the sprint, or you can add issues from your backlog by dragging the sprint marker or footer down, and all issues that are above the marker will be automatically added to the sprint. You can add issues from the backlog or other sprints that have not yet started, but not issues that are a part of an active sprint.

After creating your next sprint and including issues to be completed, you are ready to start your sprint. Perform the following steps to start a sprint:

1. Browse to your Scrum board and make sure you are in the Plan mode by clicking on **Plan** at the top-right.

2. Click on the **Start Sprint** link. This will bring up the **Start Sprint** dialog box.

3. Specify a name for the sprint if you want to change it.

4. Specify the start and end date for the sprint.

5. Click on the **Start** button to start the sprint, and you will be taken to the Work mode of the board:

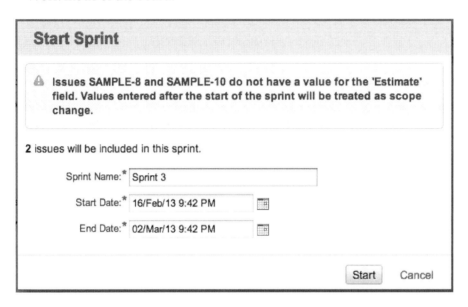

On the last day of the sprint, as specified when you started it, you can end it. Any issues that have not been completed will be returned to the backlog or the next available sprint if there is one. Perform the following steps to end a sprint:

1. Browse to your Scrum board and make sure you are in the Plan mode by clicking on **Plan** at the top-right.

2. Bring down the menu next to the name of the sprint.

3. Click on the **Complete Sprint...** button:

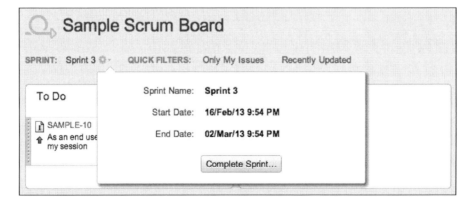

Working with Kanban boards

There is no Plan mode in Kanban boards, and you start in the Work mode directly. With Kanban, the focus is on visualizing and understanding what you and your team are working on, and also limiting the amount of work in progress.

So, with each Kanban board, you can set a minimum and maximum constraint on the number of issues that can be within each of the columns, and if the constraints are exceeded, the board will alert you of that. The following screenshot shows a Kanban board in the Work mode, and as you can see, the **In Progress** column is highlighted in red to indicate that the constraint placed on the column has been exceeded:

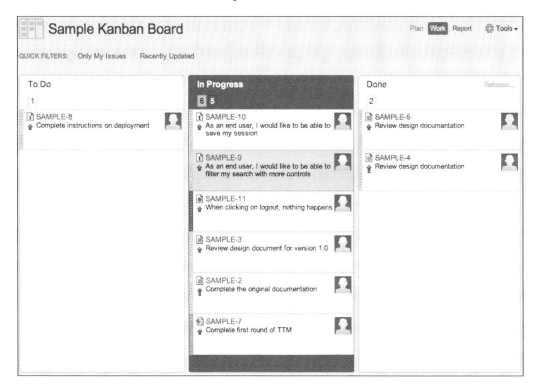

Setting up column constraints

Each column on a Kanban board can have its own minimum and maximum constraints. Perform the following steps to set up the constraints for a board:

1. Browse to your Kanban board and make sure you are in the Work mode by clicking on **Work** at the top-right.

2. Bring down the **Tools** menu and click on the **Configure** option.

3. Select the **Columns** tab.

4. Select the type of **Column Constraint**.

5. Specify the minimum and maximum constraint values for each of the columns you want to place a constraint on. The constraints will be saved automatically.

The following screenshot shows that we are limiting the maximum number of issues that can be in the **To Do** and **In Progress** columns to 10 and 5 respectively, and the minimum number of issues in the **Done** column to 5:

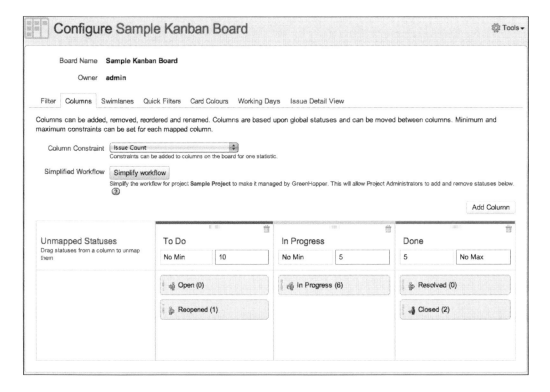

Releasing a version

Since Kanban does not have sprints, instead of ending a sprint in the Work mode, you release a version. While releasing a version from a Kanban board, a new version will be created in JIRA, and all issues that are released, as part of the version will automatically have their **Fix Version/s** field set to the new version. Perform the following steps to release a version from a Kanban board:

1. Browse to your Kanban board and make sure you are in the Work mode by clicking on **Work** at the top-right.

2. Click on the **Release** link at the top of the **Done** column.

3. Provide a new name for the new release version.

4. Specify the release date; usually today's date.

5. Provide an optional description for the release.

6. Click on the **Release** button.

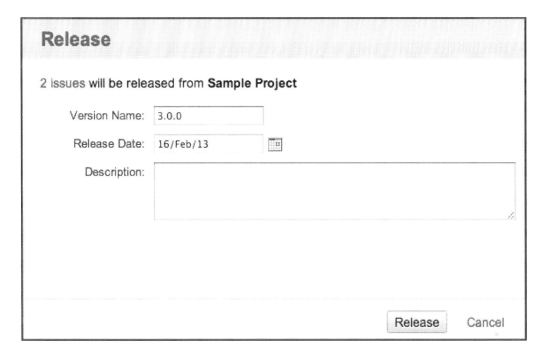

Setting GreenHopper as the home page

By default, the JIRA home page will be the dashboard. But after a while, you may find that you are working in the GreenHopper interface more and more and would like to default the home page to your board instead. You can do this by performing the following steps:

1. Click on on the triangle icon next to your name at the top right to bring down your user menu.

2. Select **Agile** under the **My JIRA Home** heading:

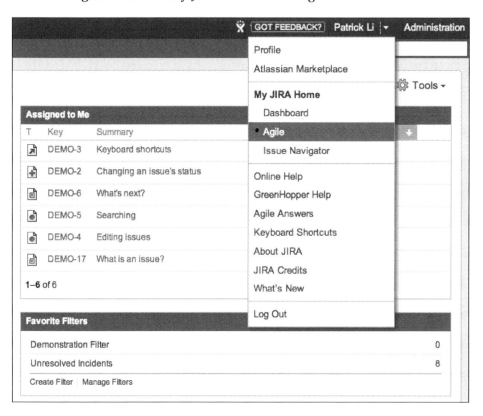

After setting your home to Agile, the next time you log in or click on the JIRA icon at the top left-corner, you will be taken to your last visited GreenHopper board instead of the standard JIRA dashboard.

Issue Collector

JIRA is a great system to track and manage issues, but one of the challenges is that it can be overwhelming at times for users who are not familiar with JIRA to get started quickly. Another challenge is that there is not a simple way to take advantage of JIRA's issue-tracking capability and making it available to other websites, such as an Intranet. Just like GreenHopper, a new add-on, the **Issue Collector** has been created to address these issues.

Issue collector is another add-on from Atlassian, and is bundled with JIRA. However, if for some reason you do not have it, you can still get it from the Marketplace and install it via the UPM.

With the issue collector, you can embed a feedback form directly in your website and collect feedback from visitors and automatically push that feedback into JIRA. The major advantages of using the issue collector are as follows:

- Visitors do not need to have a JIRA account. The extra step of having to create a new account can be a turn off for some people.
- Visitors can provide their feedback on the spot without having to go to JIRA. In fact, they do not even know that JIRA exists.
- The feedback form is very simple to use, unlike the create issue dialog box, which can be complicated.

When embedded, the feedback form is accessed via a trigger, usually a tab positioned at the edge of the web page. You can control the position of the trigger while adding an issue collector in JIRA. The following screenshot shows an issue collector with a trigger at the right edge of the page:

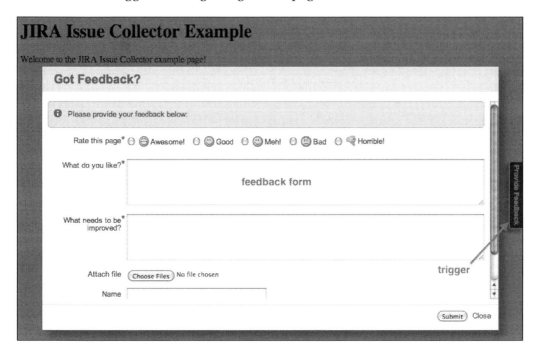

Setting up an issue collector

Issue collectors are created on a per-project basis, so when a user submits his/her feedback with the form, JIRA will know which project to create the issue in. Perform the following steps to set up a new issue collector for a project:

1. Browse to the **Project Administration** console for the project you want to use an issue collector with.
2. Select the **Issue Collectors** tab at the left.
3. Click on the **Add Issue Collector** button.
4. Fill in the form (see the following table) and click on **Submit**.

The **Add Issue Collector** page is divided into three major sections. The first section requires you to provide some basic information for the issue collector. The most important parameter is **Issue Type** and **Issue Reporter**. The following table lists all the parameters needed to create a new issue collector:

Field	Description
Name	This specifies the name of the issue collector. You should use a name that conveys the purpose of the issue collector.
Description	This specifies some more descriptive text about the issue collector.
Issue Type	This specifies the issue type for new issues created via the issue collector form.
Issue Reporter	This specifies the default user that will be used to create issues when issues are created.
Match Reporter	This specifies whether new issues should always be created with the issue reporter, or if JIRA should try to match the user with an e-mail or if there is an active session with JIRA.
Collect Browser Info	Tick this option if you want to collect additional information from the user's browser.
Trigger Text	This specifies the text that will be displayed on the **Trigger** tab.
Trigger Style	This decides where you would like the **Trigger** tab to appear on the page. If you choose the **Custom** option instead of creating a **Trigger** tab, you will get a JavaScript code snippet that will let you control and use other elements on the page as the trigger, by replacing the #myCustomTrigger text.
Template	This chooses what the feedback form will look like. You can also create your own form by choosing the **Custom** option.
Message	This specifies the message that will be displayed in the info panel on the feedback form.

For the **Trigger** and **Issue Collector Form** sections, the **Add Issue Collector** page has preview panels to help you visualize the end result of what it might look like once it is embedded into your website.

Embedding the issue collector

After creating the new issue collector, you will be able to embed it in your website. JIRA offers two options to embed an issue collector, either via HTML or JavaScript.

Embedding via HTML requires you to have the ability to modify the HTML page you want to embed your issue collector into. If you want the issue collector to appear on every page on your website, you will need to have a common HTML page that can be included in all the pages, such as a header HTML.

Embedding via JavaScript allows you to add the generated code as a part of an existing JavaScript file that is already been included in the page. Again, this requires you to have the ability to modify the JavaScript file. This option also requires the jQuery library to be available, so you will need to make sure you have included jQuery before calling the generated code, as follows:

```
<script src="http://code.jquery.com/jquery-latest.js"></script>
```

Perform the following steps to embed your issue collector in your website:

1. Select either the **Embed with HTML** or **Embed with JavaScript** option under the **Embed this Issue Collector** section.

2. Copy the contents from **Code to insert** text area, and paste the code snippet into the appropriate location of your page.

You can also click and expand the **More Instructions** section to get more details and examples on how to do this.

The following screenshot shows an example of an issue collector embedded in Atlassian Confluence, an enterprise wiki solution:

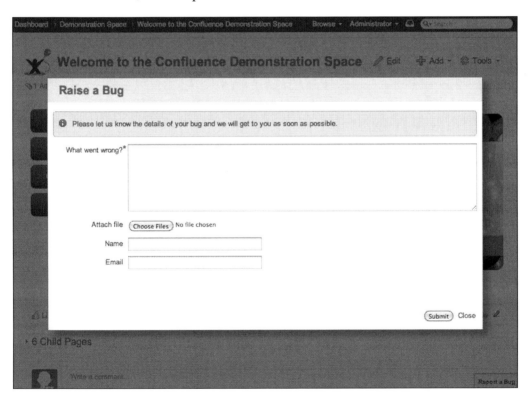

Summary

In this chapter, we have learned to expand JIRA beyond being just a simple issue-tracking system. Note that both GreenHopper and Issue Collector simply build on top of the JIRA platform, taking advantage of its already robust issue management features and present the users with new interfaces and ways to interact and use JIRA. There are many other great add-ons available in the Marketplace that will make using JIRA a much more enjoyable and productive experience for you and your team.

Index

D

dashboards
  about 298
  configuring 301
  creating 299, 300
  deleting 301
  editing 301
  layout, setting 302, 303
  managing 299
  setting up 308
  sharing 301
database drivers
  installing 30
databases
  about 13
  HSQLDB 13, 323
  Microsoft SQL Server 13
  MySQL 13
  Oracle 13
  PostgreSQL 13
database setup
  managing 30, 31
data directory 9, 10
data storage 9
date fields section 60
date picker field 97
date time field 97
date/time format
  setting 315, 316
Days per week parameter 76
default assignee field 41
Default Permission Scheme 263
Default Reporter parameter 228
Default Screen 132
Default text renderer 116
Default Unit parameter 76
Delegated LDAP 239
Delete All Attachments 261
Delete All Comments 261
Delete All Worklogs 262
Delete issues 261
delete option 45
Delete Own Attachments 261
Delete Own Comments 261
Delete Own Worklogs 262
description field 41, 96, 203, 353

developers, project role 251
directory type parameter 240
Disable Outgoing Mail button 205
draft
  publishing 166
draft status 162

E

Edit All Comments 261
Edit All Worklogs 261
Edit Issue 140, 261
Edit Own Comments 261
Edit Own Worklogs 261
Edit Workflow page 178
e-mail
  about 201, 202
  manual sending 209, 210
Email from setting 318
email prefix field 203
Enable Thumbnails option 82
Enable ZIP support option 82
epics
  about 340
  working with 344, 345
error queue 208
Escalation Level field 153, 154
Escalation List 232
events
  about 211
  custom event, adding 215
  custom event, firing 215, 216
  custom events 211
  mail template, adding 212, 213
  system events 211
Exclude email header option 321
Exit Administration link 37
export directory 10
External option 22
External password management option 320
External user management option 320

F

field
  about 34, 35, 95
  adding, to screen 136
  deleting, from screen 136, 137

association, deleting 150
association, editing 150
configuring 148
copying 147
deleting 147
editing 147
issue types tab 46
Issue Updated event 211
issue view options section 60
Issue Worklog Deleted event 212
Issue Worklog Updated event 212
iterations. *See* **sprints**

J

Java
  installing 15, 16
Java Development Kit (JDK) 12
Java Runtime Environment (JRE) 12, 15
JIRA
  about 7, 311
  administrator 37
  and e-mail 201
  and screens 129, 130
  architecture 7
  backing up 323, 324
  colors, customizing 313, 314
  configuring, as service 26
  configuring, as Windows service 25
  connecting, to LDAP 240, 241, 242
  date/time format, setting 315, 316
  events 211
  gadget colors, changing 315
  hardware, requisites 11
  hierarchy 34
  home directory 9
  installation directory 9
  installation, options 14
  installing 14, 20
  issues 58
  issues management 57
  Java, installing 15, 16
  jira-application.properties, configuring 21
  logo, changing 313
  mail queries 207
  mail servers 202
  MySQL, installing 17, 18

MySQL, preparing for JIRA 18-20
  notifications 217
  notification scheme 218, 219
  obtaining 20
  options 279
  post-installation configurations 26
  reindexing 327
  restoring 323, 324
  running, in safe mode 335
  search interface 279
  setup wizard 21, 22, 23
  software, requisites 12
  system, requisites 11
  XML, backing up 324, 325
JIRA 4.4 237
JIRA administrator
  about 36, 37
  projects, creating 38
  versus JIRA system administrator 257
jira-administrators 249
JIRA Administrators, global permission 256
jira-application.properties
  configuring 21
JIRA Configuration Tool 30
jira-developers 249
JIRA Enhancer Plugin 99
JIRA global permission 255
JIRA_HOME directory 10, 323
JIRA internal directory, user directories type 238
JIRA Misc Workflow Extensions 185
JIRA Query Language. *See* **JQL**
JIRA Suite Utilities 184
JIRA system administrator
  versus JIRA administrator 257
JIRA System Administrators, global permission 256
JIRA Toolkit Plugin 99
jira-users 249
JIRA Users, global permission 256
jira workflow 163
JIRA Workflow Bundle. *See* **workflow bundle**
JIRA Workflow Enhancer 185
JIRA Workflow Toolbox 185
JNDI location field 204

JQL
  about 282
  components 282
JQL Auto-complete option 321
JQL, components
  field 283
  functions 283
  keyword 282
  operator 283
JQL, elements
  field 283
  operator 283
  value 283
JQL syntax reference
  URL 283

K

Kanban
  about 339
  URL 339
Kanban boards
  column constraints, setting up 347
  creating, with filter 343
  version, releasing 349
  working with 347
keytool 28

L

labels field 97
labels tab, project browser 49
layout
  setting, for dashboard 302, 303
LDAP
  base DN parameter 241
  directory type parameter 240
  hostname parameter 240
  JIRA connecting to 240-242
  LDAP Permissions parameter 241
  name parameter 240
  password parameter 241
  port parameter 240
  username parameter 241
LDAP authentication 239
LDAP Connector 238
LDAP directory, user directories type 238

LDAP Permissions parameter 241
Legacy Mode parameter 76
License Key property 23
Link Active Colour option 315
Link Colour option 315
linked status 167
Link Issues 261
listeners 211
log directory 10
logging work 76, 78
Logout confirmation option 321
look and feel configuration 312

M

mail handlers
  about 227
  adding 230, 231
  comment, adding before specified marker
    230
  comment, adding before specified
    separator 230
  comment, adding from non-quoted e-mail
    body 229
  comment, adding to existing issue 228
  comment with entire e-mail body, adding
    229
  deleting 232
  new issue, creating 228
  new issue, creating from e-mail message
    229
  updating 232
mail queues
  about 207
  flushing 209
  viewing 208
mail servers
  incoming 202
  outgoing mail server 202
  setting up 233
mail templates
  about 212, 213
  HTML template file 213
  new mail template entry, registering 214
  registering, with JIRA 214
  storage 213
  subject file 212

Thank you for buying
JIRA 5.2 Essentials

About Packt Publishing

Packt, pronounced 'packed', published its first book "Mastering phpMyAdmin for Effective MySQL Management" in April 2004 and subsequently continued to specialize in publishing highly focused books on specific technologies and solutions.

Our books and publications share the experiences of your fellow IT professionals in adapting and customizing today's systems, applications, and frameworks. Our solution based books give you the knowledge and power to customize the software and technologies you're using to get the job done. Packt books are more specific and less general than the IT books you have seen in the past. Our unique business model allows us to bring you more focused information, giving you more of what you need to know, and less of what you don't.

Packt is a modern, yet unique publishing company, which focuses on producing quality, cutting-edge books for communities of developers, administrators, and newbies alike. For more information, please visit our website: www.packtpub.com.

About Packt Enterprise

In 2010, Packt launched two new brands, Packt Enterprise and Packt Open Source, in order to continue its focus on specialization. This book is part of the Packt Enterprise brand, home to books published on enterprise software – software created by major vendors, including (but not limited to) IBM, Microsoft and Oracle, often for use in other corporations. Its titles will offer information relevant to a range of users of this software, including administrators, developers, architects, and end users.

Writing for Packt

We welcome all inquiries from people who are interested in authoring. Book proposals should be sent to author@packtpub.com. If your book idea is still at an early stage and you would like to discuss it first before writing a formal book proposal, contact us; one of our commissioning editors will get in touch with you.

We're not just looking for published authors; if you have strong technical skills but no writing experience, our experienced editors can help you develop a writing career, or simply get some additional reward for your expertise.

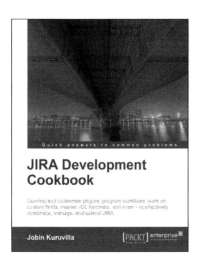

JIRA Development Cookbook

ISBN: 978-1-84968-180-3   Paperback: 476 pages

Develop and customize plugins, program workflows, work on custom fields, master JQL functions, and more – to effectively customize, manage, and extend JIRA

1. Extend and Customize JIRA--Work with custom fields, workflows, Reports & Gadgets, JQL functions, plugins, and more

2. Customize the look and feel of your JIRA User Interface by adding new tabs, web items and sections, drop down menus, and more

3. Master JQL - JIRA Query Language that enables advanced searching capabilities through which users can search for issues in their JIRA instance and then exploit all the capabilities of issue navigator

Selenium 2 Testing Tools Beginner's Guide

ISBN: 978-1-84951-830-7   Paperback: 232 pages

Learn to use Selenium testing tools from scratch

1. Automate web browsers with Selenium WebDriver to test web applications

2. Set up Java Environment for using Selenium WebDriver

3. Learn good design patterns for testing web applications

Please check **www.PacktPub.com** for information on our titles

VMware ThinApp 4.7 Essentials

ISBN: 978-1-84968-628-0   Paperback: 256 pages

Learn how to quickly and efficiently virtualize your applications with ThinApp 4.7

1. Practical book which provides the essentials of application virtualization with ThinApp 4.7

2. Learn the various methods and best practices of application packaging and deployment

3. Save money and time on your projects with this book by learning how to create portable applications

Java EE 6 Cookbook for Securing, Tuning, and Extending Enterprise Applications

ISBN: 978-1-84968-316-6   Paperback: 356 pages

Packed with comprehensive recipes to secure, tune, and extend your Java EE applications

1. Secure your Java applications using Java EE built-in features as well as the well-known Spring Security framework

2. Utilize related recipes for testing various Java EE technologies including JPA, EJB, JSF, and Web services

3. Explore various ways to extend a Java EE environment with the use of additional dynamic languages as well as frameworks

Please check **www.PacktPub.com** for information on our titles

Made in the USA
Lexington, KY
26 July 2013